T0291521

PLAY TO SUBMISSION

Tongyu Wu

Play to Submission

Gaming Capitalism in a Tech Firm

TEMPLE UNIVERSITY PRESS

Philadelphia • *Rome* • *Tokyo*

TEMPLE UNIVERSITY PRESS
Philadelphia, Pennsylvania 19122
tupress.temple.edu

Library of Congress Cataloging-in-Publication Data

Names: Wu, Tongyu, 1987– author.
Title: Play to submission : gaming capitalism in a tech firm / Tongyu Wu.
Description: Philadelphia : Temple University Press, 2024. | Includes
  bibliographical references and index. | Summary: "This book shows the
  workplace culture of the engineering department of a prominent tech
  firm, in particular how the firm uses games to promote productivity and
  buy-in. Despite high demand for their unique skills, the games
  effectively motivate the cooperation of many workers because they grew
  up developing gamer subjectivities"— Provided by publisher.
Identifiers: LCCN 2023049491 (print) | LCCN 2023049492 (ebook) | ISBN
  9781439922972 (cloth) | ISBN 9781439922989 (paperback) | ISBN
  9781439922996 (pdf)
Subjects: LCSH: Management games—Case studies. | Employee motivation—Case
  studies. | Industrial management—Case studies. | High technology
  industries—Employees—Case studies. | Gamification—Case studies.
Classification: LCC HD30.26 .W667 2024 (print) | LCC HD30.26 (ebook) |
  DDC 658.4/012—dc23/eng/20240403
LC record available at https://lccn.loc.gov/2023049491
LC ebook record available at https://lccn.loc.gov/2023049492

Printed in the United States of America

9 8 7 6 5 4 3 2 1

Contents

Acknowledgments

The realization of this book owes its existence to the support and guidance of many people. At the forefront of this journey stands Eileen Otis, my onetime teacher and a lifelong intellectual comrade. Her mentorship was the lighthouse guiding the evolution of this book—a venture that began with the endeavor of a Chinese female graduate student seeking to interpret mainstream U.S. society. Inspired by ethnographical and feminist methodologies, I was intrigued by the prospect of decoding the Western world through a non-Western lens and challenging the white, male-dominated narrative of U.S. society from the unique perspective of a woman of color. This intellectual pursuit led me to the heart of the U.S. tech industry—a field site fraught with challenges yet ripe for exploration. Eileen's support never wavered, despite fully recognizing the formidable obstacles ahead. Throughout the research and writing process, she remained my most steadfast ally. Her incisive mind relentlessly challenged my thought processes, and her rigorous academic training strengthened my scholarly resolve. Her thoughtful commentary on each lengthy email and successive draft was invaluable. In addition to Eileen, my immense gratitude extends to my committee members—Jianbin Shiao, Aaron Gullickson, and my outside member, Andrew Nelson. They have consistently offered timely guidance whenever I needed it, while also granting me the intellectual freedom to explore my thoughts and ideas. Their balance of support and autonomy has been crucial to my growth as a scholar.

The existence of this book owes much to the vital guidance and encouragement of Dingxin Zhao. Time has marched on, yet my mind often revisits the inaugural presentation of this project to him in 2018. It took place during a group interview Zhao had organized at the University of Chicago for the sociology department of Zhejiang University. Having witnessed Zhao's sharp critiques of several scholars' works, I approached the podium with trepidation and presented my work. Against all expectations, Zhao commented, "You have a good project there. Be more ambitious." In the fullness of time, I came to understand that his words were not mere casual encouragement but a resounding pledge to assist in the transformation of my project into something truly "ambitious." Indeed, over the next five years, Dingxin Zhao exemplified what it means to be ambitious in academia. He instilled in me a disdain for mediocrity and a drive for excellence. He taught me to never shy away from any intellectual combat and to maintain an unwavering belief in the transformative power of my work. Amid the tumultuous years overshadowed by the pandemic, Dingxin was the one who steered me through, not only continuously sharpening my ideas but also ensuring the survival of my manuscript writing process. Furthermore, it was Dingxin Zhao who, from scratch, fostered a vibrant and nurturing academic community at Zhejiang University. This community has become my intellectual refuge throughout the writing process.

I am deeply grateful for the substantial support I received from the labor scholar community, a sphere where my academic persona truly resides. Foremost, I must extend my heartfelt thanks to Michael Burawoy. I count myself among the fortunate, having had the invaluable opportunity to discuss my research with him during his visit to Zhejiang University. Despite his packed agenda, he generously allocated time for a comprehensive discussion on the diverse types of labor games I observed on the engineering floor. During our conversation, he underscored a point he has long insisted on: it is not enough to talk about games in general but to recognize different types of games. "And that is just what you have done! Congratulations!" were his encouraging words. Subsequently, I learned that Burawoy has been instrumental in occasionally broadcasting my research within the labor scholar community. His devotion to his students is well-known, but through this research, I have come to realize that his commitment extends beyond his own students. His dedication to the broader labor scholar community is truly legendary, and I have been fortunate to experience the empowering effects of such devotion. As I now guide PhD students specializing in labor studies, I am inspired to follow in his footsteps. Alongside my peers in labor scholarship, I aim to seize the torch he has lit and carry it forward, spreading its enduring light across our field. I owe a profound debt to Shen Yuan, the token Marxist scholar in China, for his unwavering support over the last five years as I drafted this book and sought my place within the solidarity of the Chinese labor scholar community. He demonstrates, through actions, how ethnography can be a powerful weapon for those scholars committed to voicing the struggles and stories of laborers. "Only when one pulls their feet from the mud does the true depth of their 'sinking down' come sharply into view (出水才见两腿泥)," he would often say, inspiring us to always immerse deeply in the "mud" of the laboring world. As I approached the end of writing this book, it became almost my obsession to craft a labor ethnography that is both "muddy" and "weaponful" enough to steadfastly walk the path he has paved. In addition to Burawoy and Shen Yuan, I owe a debt of gratitude to many labor scholars, including Steven Vallas, Christian Fuchs, Jamie Woodcock, and Micah Rajunov, who have provided generous support and invaluable suggestions at various stages of this book.

My profound gratitude extends to the engineers at the pseudonymous Behemoth. Bound by confidentiality, I am unable to mention them by their real names, but their stories form the very essence of this exploration into the work lives on the engineering floor. Without their generous cooperation, these pages would remain blank. Some, like ZH, would humorously express their astonishment at the lengths I have gone to in pursuing a PhD, yet their support remained steadfast. They played a crucial role in connecting me with key figures in the field and even organized gatherings to facilitate these introductions, allowing me to "hunt them all," so to speak. Others, like Xin Suo, lifted my spirits with "promises" of championing regional book sales and turning this book into a "best-seller," should their stories be featured. I am equally grateful to Danny, Michael, Peter, and Sylvia, who candidly shared their insights on such topics as gamification, "brogrammer" culture, and gender dynamics. Often, these unvarnished truths were shared in the late-night hours, after countless shots of tequila.

My friends, unwavering in their companionship, served as my bulwark against the solitude that often shadows the writing process. Intan Suwandi nourished me with "real food" and vibrant discussions about Marx, Russell, Mao, and Lu Xun, accompanied by drinks and laughter. Camila Alvarez was ever ready to help me dissolve the tribulations of the written word through hikes, camps, and travels. Brian Ott and Stephanie Raymond embraced me with open hearts from the moment I set foot in the United States. Bingqing Xia, who entered my life during the final stages of this project, infused much-needed doses of humor, cynicism, gossip, and homemade cassia wine, illuminating even the darkest, predawn stretches of my journey.

Above all, I am indebted to my husband, Jinglun Dong—an engineer and a pivotal informant for this research. Night after night, he patiently imparted the technical intricacies of engineering to me, bearing my novice frustrations with patience. His insistence on uncompromising standards sharpened my understanding of the engineering world. The insights we forged through endless discussions and debates are reflected on every page, bearing witness to his significant impact on this work. I also owe much to my parents, Xiao-dong Wu and Jinghui Ding, who have given me more love, freedom, and tolerance than I could ever hope to repay.

PLAY TO SUBMISSION

1

INTRODUCTION

L ike many fieldworkers, who spend their first on-location days glowing with the exhilaration that comes from learning about a new social setting, I experienced a palpable sense of excitement when I first entered my new research site. Unlike most research sites, though, this one did everything it could to maintain that excitement for everyone who walked in—especially for its employees. Walking into the tech firm Behemoth (a pseudonym), I discovered a veritable playground within the offices, complete with a variety of gaming TV stands and video game consoles, pinball arcade machines in most meeting rooms, Nerf guns scattered on the floor, and war-themed posters adorning every team's wall. Later that day, I mulled over my exciting Behemoth visit and tried to remind myself that these fun perks were just part of tech companies' manipulative culture. At that time, I remained fully convinced by previous organizational ethnographers' assertions that professional workers would struggle to distance themselves from corporate fun culture. My convictions, however, quickly wavered as I familiarized myself with Behemoth life: engineers seemed to genuinely enjoy the games organized around these office perks. At one point, the Knight team's tech lead, "Bloodseeker"—nicknamed after his favorite gaming hero—led his team in organizing a "defensive battle" to protect their favorite team poster from being abducted by their sister team. The poster's caption was a play on words from *Game of Thrones*—"In the Game of Security, we only play to win"—and portrayed these security engineers as tough, brave, and loyal warriors marching in a world of ice and snow, fearless in the face of a (security) battle. The

Knight engineers identified so strongly with this poster that they coordinated a defense strategy to keep displaying this monument to the company's fantasization of their work life.

That defensive battle was just the tip of the iceberg. Behemoth, it seemed, transformed reality itself into a game scene. On the first day that I was officially introduced to the Wizard team, I witnessed a terrifying game: Code Review Roulette. The game, based on Russian roulette, was designed by the engineers to solve the difficulties of delegating code review (CR) tasks. The rule was straightforward—"Whoever gets a bullet does the CR!"—and the game scene was brutal. It began with Jay loading a bullet into a toy revolver, spinning the cylinder, placing the muzzle against his temple, and pulling the trigger—but getting an empty chamber. Following Jay, Peter grabbed the gun and spun it, trembling slightly and mumbling, "Can't be me . . . The odds're low! Only one in six." Hearing this, Charlie chimed in, "Calm the fuck down! Odds're even lower." Charlie then turned to the whiteboard wall and wrote Peter's odds as an equation: "$(5/6) * (1/6) = 5/36$." As expected, Peter triggered an empty chamber. However, Charlie's quick math caused the team to realize that the respin changed players' odds, and they soon reached an agreement to not respin before continuing. Charlie took the revolver, cocked the hammer, and, unfortunately, fired the bullet. The game ended with Charlie taking on the CR task.

On the surface, this workplace had seemingly become a virtual playground for overzealous game hobbyists. Compared to the conventional corporate-fun environment that is usually staged (e.g., a sports event, a club or movie night, or a family party), the chaotic fun depicted above is undoubtedly more spontaneous and authentic, and thus more seductive. Despite the appearance of spontaneity and inclusivity in an employee-centered workplace such as Behemoth, the persistent reality is that the company reaps the reward of surplus productivity, leaving employees themselves in a highly competitive and sometimes precarious work position. The question then becomes, What is really going on behind the ludic gaming scenes? Whether and how engineers' ebullience silently creates surplus through a poster battle and Code Review Roulette remains contentious and debatable. In the tradition of previous labor ethnographies, this book—*Playing to Submission*—goes on an ethnographic adventure into the heart of a top U.S. tech company to observe its scenes on the main stage and behind the curtain, to uncover the logics, mechanics, and effects of a fun, game-playing cooperative environment. In many ways, these tech-industry workers were "avatars" for the future of work and production, and this book is situated vis-à-vis the mythic aura around the future of work.

A decade after the global financial crisis of 2008 and two decades after the dot-com bubble, capitalism has continued to evolve toward "informational capitalism," developing new modes of production, accumulation, and exploitation (Fuchs 2010). There is mounting evidence of four trends that seem to dominate informational capitalism. First, the logic of informational capitalist accumulation and competition leads to further polarization between mental and manual labor, creative and routine labor, and high-skilled and low-skilled labor (Harvey 1990; Huws 2014; Kalleberg and Vallas 2018). On the one hand, the maturing information and communication technology (ICT) and the advances in platform and algorithmic management technologies allow corporations to lower the labor cost of low-skilled workers, either through global outsourcing or presenting themselves as a "marketplace" for matchmaking between "hirer" and self-employed workers, thus completely avoiding employers' responsibilities (Gandini 2019; Prassl 2018; Rosenblat and Stark 2016). On the other hand, capitalists' increased reliance on those technologies to expropriate cheap labor significantly increases the labor value of programming and maintaining digital machinery and infrastructure, boosting corporations' demand for high-skilled engineers.

Additionally, informational capitalism opens up worldwide access to new, fast-growing companies that are unencumbered by legacy costs, labor regulations, or location constraints, creating an unprecedentedly competitive environment. To maintain their advantageous position, leading capitalists constantly try to develop new products with high technological content or complexity that cannot be easily imitated, so they are in dire need of highly skilled and creative workers (Gandini 2019; Huws 2014). These two trends—the increased polarization between high- and low-skilled labor, and capitalists' heightened demand for technology and creativity—contribute to a historical novelty in which human knowledge and innovative ideas have become the primary forces of production. The market's premium on innovation endows knowledge workers with an inherent power in the production process.

Another distinct feature of informational capitalism is that its production is mediated by a mind-boggling iteration of informational knowledge and technologies. As the bellwether of informational capitalism, the tech industry pushes iteration to an extreme, adopting a "permanently beta" ethic and promoting a never-ending innovation cycle (Neff and Stark 2004). To some extent, the tech industry's "permanent beta" status stems from the nature of software-driven products, which are characterized by an endless series of patches, updates, and developmental pivots. Last-minute pivots are common in the tech world and occasionally mythologized as "life-savers"—for example, Instagram's final pivot (eight weeks before launching) from a location-based check-in service to a photo-sharing service that ensured its dominant position in social media. Similarly, the breakthrough moment for YouTube was its pivot from video dating to video sharing—and the latest pivot legend, I guess, has to be Facebook's sudden shift to the Metaverse. The overarching problem with these legendary sea changes lies in their enchantment with eleventh-hour pivots, which have normalized an unprecedented level of flexibility, adaptability, and intensity in the tech industry.

Finally, the permanent-beta production cycle goes hand in hand with the financialization of the tech industry and the broader economy (Neff 2012; Shestakofsky 2017). The increasing "financialization" of the U.S. economy increases worker precariousness in the United States, and the tech industry, filled with firms backed by venture capital (VC), makes clear the close relationship between the power of speculative financial capital and the increasing intensity, instability, and risks borne by workers. To some extent, venture capitalists set the tone for tech's permanent-beta ethic: companies that aim to steadily develop stable products do not attract VC investment, since venture capitalists are obsessed with funding extremely flexible firms willing to take a high-risk, high-reward approach that includes a perpetual readiness to pivot. Engineers working for a financialized company, therefore, always find themselves being asked to pivot to satisfy VC expectations. Thus, financialization— coupled with the permanent-beta production cycle—has produced the endless iterations of extremely intense, flexible, and unstable development work that lies at the heart of the tech industry.

A review of these four trends exposes a paradox embedded in informational capitalism. On one hand, the informational capitalists' gamble on technological innovation gives engineers access to privileged positions in the labor market and inherent power in the production process, while their desperate demand for a constant flow of high-quality creative ideas fuels greater compromise in terms of workers' autonomy and freedom. After all, creative labor cannot be extracted coercively; it must be stimulated in a state of liberty. On the other hand, to satisfy financial capital interests, tech firms hustle to establish a permanent-beta production mode, which aims to expropriate engineers' creativity in the fastest, most intense way possible. Without the engineers' dedication to "crunch mode" (a term that describes working extra hours for extended periods), however, permanent-beta production would not exist. It is normal to see engineers in crunch mode devote seventy to one hundred work hours a week to meet a developmental project deadline or when pivoting and launching a product (Bulut 2020; Ó Riain 2009). This paradox leads to another question: Why does this seemingly powerful worker group submit to such an intense production mode? My starting point to addressing this question is labor control; namely, how is control over legions of highly skilled, often powerful workers achieved and disguised? How can creative work, usually not subject to a schedule or taskmaster, be channeled and intensified? How is the extraction of creative labor obscured?

This book draws on the information technology (IT) industry in the United States to tell the story of how production and control modes dramatically transform in informational capitalism. At first glance, the U.S. tech industry's primary ways to navigate the labor dilemma described above are simple and brutal: to lower labor costs, tech companies aggressively recruit new graduates and replace senior employees with fresh talent. High-tech companies' intense search for new blood rejuvenates the sector's labor force: the average age of the high-tech worker is thirty-eight, five years younger than the average U.S. worker (Visier 2015). The median age of employees at Google and Facebook is between twenty-eight and twenty-nine.

The aggressive recruitment of young talent can be a double-edged sword for U.S. informational capitalists. These engineers are ideal employees for a working environment characterized by high demand for innovation and intensity; tech firms prize the permanent-beta ethic and constantly hunt the next big disruptive innovation. *Disruptive innovation* captures the situation whereby a smaller company challenges established incumbents or creates a new market niche with an innovation that eclipses the current dominant product (Christensen et al. 2006; Lin, Evans, and Wu 2021). Disruptive innovation demands a very high level of intensity, and engineers often find they have to keep letting "innovation adrenaline" kick in to fuel creativity (Shestakofsky 2017). Senior employees who reach a certain life stage or burn through their supply of innovation adrenaline quickly lose their value to these informational capitalists. Moreover, young engineers usually have more leisure time for (and fewer familial responsibilities to interfere with) updating their coding skills and programming knowledge, which is crucial to working at the high speeds of technological innovation. In general, young engineers possess more advantages when adapting to the rather intense permanent-beta development cycle: they can stay up late, pull all-nighters, and be tied to their computers 24-7.

The other edge of the sword? Although tech firms can lower labor costs and enhance innovation by targeting fresh graduates, they must face the tremendous difficulties of recruiting, retaining, and—perhaps most importantly—controlling this youthful workforce. Young engineers will continue to be in demand, not only due to the tech industry's efforts to rejuvenate its labor force but also because new graduates are in short supply. In 2012, the President's Council of Advisors on Science and Technology claimed that the U.S. tech industry needed an additional 1 million STEM graduates to meet labor market demands, but institutions conferred fewer than 0.4 million STEM degrees in that same year (National Center for Education Statistics 2012). Tech firms' difficulties in attracting young tech workers is accompanied by challenges in retaining them: Silicon Valley's turnover rate can reach 20 percent, which is twice the national average (Shankar and Ghosh 2013). According to data compiled by LinkedIn in 2017, employees' job tenure in the fifteen largest Bay Area tech companies ranged from 1.8 to 7.8 years, with an average of 3.8 years (Charles 2018). Finally, although these new engineers are energetic and passionate about technological innovation, their creativity is difficult to stimulate and discipline: for example, these young employees' resentment levels rise dramatically when their prioritization of technological innovation over profits and markets conflicts with the priorities of their firm and its financial backers. New graduates' passions for technological innovation destabilize their work performance.

These circumstances force the U.S. tech industry to develop new coping mechanisms for its young laborers. One such method is for capitalists to take full advantage of a crucial characteristic embodied by these young engineers—their "gamer traits"—to squeeze out creativity. The majority of the Silicon Valley engineers I spoke with were born between 1979 and 2000, when the video game industry began its spectacular rise, and thus they are members of the "gamer generation." Many of the interviewees in this study call themselves "gamers," "game hobbyists," or "game addicts" and emphasize how it was their passion for games that propelled them to learn programming. Long-term gameplay equips the gamer generation with specific "gamer traits," like quick learning ability, fast reaction, modder (modification) traits, and a crisis mentality. Young engineers' lengthy immersion in the gaming world also lays the foundation for them to bust out disruptive innovative ideas; since gaming worlds are fictional, gamers find it easier to destroy an established world and construct a new one. To a certain extent, tech firms were compelled to explore ways in which these gamers' adventurous spirit and experimental skills cultivated via video-game play could be transformed into the principal productive force—disruptive innovation—on the engineering floor.

It seems inevitable, then, that informational capitalists developed labor games as a strategy to extract these engineers' labor power and maintain control over their behaviors. Indeed, labor games on the engineering floor can be designed to simulate video games, creating a familiar environment for engineers and mobilizing the emotions, desires, creativity, and energies inspired by those games. If such a simulation works, leisure becomes work and work becomes play—and the fuzzy boundaries between the two form a foundation for consent to long hours of intense labor. To understand these labor games on the engineering floor, this study follows the labor research tradition launched by Michael Burawoy, a Chicago School labor ethnographer who described a game of "making out" used on the manufacturing shop floor to motivate competition between workers and drive high levels of production. Burawoy (1982) illustrated that in the process of playing the "making out" game, workers experienced the game as a way in which they controlled the labor process, while in fact the game secured greater production of surplus.

Burawoy's thesis of labor games is still a classic that transformed the field of labor study. Before Burawoy, Harry Braverman's (1974) "deskilling thesis," developed on the assumption that capitalism's advanced technological apparatus can be harnessed by managers to expropriate workers' skills, dominated labor study. As a challenge to Braverman, Burawoy stood the objectivist and technological determinist tradition on its head and developed a more refined theory of labor games, which not only accounts for workers' subjectivities in organizing labor games but also highlights the critical role of workers' consent generated via game playing in securing and obscuring capitalist exploitation. Burawoy's labor game analysis synched with the course of historical development: as society moved into the post-Fordist period, labor control became more subtle, leaving behind the coercive control under Taylorism. Labor studies of the service sector further demonstrated that Burawoy's labor-as-game thesis was nimble enough to sustain new interpretation, even after society experienced another transformation and entered the era of deindustrialized service (Mears 2015; Otis 2016; Ouellet 1994; Pierce 1996; Ranganathan and Benson 2020; Sallaz 2009; Sharone 2002, 2013; Sherman 2007; Shestakofsky 2017).

This study builds on Burawoy and his followers by attempting to update these predecessors' insights, highlighting how labor games have changed dramatically, growing in both prevalence and prominence under informational capitalism. Most critically, I document a shift from a labor process defined by the rhythms and logic of a single game to one characterized by a multiplicity of games. Drawing from thirteen months of ethnographic work, this investigation advances labor game studies by documenting the development of a "field of games" that permeates every corner of engineers' work life. Work has become much more complicated and fragmented in the present day, and a single labor game may not satisfy the organizational goal of motivating workers; now, however, workers engage multiple, overlapping, and sometimes contradictory workplace games. A "field of games" serves multiple purposes: some function to increase productivity, while others may enhance creativity. As essential productive forces, innovative ideas are challenging to stimulate and control, even though informational capitalists desperately crave them. An additional wrinkle here: different games can lead to varied outcomes—while some games can garner engineers' consent and submission, other games may increase their resentment.

Compared to classic labor games, the tech industry's field of games is characterized by higher voluntarism and senses of agency. Engineers' technologically infused "gamer subjectivity" is a critical resource in shaping their gaming and working strategies; this subjectivity is leveraged on the work floor through their investment in labor games, which contributes to their submission to workplace domination. In this way, this study conceptualizes game playing not merely as a consent-generating strategy to obscure exploitation but also as a disciplining technology exercised through directing engineers to use their autonomy to develop the self-expressed subjectivity of a productivity gamer. By proposing the concept of gamer subjectivity, this book attempts to diverge from Burawoy's focus on how the shop floor generates subjectivity. Instead, this study shows that preexisting gamer subjectivities constructed by consuming games have predisposed engineers to a gaming labor process—in other words, the tech industry generates profit and exploitable subjectivities with its consumer products. Finally, this book aims to bring the critical role of technology back to labor game analysis, not as a means of deskilling but as a mechanism for individualizing power and manipulating behaviors. Facilitated by contemporary digital technology, games organized on the engineering floor can generate disciplinary power and ensure individual submission to exploitation. In taking advantage of technology's all-consuming nature, the workplace ultimately immerses engineers in a surreal gaming environment where they lose any sense of "working." In a later section, I provide more detailed discussion on how this study delivers insights into labor studies.

Methodology

This book's findings are drawn from thirteen months of ethnographic work and sixty-six interviews at Behemoth, a multinational corporation that operates a leading website, develops hardware products, and provides internet infrastructure services. Like the tech industry as a whole, its employees skew young, with an average age of just thirty-one. Employees describe Behemoth as a decentralized, flexible work environment marked by frequent reorganization. As shown in Figure 1.1, the field setting is located in the security department under the E-Commerce Group (ECG), which consists of roughly six hundred employees and is overseen by "Josh," a Level 8 manager. ECG is divided into three technical subgroups or, in Behemothspeak, "organizations." These organizations are charged with developing specific security products, putting them on the company's e-commerce platform, and allowing other Behemoth developers to use their products. This study focused on one ECG organization, Pipe Org, comprising about sixty people working on four major projects (shown in Figure 1.1 and highlighted in gray). These projects are a mix of independent products and parts of other projects, and each of the four is associated with a separate team: the Wizards, the Knights, the Assassins, and the Rangers. Each team has a Level 5 manager, who supervises between five and fifteen software engineers and reports to a Level 6 manager.

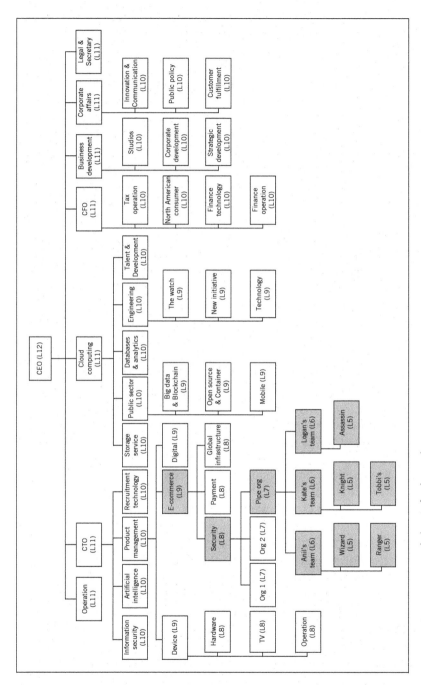

Figure 1.1 Organizational chart of Behemoth

The thirteen months of Behemoth fieldwork are divided into four phases. During my initial trip (November 2013–January 2014), I strove to understand Behemoth's localized knowledge and culture, its corporate structure, and engineers' daily routines. I also completed eleven formal interviews during this first phase. In the second phase, I spent six months (June–December 2014, excepting July) in the Pipe Org organization to observe engineers' daily activities, concentrating on the Wizard team; I also conducted twenty-seven formal, semistructured interviews. I returned to Behemoth for two months during summer 2015: this visit provided an opportunity to probe specific themes and questions that emerged from the ongoing data analysis. The third phase allowed me to explore whether the themes that emerged from my study of Pipe Org might apply to other groups within Behemoth. I visited other teams with entirely different technological foci housed outside the building where Pipe Org works, including the web design team, the cloud computing organization, and the payment solution department, and I interviewed eight engineers from outside Pipe Org. I conducted the final phase of fieldwork in July–August 2019 and completed another twenty interviews during this trip. In the end, the data consist of several hundred pages of field notes tied to approximately hundred hours of observation, informal conversations, and sixty-six formal interviews,[1] as well as supplementary materials, including internal memos and documents, brochures, posters, and information copied from key informants' Facebook pages.

Gaming at Tech: Brief Overview

At Behemoth, software engineering work can be divided into three key areas. The most important of the three entails the development of new products (e.g., apps) and features (e.g., new functions in an existing app). Behemoth uses an agile software development framework called a "scrum," which is organized around an incremental model of work.[2] The incremental model reflects tech companies' unconditional embrace of constant change and flexibility—the permanent-beta ethic. The second type of work is maintenance work, which can be further divided into two categories: routine maintenance tasks for engineers' own development teams (e.g., continuous monitoring of a product and error troubleshooting to ensure its smooth operation) and volunteering for maintenance tasks beyond their job descriptions, such as helping another team test and optimize their beta-version products. Finally, there are everyday workplace activities like meetings, email exchanges, training, and recruitment.

Different segments of engineering work require varied skills. Software development—the scrum process—relies heavily on engineers' innovation. Once an engineer fleshes out an innovative idea, this creativity allows them to develop unconventional design and save enormous computational power.[3] On average, one year of an engineer's software development work is equivalent to two years of machine computational power—but for exceptionally innovative engineers, a year of development work can easily equal three to four years of computational power.[4] Unlike scrum development, maintenance work cherishes the engineer's modder trait: "modder" usually describes video-game players' habit of helping companies improve their video games by endlessly tweaking the game system, providing feedback, and fixing bugs. In addition to its usefulness given the never-ending process of software updating, optimizing, and troubleshooting, the modder trait is a critical skill that helps ensure engineers tolerate and even enjoy maintenance tasks.

Each segment of engineering work, however, is structured by a distinct type of labor control crisis. Software development under the scrum model's unconditional embrace of change creates an implicit contradiction between the uncertainty associated with scrum development and engineers' demand for stability to establish trustworthy collaborative relationships. This contradiction can quickly generate anxiety among engineers. Uncertainty is at the core of what scrum development valorizes most—disruptive innovation—which is very difficult to initiate, measure, and control. In scrum development, engineers must develop a product that is only minimally viable, so while defects are a normal feature of this process, they easily elicit engineers' resentment and sabotage. When the minimum viable products (MVPs) are filled with unresolved issues, errors constantly occur while the system is running, so engineers responsible for maintenance at the time ("on-call" engineers) must often switch to crisis mode and troubleshoot errors as quickly as possible, which can be exhausting and stressful. Development teams engage in bricolage[5] and optimize MVPs by eagerly recruiting volunteer engineers to assist them with testing, code reviewing, and bug fixing—but while the extra help is invaluable to teams, it is not easily mobilized. Even daily interactions and communications are rife with crises: as recent graduates, these engineers are inclined to perceive work as a way of having fun, pursuing technological perfection, and expressing their competitive selves, even to more professional colleagues who have a different outlook on their working life. These distinct features of younger engineers pose enormous management challenges: while harsh control can damage worker autonomy and create resentment, a laid-back approach can harm workplace order when furious team competition creates a hostile atmosphere. Meanwhile, every workplace difficulty is accompanied by the overarching need for the firm to tap into their youthful employees' analytic and creative skills.

In light of these multifaceted control crises and dilemmas, the field-of-games development is perhaps the predictable solution. Given the nature of these particular workers, often characterized by gaming traits and student temperament, and the corporation's efforts toward constructing a "fun," "gamified" working environment, the introduction of labor games to the work process seems like a no-brainer for management. Furthermore, since engineering work breaks down into various tasks—each one of which suffers from a distinct set of problems—constructing a field of games instead of just one labor game to address those problems is more effective. At Behemoth, there is a vast array of organized games: coding games, code-review games, debugging games, training games, grinding games, hazing games, and hacking games. Some games are fleeting and spontaneous, while others are systematic and sustainable. There are games more embedded in core labor processes and others that are less embedded. And yes, while some games gradually stabilize and have more substantial labor-control effects by eliciting workers' consent, motivating extra labor, and distracting workers from the contradictions embedded in work, other activities turn into ersatz games of mock recognition that attract limited worker buy-in.

Several features define the field of games. First, through conceptualizing the field of games, this study depicts the pervasiveness of games that permeate every corner of industrial life for the purposes of control and exploitation. The field of games effectively constructs a world of no exit and deprives engineers' right to sanctuary. Second, unlike classic labor games that promote productivity, the field of games maximally appropriates engineers' innovative knowledge, which has become informational capitalism's essential resource for producing commodities. Third, as discussed below, by simulating the video-gaming world on the engineering floor, tech companies interpellate engineers' "gamer subjectivity." Here, informational capitalists mobilize the skills and traits associated with gamer subjectivity—modding attitudes, quick-learning ability, and heroic ethos—in the workplace and appropriate and exploit them as needed. The incorporation of gamer subjectivity means that the field of games is more likely to inspire engineers to self-mobilize for participation in (and initiation of) games more voluntarily than classic labor games. Finally, the field of games phenomenon blurs engineers' work and gaming time, space, life, and self to a large extent. As a result, engineers' leisure time is inevitably integrated into the labor cycle, and games and gaming relations developed on the engineering floor extend beyond company life—highlighting another difference between the field of games and classic labor games, which usually stop at the boundaries of workday and workplace.

To delineate the critical roles accomplished in a field of games, this book concentrates on four groups of labor games. *Simulation games*, which consist of battle simulations, adventure simulations, and crisis simulations, developed directly out of the scrum—the core labor process. Through adopting gamification techniques, including mythological storylines and heroic characters, managers simulate the artificial video-gaming environment in the software development process and stimulate engineers' self-fantasization of the work in terms of adventures full of change and unknowns—normalizing the uncertainty embedded in the scrum process and reducing engineers' anxiety. *Racing games*, which typically include events like debugging marathons/ hackathons, are organized when engineers need to race against the machine to troubleshoot and recover the system as fast as possible. One example of a racing game is the "ticket sprint." To address tickets (error notices), managers use a leaderboard to rank each development team's ticket-resolving performance. When engineers see their own teams' rankings drop too quickly or hit rock bottom on the leaderboard, they import similar strategies used in the video-gaming world to boost their rankings there, such as organizing weekend ticket sprints. In this case, managers successfully leverage gamification techniques (e.g., the leaderboard) to distract engineers from criticizing error-prone minimum viable products (MVPs) and redirect their attentions to winning the ticket sprint. *Crowdsourcing games*—badge-collection games, scavenger hunt games, and grinding games—are designed to crowdsource extra skills, knowledge, and labor from volunteering engineers to help the company optimize its MVPs. The badge-collection game, a typical crowdsourcing game, illustrates Behemoth's effort to adopt a video-gaming concept—the badge—as a reward to employees who complete volunteering work, like handling thousands of outstanding bricolage tasks[6] or providing feedback for other teams' products. Finally, *pranking games*, like the donut email prank, newcomers' hazing games, and other spontaneous pranks, approximate classic working-class humor and teasing. Engineers organize and patrol these pranking games to slay the "beast of monotony" in routine workplace tasks such as "standup" meetings and email communications or engage them as a way to express rebellion toward a rigid control that largely restricts engineers' freedom and autonomy.

Two attributes further determine the outcome of these games: the degree to which games interpellate engineers' productive gamer subjectivity and the depth of the alliance between managers and workers. Simulation games boast a high level of subjectivity interpellation and a strong manager-worker alliance. In other words, these games successfully conceal contradictions in the core scrum development process and lure engineers into self-mobilizing their gamer subjectivities to romanticize the software development process as a video game. This fantasizing results in engineers' internalization of the tech firm's permanent-beta ideology and ensures the coordination of interests between managers and workers. In short, simulation games construct a "gamified governmentality" in the software development process.

Racing games utilize video-game mechanics, such as leaderboards and rankings, and structure work as contests to awaken engineers' "competitive gaming selves." Engineers are thus motivated to develop gaming strategies to outperform other development teams, elevate their team's ranking, and win contests. By mobilizing engineers' competitiveness and supporting their contests, managers are able to redirect conflicts away from vertical tensions between managers' profit-driven priorities and engineers' focus on technological perfection toward horizontal ones between different teams. In other words, a medium-high level of alliance is formed between managers and engineers through the formers' successful conflict redirection. However, this alliance is less sustainable than that established in simulation games, where engineers completely internalize managers' interests. Thus, instead of formulating gamified governmentality, racing games establish a "gamified hegemony."

Pranking games typically resemble classic working-class labor games and involve a medium-to-low level of gamer subjectivity interpellation. In these games, workers' and managers' incentives overlap, and their interests can be coordinated, especially when engineers play to celebrate the chaotic fun at tech, alleviate fatigue, or to flatten the engineering floor's hierarchy. However, under certain circumstances, engineers' gamer subjectivity, which values technological freedom and autonomy, is mobilized and simulates engineers' rebellious behavior, leading to resistance pranks against manager control. Rather than coordinating interests, engineers' investment in these pranks threatens manager-worker alliances. Pranking games accordingly represent a tug-of-war between control and resistance, with "occasional hegemonic states" emerging as a result.

Finally, crowdsourcing games inspire low subjectivity interpellation and low manager-worker alliance. These games created by managers are so rigid that they allow only a low level of strategic discretion on the part of engineers, which hampers both the manager-worker alliance and the mobilization of gamer subjectivity. Ultimately, the concept of "mock hegemony" best describes this situation, and most crowdsourcing games wither on the vine.

Tech Work Control: A Labor Process Perspective

This book rests on a significant body of scholarly work. Study of the labor process dates back at least to Marx's recognition that workers sell their "labor power" (the capacity to work) rather than their "labor" (the act of working), thus begging investigation of how the labor process transforms labor power into actual work. Despite its importance, Marxist analysis of the labor process has been overshadowed by other disciplines and approaches, including management, industrial relations, and organizational theory since the 1950s.

In 1974, Harry Braverman's influential book *Labor and Monopoly Capital* revived the labor process tradition. He argued that deskilling (based on separation of the conception and execution of work) is a critical strategy used to exert maximum control over the pace and manner in which labor power translates into labor. Successive theorists developed Braverman's idea and created new control strategy typologies. Friedman (1977), for instance, proposed two broad strategies: direct control and responsible autonomy.[7] Edwards (1979) meanwhile introduced a progressive model of simple, technical, and bureaucratic control, illustrating their respective dominance at different stages of development.[8] As society shifted away from industrialization, labor process theories were extended to service sectors (Leidner 1993; Hochschild 2012; Otis 2012). Since the advent of informational capitalism and the rapid growth of the IT industry after the 1990s, labor scholars have faced a new challenging question: Do classic labor process theories effectively capture control over tech work?[9]

Scholars are divided as to whether classic theory can be applied in this newly emerging sector. A minority suggests that Taylorist control elements continue to play a crucial role in shaping the tech labor process.[10] Some studies reveal, for example, that managers strive to standardize and routinize software development processes by requesting that developers not make software from scratch but build upon existing modules. In doing so, tech capitalists narrow creative possibilities, enhance efficiency, and increase engineers' deskilling and replaceability (Kraft 1977; Woodcock 2019, 78). Similarly, fragmentation has been shown to still be present in software development in the form of dividing total software production into functionalities. This ensures that managers monopolize the conception of work and makes the development process more easily measured, controlled, and even outsourced (Kirkpatrick 2013; Ross 2004, 255; Weststar and Dubois 2022).

However, most labor scholars question the validity of Taylorist control mechanisms in disciplining hypercreative knowledge work (Andrews, Lair, and Landry 2005; Barrett 2005; Sharone 2002) and contend that standardization constrains engineers' creative freedom (Weststar and Dubois 2022). In reflecting on the unique nature of software production, researchers have illustrated that conception and execution cannot be separated since the software design and development process essentially takes place in engineers' minds (Andrews, Lair, and Landry 2005). Meanwhile, fragmentation in tech work primarily serves to increase development flexibility and not to deskill workers. Rather, specialized tools introduced to facilitate fragmentation are vital in upskilling rather than deskilling programmers (Barrett 2005; Orlikowski 1988, 108).

As the IT industry aggressively expands and constantly reinvents itself to accelerate the post-2000s innovation process, scholars generally agree that the Braverman strategy is not an efficient means of controlling tech work.[11] It is now widely thought that, in the face of heightened labor indeterminacy, normative control over creative workers proves more effective (Kunda 2006;

Peticca-Harris, Weststar, and McKenna 2015; Tse and Li, 2022; Weststar and Dubois 2022). Kunda's (2006) study of Tech, an American IT firm, has been particularly influential. He employs a Foucauldian approach to conceptualize corporate culture as a subtle form of "normative control," emphasizing how engineers internalize this culture and detailing their resultant submission to control.

Building on Kunda's theory, a number of neonormative control theories have since been proposed. Some scholars have highlighted workers' coping strategies to manage cultural discourse (Clarke et al. 2009; Fleming 2005; Fleming and Costas 2009; Fleming and Sturdy 2009; Sturges 2013). Others have explored how normative control legitimizes widespread work intensification in the tech industry (Peticca-Harris, Weststar, and McKenna 2015; Perlow 1998, 2001; Weststar and Dubois, 2022), with much discussion revolving specifically around video-game development work. Studies show how the intrinsic value that video-game developers ascribe to their work leads them to willingly put in long uncompensated working hours (O'Donnell 2009; Peticca-Harris, Weststar, and McKenna 2015; Sturges 2013; Weststar and Legault 2019; Whitson 2013). An emerging literature has begun to contextualize normative control in non-Western contexts, such as Tse and Li's (2022) study, which examines the process of recoupling corporate culture with political discourse in China's tech industry.

Yet the normative control paradigm is inadequate when it comes to interpreting the dynamics of tech work under the most recent form of informational capitalism. Namely, since the 2007–2008 financial crisis, massive outsourcing, increasing popularity of entrepreneurship rhetoric, and greater job mobility (Bulut 2020; Huws 2014; Neff 2012) have made the traditional construct of engineers' long-term commitment to a particular organizational culture unrealistic (Alvesson 2000; Capelli 2000; Rasmussen and Johansen 2005).[12] In fact, Kunda himself acknowledges that the evolving nature of the tech industry had transformed engineers from "loyal subjects" who identify with a specific organizational culture into "itinerant experts" who align more with market rhetoric (Barley and Kunda 2011, 295; Kunda and Van Maanen 1999).

Ethnographic work at Behemoth reveals a reinvention of Burawoy's theory of labor games (often considered as an alternative to Braverman's objectivist approach to labor control) as the most effective mechanism for capitalists to appropriate engineers' surplus, to motivate while at the same time disciplining engineers' work effort. Notably, the distinct nature of the software development process itself provides advantageous conditions for destabilizing many elements of classic labor games studies. In this book, I thus engage with labor game studies in two ways. On the one hand, I draw on a specific theoretical framework to investigate labor control patterns in the tech industry; on the other hand, I utilize the importance of tech work in revitalizing labor game theory. I further discuss both aspects in the next section.

Updated Labor Games Studies: Software Development Process as an Intervention

Burawoy's (1979) pioneering research laid the foundations for the study of labor games. In his ethnographic study of a South Chicago machine shop, he shows how manufacturing work was constituted as a game on the shop floor called "making out" and illustrates how, in participating, workers consented to capitalist objectives and rules. Specifically, workers were *deeply absorbed* in the game, strategizing, cooperating, and competing to beat the production quota (i.e., "make out").[13] By granting workers autonomy to "make out," managers gained their *consent* to extract surplus labor while simultaneously *obscuring that extraction*. In this process, worker *agency* was not reflected as antagonism or resentment but rather interpreted as essential coordination with capitalist interests. This phenomenon, which Burawoy calls a "hegemonic regime," emerged as a means to motivate workers during a historical period when legal protections hindered easy dismissal and replacement.

A close reading of Burawoy's work reveals that four vital elements underpin the making-out game: absorption mechanisms, practices of obscuring the extraction of surplus, worker agency and subjectivity, and the gaming outcome (i.e., hegemonic regime). According to Burawoy (1979, 87–88), one of the critical preconditions for *absorbing* workers into a game is uncertainty, though this can be neither too great nor too slight. High uncertainty means that no matter how workers strategize their making-out tactics, achieving the 125 percent goal is beyond their control. Low uncertainty meanwhile makes the 125 percent goal too easy to achieve and therefore uninteresting. Burawoy's analysis addresses a fundamental question in game and play studies—namely, why are humans absorbed into play, and what role does uncertainty play in such absorption (Huizinga 1949, 10)?[14] Yet the quantified line he uses to measure uncertainty is too precise to evaluate situations beyond manufacturing work. Later scholars who document work games have thus either neglected to discuss or ambiguously portrayed the mechanisms through which workers are drawn into games. Siciliano (2022) for instance uses a "wormhole" metaphor to describe how office staff in the digital media industry become so immersed in work activities while playing the "game of disappearing." However, he does not explain why they are drawn into it in the first place. Similarly, while Lupu and Empson (2015) do offer several explanations for why workers in accounting firms are deeply captivated by workplace games (e.g., the high stakes of giving up and lack of alternative approach to withdrawal), they are unable to prove the validity of absorption. These examples highlight the limitations of current labor game studies and the need for more rigorous analysis of absorption validity and mechanisms.

Second, Burawoy stresses that the game of making out involves *obscuring* surplus labor extraction. His ethnographic work revealed that the making-out game allowed managers to obscure the production relations between capital and labor by redirecting vertical conflicts between managers and workers to lateral ones among workers (Burawoy 1979, 66). Despite workers' belief that they were outwitting management through the game, they were inadvertently contributing to their own exploitation. In a later work, Burawoy emphasizes that this "obscuring" process furthers Antonio Gramsci's discussion of consent and calls for greater attention to the "concealment of exploitation" (Burawoy and Von Holdt 2012).[15] Indeed, the better capitalists become at obscuring their exploitation, the more durable capitalism becomes (Burawoy and Von Holdt 2012, 184).

Various labor scholars, particularly those focused on service work, have since examined the obscurity of production relations through games (Mears 2015; Sallaz 2009, 2015; Sherman 2007). Labor relations in the service sector involve a triangular pattern of relations among managers, workers, and consumers (Leidner 1993; Otis 2016), making the process of mystifying power relations more intricate than on the shop floor. Jeffery Sallaz's (2009) ethnography, for example, documents that the labor game in Nevada's casinos is built on a new mode of conflict redirection. Conflicts between dealers and management are redirected to conflicts between workers and clients, allowing managers to obscure power relations and secure the extraction of dealers' emotional labor. A variety of insightful studies furthermore demonstrate how capitalists' practices of obscuring control have evolved with the shift from an industrialized economy to a deindustrialized service society. With continual societal transformation and informational capitalism leading the new economy, production modes have undergone substantial change, and capitalists' have readjusted their obscuring strategies (Bulut 2020; Fuchs 2010; Gregg 2013; Huws 2014; Neff 2012). But have these made capitalism even more durable, as Burawoy predicted? This book explores this question through a specific case in the U.S. tech industry.

Third, *workers' subjectivity and agency* compose a critical element of Burawoy's labor games theory. He argues that previous labor scholars, such as Braverman (1974), underestimate the role of workers' agency in shaping and transforming the labor process and overly focus on structural determinants of exploitation (Burawoy 1979, 94). In contrast, his theory posits that workers' subjectivity plays a crucial role in shaping their perceptions, attitudes, and strategies of play and leads to their consent to the game. Inspired by Gramsci's observation that "hegemony was born in the factory but not in civil society," Burawoy furthermore contends that workers' subjectivity is constructed at the point of production rather than shaped by outside social structures.[16]

Though Burawoy's theorizing of workers' subjectivity is indubitably groundbreaking, it has drawn criticism for being formulated solely in class terms. Feminist labor scholars in particular have drawn attention to the importance of workers' gender subjectivities (Lee 1998; Salzinger 2003). They have also taken issue with Burawoy's emphasis on subjectivity being constructed at the point of production, showing that external resources, relations, and structures (e.g., patriarchal family and community) play equally important roles in shaping workers' subjectivities (Lee 1995; Ong 1987; Patricia Fernández 1983; Pun 2005; Wolf 1992). Finally, the fluidity and heterogeneity of gender subjectivities have also been highlighted. Salzinger (2003), for example, shows that different tropes of "productive femininity" are forged through specific labor processes under divergent production regimes.

The emergence of a gendered theoretical approach was accompanied by notable prosperity from the international division of labor.[17] With the deindustrialization process, labor scholars began to reflect on what other resources beyond the production site might shape workers' subjectivities. The literature on aesthetic labor has shown, for example, that workers' subjectivities are also molded by consumption (Otis 2012; Williams and Connell 2010; Witz, Warhust, and Nickson 2003).[18] This book accordingly explores newly emerging resources outside the workplace that can play a critical role in shaping workers' subjectivity and thus their gaming approach.

Finally, Burawoy argues that the making-out game produces both direct and indirect gaming outcomes. The direct outcome consists of increased economic profits for management, achieved by appropriating extra surplus. This surplus is measured as a percentage output (e.g., not higher than 140 percent or lower than 125 percent).[19] The indirect outcome concerns the contribution to hegemony, achieved through managers making compromises with workers and cooperating in limiting output to 140 percent in order to obtain their consent. Burawoy also stresses that the specific protective apparatuses—the internal state (union and contracts) and labor markets (job ladders and seniority)—existed at that particular historical moment, constituting vital preconditions for ensuring the emergence of such consent.

Subsequent studies have shown that direct gaming outcomes are pervasive in manufacturing settings such as machine shops, juvenile prison facilities, and garment factories, where games are organized to appropriate extra physical labor (Burawoy 1979; Ranganathan and Benson 2020; Reich 2010). In service settings, games are designed to extract emotional labor (Mears 2015; Sallaz 2009; Sherman 2007). Gaming outcomes in professional settings and knowledge industries are, however, more complex and challenging to evaluate. The limited scholarship on this issue tends to reduce the direct gaming outcome to appropriating extra labor time and general labor effort (Mc-Cabe 2014; Sharone 2003; Siciliano 2022). This is unfortunate, as the most critical issue in the new economy is how to possess the labor power of knowledge workers (Fuchs 2014; Gregg 2013; Ross, Kunda, and Neff 2012; Shestakofsky 2018).

Burawoy's investigation of the hegemonic regime broadened the impact of labor studies, and various comparative ethnographic studies have since sought to understand why hegemonic regimes can be constructed in certain contexts but not others. These investigations have helped to discern the critical apparatuses that facilitate the establishment of consent, such as wage systems, managerial practices, gender identities, labor markets, and state policies (Lee 1998; Sallaz 2009; Salzinger 2003; Sharone 2013). Yet as work becomes more complicated and production relations evolve in a more complex format, this hegemonic-regime study tradition faces new challenges. Burawoy himself reflects on this issue, identifying a new hybrid regime of "hegemonic despotism" that emerged after society moved toward neoliberalism (Burawoy 1985). Nonetheless, the production regime remains little explored, with very few attempts to resolve the limitations of the hegemonic model (Purcell and Brook 2022).[20]

This book recognizes the importance of tech work in revitalizing labor game theory and seeks to improve game theory in the four aforementioned directions—namely, absorption mechanisms, practices of obscuring the extraction of surplus, workers' subjectivity, and gaming outcomes. Before elaborating more specifically on the content of the book, I briefly discuss the unique characteristics of the engineering labor process and why their intervention can destabilize presumed aspects of labor games.

To begin, the software engineering work process is composed of several branch segments, each with its own distinct labor nature. To better understand how multiple games can coexist on the engineering floor and how their nature can vary widely, I propose the concept of a field of games. This concept does not adhere to the traditional theoretical structure of the labor game as a single-function game organized by workers. Removing this precondition allows to resolve several problematic issues identified above.

Secondly, labor games are essentially gamified labor processes aimed at maximum objectification of raw materials through efficient use of labor power. Therefore, many identified labor game elements (e.g., absorption conditions and obscuring mechanisms) are centered on this purpose. In tech work, however, labor power has changed dramatically and is primarily defined by innovative capabilities. It is thus reasonable to expect that the mechanisms of labor games have also changed. This shift provides a valuable opportunity to investigate which labor game elements are profound enough to sustain new interpretations.

Finally, engineers, as a distinct labor force, bring fresh meaning to labor games analysis. On the one hand, their emphasis on autonomy makes labor games a more adaptable control mechanism than coercive control methods. On the other hand, their highly individualistic, calculating, and rationalized occupational traits may contradict several guiding characteristics of labor games (e.g., built on collective consent, gaming behaviors cannot simply be read as a rational choice). Additionally, a distinct aspect of this generation of engineers—gamer traits—adds further complexity to the analysis of their labor game practices. This book delves into these complex characteristics and investigates whether they uncover previously uninspected features or may reinvigorate certain forgotten aspects in labor game studies.

The question therefore becomes, How can the distinct nature of the engineering labor process improve game theory in the four directions and revitalize labor game theory? With specific regard to absorption mechanisms, this book critiques the latter as having become almost a tautology of general motivation mechanisms in later labor game narratives (Lupu and Empson 2015; Siciliano 2022). Core absorption elements, such as uncertainty, are, for instance, missing. Given the gamer subjectivity of engineers, it is safe to speculate that labor games that only contain fuzzy motivation mechanisms would hardly be conceived as "games" by engineers. On the contrary, games with substantive absorptive elements (e.g., level of uncertainty, cautiously designed scoring, and ranking system) would be more effective, as engineers are likely to be addicted to and immersed in games. This study thus aims to leverage the gamer subjectivity of engineers to filter out and magnify the strictly defined absorption mechanisms in labor games.

Second, Burawoy and later labor scholars have demonstrated that an essential function of labor games is their obscuring of exploitation (Burawoy and Von Holdt 2012; Mears 2015; Sallaz 2009, 2015; Sherman 2007). As capitalism shifts toward informational capitalism, labor power is primarily defined by innovative capabilities and thus very hard to extract coercively. Given that capitalism's durability relies heavily on how effectively it can obscure the exploitation of innovation, labor scholars seek to reveal the approaches through which the latter occurs and accordingly alert society. Drawing on the case of the tech industry, this book aims to expose whether and how labor games have evolved to embody new, and perhaps slyer, approaches to obscuring exploitation.

With respect to labor subjectivity, this book adopts a feminist approach, synthesizing engineers' off-work subjectivity in the work process and examining how it affects their gaming prescription and strategies. Building on the work of scholars in the creative industry, the relevant literature suggests that engineers' video-game consumption predisposes their gamer subjectivity, which can be interpellated in playing labor games (Bulut 2021; Chess 2017;

Dyer-Witheford and de Peuter 2009; Kirkpatrick 2016; Kücklich 2005; Shaw 2012).[21] I accordingly explore important questions regarding gamer traits. How are they interpellated on the engineering floor to serve capitalist interests? What are the consequences when external subjectivity is involved in the work and game processes? Responding to these queries is essential to understanding the puzzle of labor games in contemporary society. Moreover, I compare the roles of subjectivity in different games and investigate under what conditions workers' subjectivity and gaming structure can (or cannot) be mutually adjusted and how this affects workers' investment in games.

Broadly, this book proposes three primary directions to improve the study of gaming outcomes. First, I investigate whether the organization of the labor game generates the direct outcome of appropriating extra labor power from tech workers. If so, in facing tech workers whose primary labor power is creativity, will games' extracting mechanism be different from those used to extract physical and emotional labor? Secondly, having eliminated the precondition of a single game persisting throughout the labor process, I examine how multiple games can generate varied gaming outcomes on the engineering floor and how this affects engineers' work life. Finally, given the revolutionary features of the tech labor process and workforce, I explore whether production regimes beyond hegemony emerge in the tech industry, building on Burawoy's notion of hegemonic despotism.

Up-Front Technology: Bridging Labor Game Analysis and Game Studies

Last but certainly not least, this book aims to bring the critical role of technology back to labor game analysis in a bid to reinvigorate labor game study in today's society. One central feature of information capitalism is its celebration of the pervasive role of technology: research in the fields of digital labor analysis, management and organization scholarship, creative industries studies, and critical game studies has emerged as influential in the study of the relationship between computer-mediated technology and work processes (Banks and Humphreys 2008; Deterding 2014; Dyer-Witheford and de Peuter 2009; Fuchs 2014; Gandini 2019, Gregg 2013; Kerr 2017; Rosenblat and Stark 2016; Ross 2004). Scholars have demonstrated that emergent digital technology (e.g., chat programs, social media, and platforms for digital distribution or work assemblage) and algorithmic-logic-based techniques (e.g., rating and ranking systems, crowdsourcing, and data tracking) have given rise to new regimes of labor control. Assisted by new technologies, employers strive to erase remaining boundaries between work and off-work spaces, activities, and selves (Bulut 2022; Gandini 2018; Gregg 2016); seduce employees with rather autonomous, flexible, and fun work environments (Banks and O'Connor 2017; Fleming 2014; Gregg 2016) to enhance workers' self-exploitation (Bulut 2022; Legault and Weststart 2015; Whitson 2014); normalize a "permanent upgrade culture" that largely increases workers' precarity and pressure to update skills (Bulut 2022; Dovey and Kennedy 2006; Neff 2012); and diminish the line between work and play to legitimize uncompensated hours of overtime or unpaid labor (Banks and Potts 2010; Kücklich, 2005, 2009).

Among these prevalent studies on technologically driven labor process and control, an approach centered on gamification analysis has attracted a robust discussion (Bogost 2007, 2014; O'Donnell 2014; Whitson 2019). This approach focuses on how employers adopt gamification techniques (e.g., real-time feedback, leveling up, data visualization, and badge collection) to incentivize workers' engagement and passion, increase workers' self-discipline and governance, and enhance their productivity. The rise of the "gamer generation" (or the larger cohort of digital natives) has drastically enlivened critical studies on gamification (Beck and Wade 2006; Bunchball 2010); members of this group grew up computer literate and device empowered, and they expect to work in a gamified environment (Colbert, Tee, and George 2016; Deterding 2014; Yee 2006). Gamified workplaces use video-game elements to engage younger workers, so their work activities are very nonlinear and unpredictable (McGonigal 2011; Rangaswami 2014). Given these contexts, it is unsurprising that critiques on gamification have become prevalent.

The strength of gamification analysis lies in its emphasis on technology, the mechanisms through which technology assists the formation of gamification techniques, and the role of those techniques in individualizing power and manipulating people's behaviors. Whitson (2014), for example, illustrated a major gamification mechanism that entails setting challenges or goals and then rewarding or "leveling up" the worker once they accomplish those goals. This kind of gamification mechanism must be supported by advanced technology through its capacity for perpetually amassing and analyzing large quantities of data in real time—and its ready ability to simplify data into easily digestible illustrations, like progress bars, graphs, and charts (348). Scholars also stress that successful gamification practices rely on behavioral manipulation and monitoring and locate the seeds of that behavioral modification as being planted in the structures of technologically assisted games. For instance, gamification mechanisms like scorekeeping inspire players' competitive behaviors. Unlike traditional labor games that rely on building consent to motivate employee commitment, gamification circumvents this persuasion process by employing technologically enhanced gaming mechanisms that "nudge" individual worker behaviors or, as Scharpe (2014, 21) puts it, develop a "new mode of governmentality" (Bogost 2007; Zuboff 2019). Scholars furthermore caution that gamification is not a neutral technology but is instead designed by "gamification experts" who work for capitalists. The implementation of gamification technology thus essentially serves managerial interests, such as improving efficiency, enabling surveillance, and driving revenue. It also reinforces the economic relations of neoliberal capitalism by diverting workers' attention away from their precarious employment situation (Kelly 2012; Woodcock and Johnson 2018).

Critical studies on gamification offer inspiring insights that reflect on how the incorporation of technology transforms game-playing mechanisms and forms of power domination. Through the lens of game studies, this study explores alternative explanations for labor games on the engineering floor and investigates under what conditions technologically infused labor games facilitate worker discipline not by generating hegemony so much as through behavioral engineering. Inspired by gamification studies, this study underlines the significance of video games in attracting young workers to develop their playing strategies—improving young workers' performance, advancing organizational goals, and "video-gamifying" a post-industrial work environment (Mollick and Rothbard 2014; Mollick and Werback 2014; Seaborn and Fels 2015; Walz and Deterding 2014).

Although labor game studies on gamification present the new and radically disruptive characteristics of technologically centered work control, they still contain a few weaknesses. For instance, several researchers are puzzled by why many technologically enabled gamification mechanisms can only generate prescribed and inhibited fun, have a short shelf life, and are eventually trivialized for their inability to attract workers' interests and consent (Mollick and Rothbard 2014; Statler, Heracleous, and Jacobs 2011; Tritten, Fieseler, and Maltseva 2019). Woodcock and Johnson (2018) explains the unsustainability of most gamification mechanisms as due to the fact that they all belong to the "game-from-above" category, where management imposes gaming elements on work to promote regulation and surveillance. He urges instead a focus on "gamification-from-below," where workers transform work into real games through subversion and ridicule rather than simply incorporating gaming elements into work (Woodcock and Johnson 2018, 543). Woodcock and Johnson suggest that this perspective allows workers to discover the "true gamification of everyday life," which is more authentic, sustainable, and ingrained.

This study suggests, however, that marrying labor game studies and gamification analysis can significantly enrich our understanding and offer a more nuanced analysis of these newly adopted game setups and mechanics. As labor game theorists report, the balanced level of a game's uncertainty plays a crucial role in ensuring the game's absorption: when workers perceive the game's outcome to be beyond their control (i.e., either too certain or too uncertain), they lose interest in investing in the game and strategizing their play. Following this train of thought, one can infer that many managerially im-

posed games fail to capture workers' interest because of their rigid gamification setup, which leaves little room for uncertainty, unpredictability, and
spontaneity. Integrating both game studies and labor game analysis furthermore allows us to recognize that the two approaches differently perceive the
role of management in games. Classic labor game analysis highlights the role
of lower-level management in organizing labor games on the shop floor, while
upper management largely avoids intervening or even disapproves of these
games due to their rebellious and output-restrictive nature (Burawoy 1979;
Clawson and Fantasia 1983). In contrast, the gamification literature emphasizes the critical role of upper-level management in designing and implementing gamification mechanics and the lesser involvement of lower-level management (Deterding 2014; Crain, Poster, and Cherry 2016). Consolidating these
two perspectives reminds us of the pertinent roles of both upper and lower
levels of management in games and the need to explore their different natures.

In sum, bridging two approaches—game studies and labor game analysis—allows this study to surface the essential preconditions that ensure gamification's success (and without which it can barely impact workers at all). In
the meantime, by reinvigorating labor game studies, this book hopes to challenge the notion that classic labor game studies are ill-equipped to engage
these new labor phenomena (Crain, Poster, and Cherry 2016; Thompson and
Smith 2009).

Book Structure and Chapter Outline

Chapter 2. Welcoming Gamers to the Wonderland— A Workplace Permeated with Games

Chapter 2 outlines the "gamer generation" and how gamers are imported into
the tech industry. The story begins with the formation of gamer subjectivity
in informational capitalism, sketching the image of gamers in the tech industry: how gamers are constructed along race, gender, and age lines; how
gamer traits—ties between gaming and programming passion, modding attitudes, and heroic ethos—are valorized in defining the ideal gamer image.
The lens moves onto the engineering floor in the second half of the chapter,
examining how the field of games has become a contested terrain for managers and workers. Thus, Chapter 2 offers a comprehensive description of more
than fifty games played on the work floor, such as coding games, code-review
games, debugging games, training games, grinding games, hazing games, and
hacking games. To illustrate the playing field, I categorize these games into
four game groups—simulation games, racing games, crowdsourcing games,
and pranking games—and further divide each group into dominant and scat-

tered games. This chapter offers a brief overview of these dominant and scattered games, including their basic playing rules, their embeddedness (if any) into specific labor processes, and their functions and outcomes.

Chapter 3. Simulation Games and the Establishment of Gamified Governmentality

Chapters 3 through 5 make up the story's ethnographic heart and discuss the four most representative games. Each game represents a unique configuration of managers' and workers' efforts to negotiate, invest, and strive for control over production processes. These chapters cover why games are constructed in such formats, what playing strategies engineers adopt for them, and how the productive gamer subjectivity is constituted via games.

Unlike other games that aim to establish a hegemonic production relationship, the simulation game stands out for its effort to construct a regime beyond hegemony: "gamified governmentality." Chapter 3 starts by delineating the scrum software development process—the vessel of the simulation game—and describes how the contradiction between the instability associated with the permanent-beta development process and engineers' demand for stability to establish trustworthy collaborative relationships presents an internal paradox to scrum development.

The chapter then moves on to depict how simulation games are organized to conceal this contradiction, normalize the uncertainty, and reduce anxiety. Drawing on such examples as Dungeons and Dragons (D&D) scrum games and the *Game of Thrones* (*GoT*) metaphor game, this chapter shows how managers draw on video-game narratives, procedures, characters, themes, and artifacts to simulate the mythical video-gaming environment and glorify the sense of uncertainty inherent in the tech environment, framing it as a feeling of adventure as experienced in most video games. Echoing managers' metaphorical reference to software development as an adventure, these engineers imagine themselves as "saviors" for their team as they successfully pull the team through a "life-and-death" crisis. Consequently, engineers' productivity is boosted and a "productive gamer subjectivity" is constituted as well. After detailing the organization of the simulation game, this chapter wraps up by illustrating that the simulation game represents the future of workplace games, which seek to constitute a gamified governmentality.

Chapter 4. Hegemony or Not: The Comparison between the Collection and the Ticket Game

Chapter 4 presents the comparative cases of two hegemonic games: crowdsourcing games and racing games. This chapter begins by asking why racing games successfully establish a "gamified hegemony" in the on-call work process while crowdsourcing games fail to elicit workers' consent to participate, ultimately leading to a "mock hegemony." Chapter 4 first unpacks the game of collection, viewed as the most representative crowdsourcing game, which is designed to attract engineers to contribute extra efforts to bricolage tasks. In theory, this game design should appeal to engineers' modder traits—a reference to gamers' habits of voluntarily helping video-game companies modify their games' design and setup. However, the strong rigidity of the gamification setup causes the collection game to fail at reproducing the fun of video gaming and renders the game incapable of mobilizing engineers' gaming subjectivity. Questioning and contesting the collection game, engineers adopt three coping strategies: practical tactics, performance strategy, and perfunctory approach.

Building on the analysis of the collection game, the chapter proceeds to discuss racing games and explains how they differ from crowdsourcing games. As one of the most typical racing games, the ticket game successfully induces a sense of urgency and competitiveness in engineers' maintenance tasks. The narrative of the ticket game begins with how it abandons the gamification approach pursued by the collection game, which is characterized by a strict adherence to the gamification setup to modify engineers' behaviors. The description of the ticket game highlights that the classic labor game rule to intensify competition is at the heart of the game. Following the general portrayal of the organization of ticket games, this chapter diverts its attention to the role of engineers' gamer subjectivity: it is this subjectivity that ensures engineers closely monitor their team's every move up and down the leaderboard and inspires them to develop gaming strategies, such as ticket marathons, weekend ticket sprints, or hackathons to boost their team's rank. Chapter 4 concludes by illustrating how the comparison of two games demonstrates varying approaches to gamification, evident in aspects like setup, middle-level management involvement, and gamer subjectivity mobilization, leading to the constitution of different regimes.

Chapter 5. The Donut Email Game and the Construction of Chaotic Fun

Chapter 5 presents a different type of game—pranking games. Pranking games approximate classic working-class labor games. They barely mobilize engineers' gamer subjectivity and hardly incorporate any gamification techniques; the fun culture constructed is closer to blue-collar horseplay fun than the video-gaming fun created in other tech workplace games. On the surface, pranking games like those that haze newcomers contribute another layer of chaos to Behemoth; however, these games contain the hidden order beneath this anarchy. The corporate culture—as manifested through "fun, freedom, and casualness"—is articulated through these culture games and becomes the key force that guides workers' behaviors as shown in work scheduling, participating in the virtual community, and even maintaining dress codes.

After depicting some frequently played pranking games, this chapter moves on to narrate the organization of the donut game, the most typical and systematically organized pranking game. Documenting engineers' playing performance in the donut game allows this chapter to explore the divisions within the labor force. Game supporters' playing strategies show how the donut game operates as a means of confirming workplace culture and conducting mutual surveillance. Conversely, game challengers utilize the game as a way to express their resistance to the company's senses of penalty, surveillance, and humiliation. Challengers' strategies, such as "creating a false alarm," are analyzed in this section. Chapter 5 also points out that in the gaming field, pranking games are indispensable for ensuring the permeation of hegemony. Indeed, while racing games ensure hegemony in maintenance work and simulation games establish hegemony in software development, pranking games guarantee hegemony in engineers' daily interactions. However, unlike racing games or simulation games that produce a relatively stable hegemonic state in the engineering work process, pranking games can only form "occasional hegemonic states."

Chapter 6. Out of the Game: Peasant Coders' Suffering under Behemoth's Gamification

Chapter 6 focuses on Asian migrant engineers in the U.S. tech industry, who are considered "outsiders" for most games organized on the engineering floor. The chapter starts by depicting the influx of Asian migrant workers in the tech industry and then illustrates how these engineers' lack of gamer subjectivity determines their difficulties in integrating into Behemoth's gameful environment. In fact, Asian engineers' "peasant coder subjectivity," characterized by the "precarious self," "hardworking self," and "providing self," profoundly contradicts white engineers' gamer subjectivity.

After sketching a general image of "peasant coders," this chapter moves on to analyze peasant coders' game-playing strategies, which are quite different from those of their white counterparts. Peasant coders' attitudes to simulation games are complicated: some embrace simulation games wholeheartedly and blur the boundaries between video-gaming and work activities, relationships, and spaces; however, this group of peasant coders then encounters a dilemma in which their white colleagues conflate their aggressive gaming characters with their working characters. Other groups of peasant coders, on the other hand, try to resist white engineers' conflation of working and playing strategies by completely separating their video-gaming relationships from their working relationships. If peasant coders' attitudes toward the simulation game can be interpreted as ambiguous, their attitudes to the badge game and ticket game are much more straightforward: doubt and criticism. Peasant coders draw on their "hardworking self" and refuse to romanticize serious maintenance working processes into collecting and sprinting games. Finally, peasant coders worry that participation in pranks creates hostility toward colleagues and emphasizes their precarious status; therefore, these coders develop a perfunctory approach to coping with pranking games, one that attempts to minimize the humiliation of their colleagues.

Chapter 7. Conclusion

The conclusion sums up the empirical findings of the study and discusses their relevance to labor studies. The concluding chapter also offers a space for reflection: here, I turn from process to cause and reflect on key issues: Why have games transformed and reformed under informational capitalism? Why does gamer subjectivity matter? Why do some games become self-sustaining and effective controlling mechanisms while others become increasingly hollow and eventually fail? In other words, the conclusion shifts from a narrative of the game-organization processes to an account of why games matter. This study is an effort to update labor game study for a modern work environment under informational capitalism, not only through recognizing the formation of a field of games but also by highlighting how various games themselves have dramatically changed—as have their roles, mechanisms, and influence over how work gets done. Labor games are no longer a single-function control method to elicit consent; instead, modern tech workplaces employ a field of games in which games function as a new type of governmentality that permeates every corner of industrial life, one that ultimately turns the powerful gamer generation into a powerless labor force.

2

WELCOMING GAMERS TO THE WONDERLAND—A WORKPLACE PERMEATED WITH GAMES

Rumor had it that Mark was going to quit playing *Counter-Strike: Global Offensive (CS:GO)*—one of his favorite games—and he had been so dedicated to getting all his work teammates onboard with playing it together. Even more shocking was that Mark seemed to quit playing video games altogether. Not that it was abnormal for a gamer to quit video games; on the contrary, it was common to spot gamers quitting, even though most of them returned to play all over again sooner or later.

Nevertheless, no one would imagine Mark quitting playing; he was widely known as the most hardcore gamer in Pipe Org. Pipe Org was rife with gossip about Mark's obsession with video games. To name a few, Mark grew up in a broken family—his father ditched his family when he was a baby in a swaddle, and his big brothers were all in jail. According to Mark, if he hadn't found bliss in video games, he would have committed suicide long ago. Gaming also led Mark to realize that he was gifted in computing and programming. After graduating from the University of Michigan and while working at Behemoth, Mark's life remained defined by video games. For example, his mother bonded with him through video games; whenever Mark readied to start a newly released game, his mother would send him home-made brownies with a sticky note on the box that read, "Eat these when you are playing the latest version of Final Fantasy!!" or "Brownies go well with the new CS:GO!" Not only that but, to Mark, buying gaming gear was the whole point of earning a salary: he slept on a $30 inflatable bed but sat on a $4,000 gaming chair.

His gaming TV screen was worth more than $5,000—and the gaming PC cost more than $6,000.

Before long, the puzzle behind why Mark quit gaming was cracked by his fellow workers on the Wizard team. It turned out that Mark's colleague Amir reached the level of "Master Guardian Elite" in *CS:GO*—two levels higher than Mark—in an unbelievably short time. It was indeed quite an achievement: Amir had just started to play *CS:GO* with the Wizard team less than three weeks prior. Mark, on the other hand, had played *CS:GO* for many years and was stuck at the "Master Guardian I" level.

Mark's Wizard teammates sympathized with his situation to a large degree and worried that abandoning video games did him no good. Wizard team engineers seized every opportunity to encourage Mark to come back and play with them. I encountered one such persuasive occasion. It was lunchtime, and several engineers—most from the Wizard team, plus Ben and Philip from the Knights—sat around the bar table in the public kitchen, eating together and comforting Mark. Danny took the lead and told Mark he enjoyed playing with him much more than Amir. Moreover, Danny emphasized that he did not think Amir was a good player no matter his ranking. Other wizard team engineers interjected:

> "Danny's right. . . . Amir is always like, when everyone decided to go one direction, he would definitely go in the opposite direction."

> "And I remember he quitted in the middle of our game one time. . . . We lost the game just for that. . . . So ridiculous."

> "Wasn't he banned from another game before? Like he changed at least three account numbers?"

> "Seriously . . . he is so self-centered . . . like a spoiled child. . . . I heard his dad is a general in Pakistan . . . and they even had servants there. . . . Maybe that's the reason . . . he is so used to being served."

> "Yeah, tell me about it. . . . I worked with him on the 'demon project.' I felt like I was his servant."

> "Peter's right. He doesn't just play solo. . . . He is not a very good co-operator at work either."

I could not know whether Mark was being soothed by his teammates, but I was clearly aware that Amir was not very popular among his team. Amir's unpopularity was underlined in the Wizard team's retrospective meeting. Often, the development team incorporated a team-optimizing game into the retrospective meeting, which was used to encourage engineers to propose fun ideas to "patch" the team setup. On that day, the manager, Vikram, collected patching ideas and posed them as "action items" during the meeting. Led by Peter, the Wizard team proposed two action items: "finding Mark a new game" and "trading Amir for Ben."[1] The second action item—trading Amir for Ben—had a double meaning. It implied the Wizard team wanted Ben to replace Amir in their team's *CS:GO* game—and hinted that the development team wanted to trade him for Ben, too. Amir became visibly uncomfortable at that moment. Seeing this, Vikram immediately smoothed things over by proposing to put "finding Mark a new game" on the whiteboard as an action item for the next sprint.

At first glance, Mark's story seemed reasonably logical. After all, any workplace can have obsessive and competitive gamers like Mark and Amir. Any workplace can have sympathetic colleagues like the Wizard teammates, who would go the extra mile for their coworker. However, mulling over the story stripped away the surface normality and revealed the puzzles lurking beneath. Can *any* workplace be filled with gamers? Is it typical for work teammates in the daytime to all transform into battle comrades at night? Also, why can off-hours gaming activities be seamlessly brought up in work meetings and even encouraged by managers?

A Glimpse of the Gamers at Behemoth

To get a handle on these puzzles, it is necessary to first examine who these engineers are and how their gaming behaviors relate to their engineering work. Chapter 2 is divided into two parts, which attempt to investigate these workers and their behaviors. The first part of the chapter elaborates on who the gamers are; how gamer identity is constructed along gendered, racialized, and age lines; and what gamer traits these engineers embody. To give an overview of the gamer image, I start by providing a demographic description of interviewees at my field site.

I divide my interviewees into two groups: gamers and nongamers. Among sixty-six interviewees, there were twenty-nine gamers and thirty-seven nongamers (see Table 2.1). One thing that needs highlighting is that nongamers are very likely to be video-game players in the tech context, even though they do not self-identify as gamers and generally invest less time and intensity into their gameplay than those who identify as gamers.[2] While 43.9 percent of my informants were gamers, take note that the gamers have been further divided into two groups: self-identified gamers, or "explicit gamers," and "implicit gamers"—the other group of engineers who do not self-identify as gamers but possess prominent gamer traits. When interviewees explicitly self-identify as "gamer," "game hobbyist," "MMO addict,"[3] "hardcore gamer," "PCf*g,"[4]

TABLE 2.1 A PROFILE OF INTERVIEWEES					
	Nongamer engineers	Implicit gamer engineers	Explicit gamer engineers	All gamer engineers	All engineers
Race (number)					
White	11	4	11 (73.3%)	15 (57.7%)	26
Asian	23	11	3 (21.4%)	14 (37.8%)	37
Hispanic	3	0	0	0	3
Gender (number)					
Male	26	12	13 (52.0%)	25 (43.9%)	51
Female	11	3	1 (25.0%)	4 (26.7%)	15
Age (year)					
Mean	28.9	26.5	27.2	27.5	28.2
Median	28	26	25	26	27
Total (number)	37	15 (51.7%)	14 (48.2%)	29 (43.9%)	66

or "sort-of gamer," I categorize them as "explicit gamers" (see Table 2.1 and Appendix B). According to this categorization, fourteen engineers self-identify as gamers and account for 48.2 percent of gamers. Those engineers who do not call themselves gamers but still possess predominant gaming traits—implicit gamers[5]—merit equal attention. After all, implicit gamers' traits remain interpellated and converted into "productive gamer subjectivity" in the gamified workplace under certain circumstances. According to my observation, at least fifteen engineers were "implicit gamers," accounting for 51.7 percent of all gamers in my informant cohort.

One should be aware that structural factors such as race and gender play vital roles in shaping gamer identities and gaming behaviors. The demographic information of my interviewees offers a glimpse into the relationship between race and gamer identity. The percentage of white gamers in their white cohort is higher when compared to Asian gamers among Asians (57.7% vs. 37.8%). Also, white gamers are more likely to self-identify as a gamer than Asian engineers: while 73.3 percent of white gamers are self-labeled, only 21.4 percent of Asian engineers self-identify as gamers.

But why is there such a racial divergence? In Western society, passions for programming and video gaming highly overlap, and video-game players seem more likely and motivated to do programming work. Such an overlap is the legacy of the earlier development of the Western gaming industry. In the 1990s, video-game players brought home games as well as programming manuals, and players were very accustomed to typing in codes to start and modify games (Kirkpatrick 2012). This blurring of boundaries between gaming and programming as separate hobbies, activities, and identities dominated at Behemoth. For example, three white gamers—Danny, Mark, and Matt—formed the so-called Michigan Gang within the Wizard team. The Michigan Gang was very close-knit, not because they graduated from the same university but because they all dared to take an extremely tough game design course at a certain point in their undergraduate study. As Danny explained, "We took the course not for the credit. If we were doing it for the credit, we'd take some course less risky [an easier class]. We took it . . . more like chasing a childhood dream. We all have the experience tweaking around computers, making games as kids. Taking an actual game design course . . . it's like a dream come true." Behemoth abounded with white engineers like the Michigan Gang, people who were gamers before becoming engineers and whose gaming passion propelled them into programming jobs. Indeed, gamers are the ideal job candidates for the tech industry. As Paul, the Ranger team manager, explained, "The guy you want to hire is the guy who's been in his basement playing with his computer his whole life." In other words, white video-game players who go into programming work are likely to be gamers.

However, I want to emphasize that the "gamer-programmer" is not a disembodied worker. This gamer-programmer is actually a white man: white men's gaming identity and the memories produced by the gaming industry specific to the neoliberal Western society are subsumed into the image of the gamer-programmer. Asian engineers, for instance, belong to a completely different gaming and social context. For one thing, Asian video-game players did not grow up in the gaming development phase when gaming was very technical and approximated to programming, leading games to be apprehended as a piece of code. Instead, Asian players grew up in a different era: the online video-game industry has been booming in India and China since 2005, accompanied by the rapid proliferation of internet cafés in both countries (Messner 2019; Singh 2020; Stang and Hoftun 2007). The blurring of gaming and programming memories hardly happened among Asians.

Divergent social context further separated the gaming and programming identities of white and Asian engineers. As is detailed in Chapter 6, Asian engineers' choice to study computer science is embedded in a completely different higher educational ideology: instead of chasing individualist interests like their white peers, Asian engineers adopt a pragmatic approach and believe the ultimate goal of higher education is to secure a job (Ma 2020). This contrast was made clear when Guang, a twenty-seven-year-old engineer, talked about his choice of major. When we first met, he told me he had actually preferred the humanities to science: "I wanted to choose the humanities track [*xuan wen ke*] for Gaokao [the National College Entrance Examination] back then . . . but my parents told me that 'there is no future in studying humanities' and they warned me that it would be very difficult to get a job if I studied humanities . . . so I chose to go the science track for Gaokao . . . and after that, I majored in math and then computer science. . . . Then everything after that seemed very natural." It is not uncommon to see Asian engineers who have no interest in video games or programming choose to major in computer science. In light of the different social contexts, the proportions of gamers among Asian and white engineers makes more sense.

Equally remarkable is the self-identification gap between white and Asian engineers (73.3% of white engineers identified as gamers vs. 21.4% of Asian engineers), meaning that Asians are much more hesitant to label themselves as gamers than their white colleagues. This phenomenon can be attributed to two factors. First, Asian engineers questioned the valorization of the gamer identity on the engineering floor. For example, Fang, a twenty-seven-year-old Chinese engineer, pointed out that many of his white colleagues viewed programming as an extension of their gaming hobby. Just like gamers who obsessed over their favorite games, these white engineers "devoted 100 percent or 150 percent of their energy to work" once the coding projects interested them. However, when these gamers caught a project that they were not passionate about, they "asked for OOTO [out of the office] straight for two days." To Fang, when white gamers' productivity relied on their passion, they became less professional. And like Fang, a majority of Asian engineers tried to disassociate themselves from such a gamer image, attempting instead to establish a "professional" image in the workplace.

Additionally, Asian engineers distanced themselves from the gamer identity out of consideration for the negative stereotype associated with Asian gamers. Like their white peers, many Asian engineers were intensive and hardcore players; the problem was that the aggressiveness, dominance, and competitiveness displayed in games by these engineers did not match the stereotypical traits perceived to be associated with Asian engineers (e.g., humble, modest, conservative, and submissive). This dissonance stirred up white engineers' resentment. Some white engineers commented on Asian engineers' playing styles as "crazy fights," "aggressive as fuck," or "as if in a deathmatch." During my field trip, I encountered a couple of times when white engineers "joked" about how "domineering" and "self-centered" these Asian engineers were. Matt once even associated his Asian colleague's "self-centeredness" with the "one-child policy." Another white gamer, Peter, challenged me to play *League of Legends* (*LOL*) with two Asian engineers; he bet I would curse at them, as "it's just so damn hard to not curse at them because of how aggressive they are." In other words, once Asian engineers emphasized their gamer identity, they were very likely to be associated with these negative stereotypical images. In response, Asian engineers understandably refused to reveal their gamer identity.

Gender was another factor contributing to the shape of gaming culture and gamer identity. In general, female engineers' gender identity seems to conflict with the gamer identity at Behemoth. My informants' demographic records and my interviewees' narratives support this phenomenon. Statistically, only four out of fifteen female interviewees can be counted as gamers (26.7%; see Table 2.1). In comparison, among fifty-one male interviewees, twenty-five counted as gamers (43.9%). Only 25 percent of female engineers self-identified as gamers, whereas 52 percent of male gamers self-identified as such.

To some extent, the gamer identity became a critical factor that increased the exclusion of women engineers at Behemoth. Female engineers who were not gamers tended to view gamers' obsessive play as unhealthy. GY, a twenty-five-year-old Chinese engineer who studied computer science at Indiana University and worked on the Assassin team, commented that she felt confused about why those guys wanted to spend all their spare time playing video games. She told me she filled her spare time with different activities, such as taking care of her pets, kayaking, and hiking. GY had many social circles—she frequently video chatted with her old friends from Indiana about food, pets, even hairstyles—and she kept making new friends during her outdoor activities. She pointed out, very modestly, that she thought one reason these gamers were so "obsessed" and "cared so much about winning games" was their lack of other hobbies and social circles.

Compared to GY's modesty, Andi was more straightforward in her criticism of gamers and how gaming culture and gamer identities were entrenched at Behemoth. Andi was a twenty-eight-year-old white engineer who used to work at Starbucks. In 2011, Andi started to learn computer science, following her husband, a software engineer. In 2014, Andi joined Behemoth. When we talked about her team's gamers, she told me that she found that they had a particular game/work schedule: they usually stayed up until 2:00 A.M. playing games. Some of these night owls would get so excited after playing games at midnight that they ended up wide awake, so they would start coding or send out code reviews—sometimes at 3:00 A.M. Of course, these gamers would then come to the office very late, at around eleven in the morning. Andi complained that this made communication with these gamers very difficult. As an early bird, Andi got up at 6:30 A.M., arrived at work at 8:00, and usually tried to leave work before 4:00 P.M. to avoid traffic. As a result, the overlapping working time between her and her teams' gamers was regularly less than four hours long. Once, Andi raised this issue with her manager during their one-on-one meeting—but inexplicably, the manager persuaded her to try harder to understand and support these gamers. As Andi narrated: "My manager told me that he used to play games till midnight. . . . He said something like, 'Their brains get excited after gaming.' . . . 'They can work more focused then.' . . . I just don't buy it. Most ridiculously, he asked me to try harder to *fit in*." When I ran into Andi a few weeks later, she told me that she transferred to the Assassin team, which she considered less "exclusive" than her old team. Andi's encounter was not unique: other female interviewees expressed that the valorization of gaming culture created a relatively unfriendly work environment and marked their outsider status. Other studies have also warned that celebrating gamer identity could lower female engineers' sense of commitment to the engineering workplace and the STEM field overall (Cheryan et al. 2009).

For female gamers at Behemoth, their general gaming practices approximate those of typical female gamers depicted by game scholars (e.g., underestimating playing time and sometimes distancing themselves from gamer identification). This gaming approach is considered a display of femininity (Lucas and Sherry 2004; Shaw 2012). However, some female engineers' gaming choices, it should be noted, contradict those of typical female gamers: some female engineers show great enthusiasm for hardcore, hypercompetitive video games.

Elizabeth, a twenty-seven-year-old female engineer, illustrates this contradiction. She graduated from UCLA and worked in the Unified team at Behemoth. We met in Las Vegas when Elizabeth participated in a global cloud computing conference. When we met during the daytime, Elizabeth wore her hair short, with no makeup, and dressed in a hoodie sweatshirt with rolled-up sleeves, exposing her arm tattoos. Elizabeth was very straightforward about her "hardcore gamer" identity; she frequently stayed up all night playing games. She told me that she was distinctly aware that her gaming performance improved after these overnights. Elaborating on her gaming preference, Elizabeth said she just played multiplayer online battle arena (MOBA) games such as *League of Legends* (*LOL*) and *Defense of the Ancients 2* (*DOTA 2*). MOBA games usually involve two teams of players fighting each other on a predefined battlefield while trying to destroy the opposing team's base within a limited time (e.g., twenty to forty minutes). MOBA games are considered one of the most hardcore, as they are very aggressive, intense, and competitive.

Then, I asked Elizabeth what the most attractive thing about MOBA games was. Elizabeth replied promptly that the feeling of conquering something within a very tight timeline made the game very appealing. At the end of our conversation, I was so encouraged by Elizabeth's frankness that I even tried to ask her why she stressed her "hardcore" player identity. Elizabeth paused for a moment and then told me that she liked anything hardcore, not just video games: she had always been a fan of hardcore science. After entering tech, she found she liked hardcore coding, preferred backstage to frontstage projects, and loved dealing with underlying code—the more underlying, the better.

In general, Elizabeth's narrative demonstrates her cultural "passing" as just one of the guys not only manifested in how she played games but also in how her gaming habits paralleled her working style (e.g., a preference for hardcore science, projects, and coding). Elizabeth's contrast between hard and soft science has a clear gender implication: previous research proves that people stereotypically associate hard science (e.g., physics, chemistry, biology) with masculinity while attaching soft science (e.g., psychology, sociology, political science) to femininity (Carli et al. 2017; Munro and Munro 2014). In other words, by self-identifying as a hardcore player and programmer, Elizabeth distances herself from traditional heterosexual femininity. From another perspective, the highlight of her gamer identity is a gendering strategy, one that has been touched upon by other scholars who investigate gender issues in the tech industry. For example, Alfrey and Twine (2017) observed that some female engineers tried to downplay their femininity and emphasize their geekiness as associated with computer-related hobbies (e.g., video gaming, watching *Star Trek*).

Turning to the age profiles of my interviewees, I find that gamers are slightly younger than nongamers. The average age for gamers is 27.5, which is about 1.5 years younger than nongamers (28.9 years), and gamers' median age (26 years old) is 2 years younger than that of nongamers (28 years old). However, as shown by the age profiles of this study, age does not constitute a vital variable in differentiating explicit gamers and implicit gamers. This observation supports other scholars' statements, in which most gamers are described as young (e.g., Shaw 2012). It is not difficult to speculate why gamers skew young; after all, gaming gradually becomes less important in these engineers' lives once they transition from boyhood to manhood and their life cycle moves to the next stage (e.g., getting married and raising children). For example, Dujuan, the wife of an engineer named Liang, once told me that she was delighted that Liang had replaced his old hobby of tweaking PCs and game consoles with a new hobby of building fences for their house. Liang later explained to me that there was an internal connection between these activities: "Look, I like tuning a machine or modding hardware because I like the feeling of tweaking around and building stuff. Now I try fence building. It still involves building something new and experimenting. So it's still quite fun and rewarding." Liang's trajectory revealed a rather common pattern among several interviewees, who reported that after marriage they had more or less experienced a switch in leisure time activities from gameplay to more family-oriented activities.

On a final note, my sample is not diverse enough to generalize any pattern about the relationship between sexuality and gamer identity. Among sixty-six interviewees, only one male engineer identified as gay; he also identified himself as an explicit gamer. Of course, this one instance of an interviewee does not rule out the possibility that some interviewees who identified as gamers were inclined to be silent about their sexual orientation.

Constructing Ideal Gamers on the Engineering Floor

The gamer identity discussed in this book is not static; it is produced on the engineering floor. In fact, it is striking to me how much work is involved in building and enacting an "ideal" gamer image in the office: gamers are constituted as the desirable subjects who embody the exemplary gamer traits. As is illustrated in the following chapters, such gamer traits are constructed and forged in the field of games. Indeed, through investing in these labor games, most engineers—implicit and explicit gamers, and engineers who are video-game players in a general sense—enact these traits and transform into "productive gamers."

Programming or Gaming? Work or Habit?
It's So Difficult to Tell

An important gamer trait that most gamers bring up repeatedly is the blurring between gaming and programming memories, skills, and feelings of achievement. Many gamers admitted that their passion for programming started with playing video games. Bill's recollection was typical:

> I grew up in a farmhouse, kind of in the middle of nowhere. I guess I had always played a lot of video games as a kid . . . playing like Nintendo . . . or tweaking around on the computer. . . . Back then . . . when you bought the Commodore 64, it came with a basic programming book. . . . So the assumption was that . . . you bought it because you wanted to write your own software. . . . Then I just . . . I remember working with my dad. We made a game where . . . there's a little jet that flies across the screen, and there's like a dam. And when you press the spacebar, it drops like a little bomb . . . and ever since . . . I was teaching myself to program just as a hobby, for fun, and then I got to do an internship. . . . I feel like I just kind of ended up doing programming ever since.

Bill, a twenty-nine-year-old white male engineer, self-identified as a gamer. From his narrative, one can see his memories of his gaming activities (i.e., playing Nintendo games[6]) happened alongside his memories of programming a new bomb-dropping game. This pattern is very common among many gamers, who all expressed a feeling of accomplishment from playing games they programmed themselves. To some extent, this blurring of gaming and programming joy is a distinct trait of the gamer generation: as Kirkpatrick (2012) analyzed, members of the gamer generation—those who typically had experience playing video games on home computers before the 1990s—were more likely to apprehend the game object as a piece of code/software, and they were accustomed to coding in order to start or modify a game.

As discussed briefly above, this gamer trait—the blurring of gaming and programming skills—was racialized to a large degree and localized in a Western context. It was not until the beginning of the twenty-first century that a majority of Asian children were able to play video games. By then, video games had evolved to become much more user-friendly; they were not sold "with a programming book" and did not ask players to develop programming skills in order to play them. During my conversations with Asian engineers, it was clear that most of them do not have memories that intertwine gaming and programming experience—and their lack of these memories also marks their lack of gaming traits.

In Bill's narrative, he identified that his isolated childhood (e.g., "I grew up in a farmhouse . . . in the middle of nowhere") was an important factor behind his concentration on video games. Other gamers further associated their isolated childhood with their introverted personality and asserted that this type of personality underlies the gaming and programming culture. Tony (white male engineer, twenty-four years old, implicit gamer) in Pipe Org explained, "A lot of the programming culture . . . stems from young people who are gamers . . . who socially not so—they are not socially ready. . . . A lot of programmers don't know how to properly talk to . . . interact with others as coworkers, as friends . . . but they feel more comfortable when playing games with each other . . . because they grow up in an isolated-type environment." Many gamers echoed Tony's explanation and said that their isolated childhood and introverted personality pushed them to retreat to the virtual world and channel all their passion into video games.

Over time, the virtual gaming community became the foundation of these gamers' lives, even to the extent that sometimes gamers relied on their gaming community to overcome their struggles with real-life social activities. For example, Danny shared that it took him three weeks to open his mouth to say "Hi" to Little Zach, an engineer from another team. He eventually felt comfortable talking with Little Zach in real life after running into him on the Steam platform,[7] and they played *Final Fantasy* together for several nights. Their first in-person conversations at Behemoth consisted of chatting about the game and only later broadened to include work topics.

One thing to note is that Danny's social practices would not have been feasible in non-tech-firm settings. In other workplaces, a reliance on video games for socialization with colleagues would be considered "nerdy," "geeky," and "socially awkward"—but at Behemoth, this "gaming-social" strategy is celebrated. In addition, Behemoth raises the status of gamers like Danny, who excelled at gaming and tended to use those skills to make up for other short-comings: the company upholds the gamer image during the recruiting process and stresses that gamers are ideal candidates. As Paul, the Ranger team manager, put it:

> I would definitely . . . I mean, I have a personal bias towards . . . The people that, as kids, just felt compelled to experiment and play and teach themselves the computer—those are the guys that are going to be the good engineers. You don't want . . . people [who] are like, "Oh, I want to be an engineer because it pays me money" and start learning in college. The guy you want to hire is the guy who's been in his basement playing with his computer his whole life.

Here, Paul makes it very clear who the ideal job candidates for Behemoth are: gamers—who tend to view "experimenting" and "playing" with computers as synonymous and who are so obsessed with games that they would rather stay in the basement to play them—are going to be "the good engineers." People motivated to enter the industry by monetary rewards, on the other hand, are not ideal candidates. This discourse is widely agreed upon at Behemoth; many gamers express the idea that "true gamers" enter the industry not for money but for meeting like-minded friends and learning cutting-edge technology. Monetary rewards have never been gamers' priority, and some gamers told me they did not know how to spend their salary beyond constantly updating their gaming consoles, mechanical keyboards, gaming mice, and headphones. The problem with this perspective is that such a strong emphasis on gaming culture—and gamers' "pure" interests and motivations—largely excludes Asian and female engineers, as discussed above.

True Gamers as the "Playbor": Modding New Products for Fun

Another gamer trait is the adoption of modding as a hobby.[8] Modding, which refers to the act of modifying or creating alternate game content, is an important part of gaming culture (Kücklich 2005). While not all gamers self-label as modders outright, many of them have rich modding experiences, such as adding new code or elements to existing games, taking advantage of game bugs, publishing new mods, and tweaking gaming hardware (e.g., consoles). Modding is a time-consuming hobby and takes up most of the modders' leisure time. Mark, the engineer who tattooed his name in binary on his arm and claimed to be an enthusiastic *CS:GO* modder, discussed his hobby of "building video-game mods" and parallelized it with his newly developed habit of "testing out new frameworks at Behemoth":

> Well, I guess it's like . . . I just love tweaking around. . . . I used to build [video-game] mods in my spare time as a hobby, for fun. . . . But now [that] I am at Behemoth, there's a lot of projects I can do. . . . I might want to test out some new framework.[9] . . . Or just . . . I don't know . . . Behemoth is nice because there's so many problems to solve and it provides enough tools and resources for me to play.

Mark perceived his efforts of testing out new frameworks as a continuation of his old modding hobby. Notice that the sense of "playfulness" is an important factor Mark drew on to link his game-modding and framework-testing activities; he builds mods for "fun," and Behemoth provides many projects for him to "play" with. The problem with this perception is that since playfulness derives from modding, gamers are vulnerable to exploitation. As Kücklich (2005) claims, the key to modders' precarity is that modding is always perceived as a type of "leisure play" but rarely constructed as a type of "productive work." However, modders' hobby of choice contains significant innovative value and a commercial nature, which can be effortlessly appropriated by the video-game industry. More problematically, gamers' perception of modding—as a way of having fun, not work per se—is imported wholesale onto the engineering floor. As shown from Mark's quotes, whenever Behemoth's gamers interpret a "test out" of the firm's new framework from a modders' perspective, they highlight the playfulness of it as a leisure activity. To Behemoth, however, this leisure activity is highly productive and contains enormous business opportunities.

Mark identified another factor contributing to his unabated enthusiasm for modding Behemoth's projects: Behemoth "provides enough tools and resources" to facilitate his "play." As discussed in Chapter 4, Behemoth is skilled in establishing crowdsourcing platforms to aggregate bricolage tasks[10] or projects, provide useful resources (e.g., modding tools, programs, tutorials, FAQs), and ease connections between volunteers and development teams in need of modding efforts. Several other gamers also expressed their gratitude to Behemoth for giving them such a platform, which is similar to mod distribution platforms like Nexus Mods, CurseForge, and Mod DB.[11] To gamers, Behemoth's platform is important in reinforcing their modder identity; it mimics a modding community and increases their sense of bonding and belonging.

Furthermore, the modding skills cultivated from tweaking one particular game are often transferable to projects in other games. Through talking with my interviewees, I found that diving deep, creativity, and quick learning are valued modding skills. Peter, a twenty-five-year-old white engineer acknowledged as one of Pipe Org's hardcore modders, reported that modding's creative and explorative nature plays a vital role in motivating him to endlessly make new mods. When I interviewed Peter, he had just finished doing a hard mod[12] to get OpenMW (an open-source game engine)[13] to run on his legacy gaming PC. It was hard for him to hide his excitement, and he explained his modding process to me at length. Peter's description vividly displayed how gamers can really get into the process: after he did a little research, he realized that his processor could not run the ready-made OpenMW—so he decided to build his own. Once he took a deep dive into the building process, Peter found a "Gentoo package"[14] that allowed him to compile everything he needed for his handmade OpenMW. This discovery was just the first step of his experiment.

After listening to Peter's half-hour-plus description of his "exciting" project, I could not help but ask what the most fun part of this modding practice was. Peter quickly replied, "Come up with something creative—and really digging into it . . . think about some ideas and pick the one that from your perspective is, you know, like, the most creative . . . and see what you can do with it." Like Peter, many gamers emphasized that "digging into the code file" and "digging into the technical underpinnings" brought them enormous fun and prompted them to devote massive energy and long hours to modding.

Many scholars have asserted that modding is a vital source of innovation in the digital games industry. Compared to actual game developers, modders have more freedom and fewer risks when testing new ideas; therefore, the appropriation of their "free" mods can significantly reduce the game industry's research-and-development costs and heighten its innovation frequency (Kücklich 2005; Milburn 2018; Sihvonen 2011). Similar to game development firms, Behemoth's successful interpellation of gamers' modding traits benefits their innovative capacity: one can see from the analysis in Chapter 3 and Chapter 4 that gamification of the work process has become an important mechanism through which Behemoth promotes gamers' modder traits and innovative impulses. In general, it is not a coincidence that modders' traits are a natural match with Behemoth's engineering work process; the company deliberately constructed that process to allow modders to unleash their experimental spirit and deep-diving skills.

A final characteristic of modders is their great appreciation for quick learning skills and hands-on experiences. Matt, in his responses, identifies the significance of these traits for modders. He is one organizer of a Behemoth interest group named PC Building Shenanigans, and he has led the group in making many game mods, such as the "doomguy mods" for *Doom* and the Wii sensor-bar mod. I once talked with him about how he could build so many different game mods. He replied that he believed being quick to learn is the key skill for a good modder, which in turn can help one become a good engineer:

> You really have to kind of make time to learn it on your own. Like, I'm really interested in cryptography, so I'm checking out a lot of tips related to this . . . like every day . . . just kind of as a hobby. . . . I also do the same thing for video games. . . . I keep on top of things like . . . you know, read gaming tips on Reddit like . . . almost everyone else on the team. . . . There's a GameMods subreddit that I check out. . . . It's got a lot of different stuff. A lot of it . . . kind of not in-depth . . . but very practical.

As Matt's response demonstrates, modders like to "keep on top of things"; cutting-edge technologies and modding tools have always been a source of excitement for them. In addition, modders are propelled to master these new techniques in a "very practical" way so that they can put them to use in the next modding round. We can see from Matt's narrative that reading about tips is a critical way for tech hobbyists to "keep on top of things," so platforms or forums that aggregate these tips (e.g., the GameMods subreddit) will capture modders' attention. This kind of hobbyist forum offers diverse knowledge that is "not in-depth but very practical" and explains why the tip-distributing badge is a very popular reward in the badge-collection game (see Chapter 4).

This discussion leads to another question: Why do modders emphasize "practical" learning? Mod making is a highly innovative activity that involves testing out territories that the game developers left unexplored, so modders have to get used to learning while exploring the frontier. One modder once highly recommended that I head over to the GameMods subreddit and assured me that I would then see how often "necessity has become the mother of invention." In other words, the reason why modders are quick learners for something new is that they only learn the most practical elements that are helpful for a particular mod. These practical, quick-learning strategies are suitable for not only modders in particular but also gamers in general. Many gamers revealed that their video-gaming experiences teach them that no matter how well they understand a gaming strategy (e.g., killing, battling, and dueling), it means nothing until they begin practicing these strategies on the battlefield. Interestingly enough, the same experience works for programming skills: instead of spending a long time reading an entire book or chapter to learn a coding skill, they can get started after a brief scan of a tip forum and read about more tips that target particular problems they encounter when they implement the codes.

Be a Hero and Kill the Bugs

A heroic ethos occupies an important position in defining gamers' identity. Since the first *Superman* cartridge appeared for the Atari 2600 in 1978,[15] the video-game industry has produced decades of long-lasting superhero experiences. Games such as *Batman: Arkham Asylum, Injustice: Gods among Us, The Wonderful 101*, and the *inFAMOUS* series all created fantasy worlds that allowed players to not only perform feats of derring-do but also internalize the idea that any player can be a superhero and save the world. Indeed, video games have naturalized the heroic ethos and profoundly shaped gamers' identity (Milburn 2018).

The heroic ethos manifests in the gamer identity in a number of ways. For one thing, gamers are obsessed with drawing on video-game heroes or fantasy novel characters to nickname each other. For example, Jack's nickname is "Jack the North," which references one character in *Game of Thrones*—the King of the North. The King of the North is portrayed as the loyal warrior marching in the world of ice and snow, one who has never been afraid of fighting battles even if the chances of winning were slim. For another, it seems like every gamer wants to be a super "man" at Behemoth: in Pipe Org, I constantly heard engineers call their colleagues "Deathman," "Bugman," or "Deadlineman." I consulted with Danny about the origin of these nicknames; he suspected it had something to do with the story of Batman's name—he named himself Batman because of his childhood fear of bats, thus using his greatest phobia against his enemies. Finally, if one skims through Behemoth engineers' IM (instant messaging) IDs, one finds a bunch related to evil creatures, such as "monster terminator," "ghosthunter," and "vampire killer." After all, a typical heroic gamer action is to kill the evil monsters.

Gamers' heroic ethos—reflected in their nicknames—also feeds into daily work practices, in which superhero-game characters, tropes, and plotlines become compelling templates that gamers draw on to make sense of their work activities. For example, Amir used a monster truck to metaphorize disaster-level errors emerging in their team products by drawing a picture on his office wall that consisted of two key figures: (1) a warrior with the words "I am totally 'Tier 1'" on his head, carrying a sword and a shield just outside the gate of a fortress, and (2) an evil monster truck with three skylights and at least seven or eight doors that was driving straight at the warrior. When asked about his drawing, Amir explained that demonizing the errors helped him stay alert and keep his spirits high: a self-portrait as a well-weaponized warrior could prepare him for the onslaught of errors in Q4.[16]

Amir's case is very representative. On the one hand, in my conversations with many gamers, I found they often imagined and described work difficulties in terms of "villains," "demons," "pirates," and "monsters." From the heroic perspective, these gamers' tasks are very simple and straightforward: be a hero, kill the evil creatures, and save the world. Indeed, long immersion in superhero games trains these gamers to imagine themselves as heroes and habituates them to quickly find enemies to kill them, complete the mission, and level up their characters. On the other hand, the image of a well-weaponized, well-trained warrior—or ninja, killer, or hunter—is constantly interpellated in gamers' narratives. Gamers believe that their best weapon is their technological ability, and this belief is reinforced by year-round video-game playing. Indeed, gaming culture creates power fantasies: gamers can become superheroes as long as they know their way around the hardware and possess the right technical expertise. Technological excellence allows gamers to control the in-game situation, giving them a strong sense of power in reality (Cavallero 2017; Kirkpatrick 2012; Milburn 2018).

A final thing to point out is that masculinity is deeply embedded in this heroic discourse, which explains why gamer identity is highly gendered (Dyer-Witheford and de Peuter 2006). Whether the hero image is Batman or Superman, it has to be a male hero who crushes the evil enemy with his weapons and saves the world. Female characters in superhero video-game storylines, if they are shown at all, have to wait for male heroes to rescue them (Jansz and Martis 2007).

The Field of Games: A Critical Terrain Where Gamer Identity Is Interpellated

After sketching the image of gamers at Behemoth, this chapter now moves onto the engineering floor, examining how the field of games has become a critical terrain where gamer identity is interpellated to serve tech capitalist interests. Table 2.2 offers a glimpse into this field; ethnographic observation brings light to four analytically distinct but empirically interrelated groups of games (see also Appendix A). As shown by Table 2.2, the field of games at Behemoth comprises four major types of games: simulation games, racing games, crowdsourcing games, and pranking games. Each type penetrates deeply into a specific labor process; for example, while simulation games are embedded in the software development process, most racing games are incorporated into routine software maintenance. Additionally, each kind of game is divided into "dominant" and "scattered" games. Dominant games are systematically organized and frequently played at Behemoth; scattered games, however, are less systematically organized and exist in a random state. This section briefly surveys dominant and scattered games; the following empirical chapters provide a detailed description and analysis of the dominant games. Further discussion of the scattered games is presented in Ap-

TABLE 2.2 THE FIELD OF GAMES		
Simulation games	Dominant	Game of Security; video-gamifying work teams; nicknaming; weaponizing the team; project-naming games; Code Review Roulette
	Scattered	Code Ninja Chronicles; Four-Hour Ninja Contest; Ninja CodeSprint; Monkey Master dice game; trading games; Anti Corporate Borg games; encrypting games (Crack the Code!); customizing Cards against Humanity; Nerf gun shooting / laser attack
Racing games	Dominant	Ticket-sprint marathons; ticket-ranking competition
	Scattered	Behemoth Hackathons; Coding-Testing-Debugging Triathlon; dart-challenge games; board game tournaments; Texas Hold'em poker tournaments; betting on-call hours; pumpkin pie scalability dilemma; snatching party; Pipe Org Cup; Ping-Pong competitions; cricket matches; eating challenges; drinking challenges
Crowdsourcing games	Dominant	Phone-tool icon collection
	Scattered	PC-Building "Shenanigans"; reverse virtual reality (VR); team optimization projects; puzzle trophy collection; collecting funny causes of errors (COEs); tier 1 resolver games; online voting games; all-hands live polls; scavenger hunt; Meowstanding Achievement Award
Pranking games	Dominant	Donut email pranks
	Scattered	Newcomer hazing; welcome-back games; funny skits; farewell pranks; detective games ("Who is the traitor?"); "Who is the latest to come to work?" game; snapping a napping picture; ridiculing patent ideas; ridiculing action items; costume play; joking mentor-mentee relationships; challenges like "going to bars five days in a row"

pendix A, which lists them with in-depth information about their rules, gaming elements, gamer traits required, and outcomes. These scattered games sometimes represent a combination of dominant game types, with empirical reality assuming a complexity that outstripped the general categories of the four groups introduced here.

Simulation Games: Constructing the Omnipresent Gaming World

Simulation games are firmly embedded in the core labor process of software development. In these games, managers attempt to simulate the artificial video-gaming environment within the software development process to steer engineers' passion and promote disruptive innovation. To this end, Behemoth organizes numerous games: in Table 2.2, there are at least sixteen kinds of simulation games. Dominant games, which I detail in Chapter 3, are systematically organized and incorporated into each step of the development process. For example, Pipe Org draws on mythological narratives and storylines to develop the Game of Security, romanticizing security engineers' work as "a fight of security" in which they are charged with "maintaining security in a hostile world" and thus creating battle and adventure simulations in that framework. Battle and adventure simulations are consistent gamification techniques found in most dominant simulation games, such as weaponizing the team and project-naming or nicknaming games. As shown from Amir's self-fantasizing as a "tier 1 warrior" fighting against the monster truck presented earlier, these types of simulation games can dramatically simulate gamers' heroic ethos and provide them with tropes, narratives, and even props to heroize their work activities.

As discussed previously, one gamer trait is the boundary blurring between gaming and programming. Some simulation games mobilize this gamer characteristic by deliberately blurring gaming and programming activities, characters, and skills. For example, by video-gamifying work teams, engineers intentionally overlap their work and game team so that they can build rapport in the gaming space and extend their gaming relationship into the workplace. This blurring between work tasks and video games effectively mobilizes engineers' gaming identities and skills (e.g., "theorycraft,"[17] rapid adaptability, quick learning) and can be found in the project-naming, nicknaming, and weaponizing games as well. As discussed in the following chapters, this mobilization is vital in enticing engineers' participation in simulation games and their submission to the video-gamified development process.

The last dominant simulation game in Table 2.2—Code Review Roulette—represents a different genre of simulation game. Code Review Roulette uses the concept of Russian roulette to decide who performs code-review tasks for coworkers ("Who gets the bullets will do the code review"). By allowing engineers to organize a game of chance to solve labor-division problems, Behemoth vastly increases engineers' sense of autonomy—and highlights the fairness and equality of Behemoth's labor division.

In addition to these frequently played simulation games, many similar games are scattered across the engineering floor, as shown in the second row of Table 2.2. For example, to interpellate engineers' heroic and adventurous characters, Behemoth portrays their engineers as "an army of ruthless code ninjas with unique killing skills" and organizes a series of ninja coding games. Specifically, the Code Ninja Chronicles are organized to recruit the Code Ninja Army—if participants pass the test, they will be rewarded with onsite interviews at Behemoth. In the Four-Hour Ninja Contest, participants are encouraged to solve as many technical issues as possible within that timeframe, while the Ninja CodeSprint encourages engineers to reach beyond their departments, organize teams, and tackle Behemoth's most challenging technical issues. To immerse engineers in the ninja world, Behemoth draws on many techniques, such as utilizing tutorial videos to construct mythological storylines and building platforms that provide programming resources and timely feedback.

In addition to Code Review Roulette, engineers develop other simulation games to facilitate labor division. The Wizard team regularly plays Monkey Master dice games to decide who will take charge of organizing and taking notes in the standup meeting: in this game, teammates roll the dice to find out who will be the Monkey Master—the monkey, here, is a screaming toy that reminds engineers about standup meetings. Similarly, engineers design trading games to address other minor labor-division issues. Trading is a crucial video-game activity, in which players trade game items (e.g., characters skins, gaming gears, and weapons) they do not need for items in demand, and these activities are key engagement factors in some video games. Engineers import video-game trading into the workplace and develop similar games on the floor, trading on-call hours and team players, which ensures flexibility in addressing labor-division problems in certain circumstances (e.g., covering on-call engineers who temporarily cannot take their shift due to an emergency). They also make the working process exciting by developing an informal market where engineers can do insider trading.

Other simulation games, such as Anti Corporate Borg games, are organized to promote chaotic fun. "Corporate Borg"[18] borrows from a *Star Trek* storyline and refers to the evil corporate entity that removes worker individuality. Behemoth regularly encourages engineers to organize Anti Corporate Borg groups (e.g., email lists) to propose Anti Corporate Borg game ideas, and by using imagery from a well-known sci-fi discourse, they promote a corporate culture that valorizes chaotic fun. Also, many simulation games are organized to solve the paradox between engineers' high demand for team rapport and the constant company reorganization that destroys team rapport. Many teams in Pipe Org use encrypting games, for instance: while some teams communicate messages using encrypted code, others create codes to encrypt team members' names. These games establish "insider stories" within development teams and largely enhance team cohesion and members' sense of belonging.

Racing Games: Enhancing Urgency of Maintenance Process

The second category in the field of games is racing games, as shown in the third and fourth rows of Table 2.2. Speed, efficiency, and competition are at the heart of racing games: the ticket-sprint marathon is a dominant racing game organized by engineers when they need to race against the machine to solve tickets and recover systems in as short a time as possible. What mobilizes the engineers' ticket-sprint marathons, however, is the ticket-ranking competition set up by managers. Managers use a leaderboard gamification technique to rank each development team's ticket-solving performance and publicly display the results, which transforms Behemoth's ticket-solving process into a ticket-ranking competition and effectively mobilizes gamers' competitive traits, spurring them to organize ticket-sprint marathons, boost their own teams' ranking, and beat other teams. Once engineers are absorbed in the ticket games, they draw on their gaming skills and go all out to win the competition. Ticket-ranking competitions and Ticket-Sprint marathons are the dominant racing games, and these racing games penetrate daily work life: engineers develop various strategies (e.g., defending and attacking) to win these games. Chapter 4 provides a more detailed discussion on how these dominant games worked out.

Thirteen scattered racing games litter the engineering floors as well, as shown in Table 2.2 and Appendix A. Although these games are less embedded in the ticket-solving process and played less frequently, they still possess a racing-game essence and are similar to sports games in that they primarily focus on stimulating engineers' competitiveness and aggressiveness. The Behemoth Hackathons and the Coding-Testing-Debugging Triathlon are typical examples of a scattered racing game. For example, the Behemoth Hackathons are organized to encourage engineers to team up with their coworkers to develop functioning software within a limited time (usually seventy-two hours). Finalist teams are rewarded with a virtual trophy and are likely to receive extra resources to carry out their software deployment. The feelings of accomplishment that emerge from hackathons—the pride in achieving something within a limited time—are especially attractive to hardcore gamers. Recall the narrative of Elizabeth, the hardcore female gamer: when I asked her why she was so into the MOBA game, she replied that it was the feeling of conquering something within a very tight schedule that made the game very attractive.

When engineers invest in these racing games, they battle for ultimate victory and pit their talents in competition against each other; for them, their strengths are their mathematical and calculative skills. Therefore, at Behemoth, engineers tend to be attracted to games that let them draw on their mathematical skills to algorithmize the competition and enhance their winning chances. These games consist of the second type of scattered racing game, which I call algorithmic games, exemplified by the dart-challenge games, board game tournaments, and Texas Hold'em poker tournament. The key to playing a dart game on the engineering floor, for example, is to transform a dart-challenge game into a math competition in which engineers carefully calculate the dart-shooting speed, angle, and distance to enhance their chance of winning. Similarly, engineers organize board game nights and Texas Hold'em poker tournaments, where they compete for card-counting skills (i.e., rewards are not given to game winners but to the players who made a good play with poor hands).

The final type of racing games are the actual sports competitions organized at different levels at Behemoth, such as the Pipe Org Cup, Ping-Pong competitions, and cricket matches. However, compared to other racing games, these events attract less attention from engineers: these games approximate classic sports competitions, which require more physical strength and less mathematical and algorithmic skill.

Crowdsourcing Games: Task-Rabbiting the Tech Workplace

Crowdsourcing games are designed to collect engineers' extra skills, knowledge, and labor.[19] Unfortunately, these games are so rigidly constructed that they garner minimal interest from engineers and hardly interpellate gamer subjectivity. Take the dominant format of crowdsourcing games—phone-tool icon collection—for example. The phone-tool icon, a type of virtual badge, is designed to reward engineers who complete volunteering work, such as solving thousands of outstanding bricolage tasks and providing feedback to other teams. Ideally, this game should have appealed to gamers' modder traits and inspired engineers to devote much spare time to "grinding out" these bricolage tasks. However, it turns out that engineers are generally indifferent toward this badge-collection game. As demonstrated in Chapter 4, most engineers adopt a rather perfunctory approach to participation in this badge-collection game.

Ten other crowdfunding games also exist on the engineering floor (see Table 2.2 and Appendix A). Compared to the phone-tool icon collection game, crowdfunding games are organized much less frequently and thus are described as scattered games. I have roughly divided these games into four categories: modding games, collecting games, voting games, and non-work-related crowdfunding games. A brief introduction of these games is offered in the following paragraphs, and more detailed descriptions of these games' rules, gamification mechanisms, and outcomes appear in Appendix A.

I adopt "modding" to define the first category of scattered games. As discussed above, modding refers to players' modifications of video games; these modification behaviors capture the standard features of all three modding games here. For example, in the PC-Building "Shenanigans" game, engineers voluntarily organize interest groups to custom rebuild computers or tweak hardware at work. Similarly, engineers invent reverse virtual reality (VR) games to promote the fun of materializing elements in Behemoth's virtual world and bringing them back to the real world. For example, Behemoth has a "flip a coin" button as one of its company's internal plugins, designed to assist engineers in making minor decisions by flipping a coin. A development team once converted this plugin into a real machine.

Similarly, engineers also use a Nixie tube clock[20] to materialize Behemoth's virtual countdown timer. Finally, development teams promote team-optimizing games and encourage engineers to propose fun and unique ideas to "patch" team setups. Team managers occasionally collect these patching ideas and pose them as "action items" to be discussed in their retrospective meetings. During my fieldwork, I witnessed several patching ideas proposed by Wizard team engineers. For example, the Wizard team's dog fence can easily block engineers' line of sight and lock visitors out; in response, Danny proposed setting up an infrared detector to notify the team of guests. Unlike the simulation games that aim to blur the worlds of work and game or the racing games that aim to enhance competition, modding games concentrate on crowdfunding. In other words, these games are designed to collect engineers' modding ideas, skills, and practices. Of course, to support the mobilization of engineers' modding skills and modder selves, several gamification elements are adopted in modding games, such as timely feedback.

In addition to these games that specify crowdfunding modding practices, there are more general collecting games, including puzzle trophy collections, collecting causes of errors (COEs), and tier 1 resolvers. The puzzle trophy is a trophy in the shape of a puzzle piece and is awarded to engineers for their patent ideas. The puzzle trophy collection game adopts a "leveling-up" gamification mechanism—the more patent ideas engineers submit, the more trophies they can collect and piece together. The game of collecting funny causes of errors (COEs) is organized on the Behemoth COEs forum.[21] In the COEs forum, engineers can search for, contribute, and discuss funny COEs. Similarly, the tier 1 resolver game is also based in an online forum, where engineers can share tips to help solve technical problems and hardware issues. Both COEs collection and tip-collection games draw on the forum discussion setup and aim to mobilize engineers' gamer traits such as quick learning and knowledge sharing. If engineers bought into these games, they would be helpful in making it easy for them to contribute their knowledge and familiarize themselves with Behemoth's products and services. Unfortunately, engineers are indifferent to these games, as they are relatively rigidly structured and very distant from the core work process.

Voting games are designed to collect votes from engineers. Online voting games refer to polling on the organization's dashboard, where votes are collected to help make organizational decisions in terms of such things as department logo styles, picnic sites, and holiday party activities. There are also live polls: for example, Behemoth sometimes incorporates a voting session in all-hands meetings and uses a live poll app to collect votes and assist in decision-making. To some extent, the voting games demonstrate Behemoth's embrace of democratic decision-making and simultaneously increase engineers' engagement with the community. Finally, there are non-work-related crowdfunding games, such as scavenger hunts and the Meowstanding Achievement Award. Behemoth organizes scavenger hunt games from time to time for a variety of reasons: for instance, the company will ask development teams to gather a set of hidden items around campus to help engineers familiarize themselves with the layout.

Pranking Games: Normalize the Chaotic Fun at Behemoth

Pranking games are a unique instance in the field of games. Unlike the other three categories of games, pranking games barely rely on gamification mechanisms or mobilize engineers' gamer subjectivities (see Table A.4 in Appendix A). Instead, pranking games essentially approximate old-fashioned labor games, organized not to enhance software development so much as slay the "beast of monotony" in daily routine tasks. Additionally, when these pranking games fail to garner engineers' consent, they elect to play the games in their own way to express a degree of resistance. In other words, pranking games are excellent illustrations of how games themselves can become a way to communicate resistance and present us with a possible interpretation of games as tugs-of-war between control and resistance.

To begin with, the most systematically organized and frequently played pranking game is the donut email prank, which is designed to increase engineers' sense of security and popular among all Behemoth development teams. The rule of this game is simple: when engineers fail to lock their computers upon leaving their desks, colleagues can hijack their email accounts and send embarrassing emails. As a penalty, the one who forgot to lock their computer buys donuts for their colleagues. As described in Chapter 5, although donut emails largely motivate engineers to play, they barely adopt any gamification mechanisms; nor do they really interpellate gamer traits. Engineers playing the donut email game can be divided into two camps. *Game supporters* have never been satisfied with using donut emails to just expose their teammates' lack of security consciousness; supporters mock every aspect of their coworkers via donut emails, from the quality of their code to their work absences. In this way, these engineers transform the donut email platform into an arena for conducting panoptic surveillance. Conversely, a smaller group of *game challengers* criticizes the surveillance embedded in the donut pranks and develop alternative playing strategies to challenge the game's validity and authority (e.g., by creating a false alarm). Chapter 5 discusses donut email pranks in detail.

The dominant donut email pranking game is accompanied by other pranking games, which are ubiquitous on the engineering floors. I generally divide the rest of the pranking games into four groups: ritual pranks, normative pranks, ridiculing pranks, and spontaneous pranks. Ritual pranks are usually organized during specific occasions and have become an important "rite of passage" at Behemoth. Sometimes, going through the pranks symbolizes participants' transformation of their identity. Other times, undergoing the pranks implies participants' further confirmation of Behemoth's organizational culture. For example, newcomer hazing pranks are organized to highlight the company culture, which is characterized by chaotic fun—these pranks instruct newcomers to familiarize themselves with this culture. Sometimes, engineers' design pranks, such as redecorating offices with tinfoil or snatching computers, welcome back engineers who return to the office after a long vacation. These welcome-back pranks become a critical rite of passage that quickly transforms the vacationers' identities back to those of team players. On special occasions (e.g., all-hands meetings, postholiday parties), managers come under the prank spotlight; top managers perform funny skits, such as wearing miniskirts and dancing, to display their folksy charm and demonstrate Behemoth's "casual and fun" culture. Finally, when engineers leave Behemoth, they sometimes ritually pull a last prank on their teams as a way to say good-bye: these are farewell pranks. A few times, farewell pranks have been used as a channel through which engineers express their grievances to Behemoth for the last time. For example, an interviewee once told me that one of his colleagues "cut" the trickiest ticket to their sister team during his last day at work as revenge for the sister team's previous torturing of him regarding a ticket.

If ritual pranks can be understood as ways to reinforce engineers' cultural membership, then normative pranks should be considered a type of soft control that disguises its discipline under consent and horseplay. For example, engineers—inspired by board games like *Hunt a Killer* or *Clue*—organized the detective game to screen potential job hoppers. When playing the game, engineers follow a game script, naming the suspect (the traitor / job hopper) and listing the clues that led them to make such a deduction (e.g., "I suspect Kevin because he wears another company's logoed T-shirt"). Similarly, the Wizard team organized the "Who is the latest to come to work?" game to monitor latecomers; they keep a list on a whiteboard to document and rank those who arrive late to work. The game of snapping a napping picture, popular in Pipe Org, uses the same logic to catch engineers going to a conference room for a nap. Sometimes, these engineers will be photographed by their teammates, who send the photos to team email lists for public humiliation. Apparently, both games serve to discipline misbehavior.

The third group of games is labeled ridiculing pranks, as they involve mocking some aspects of the labor process. Ridiculing patent ideas is a game invented by engineers to mess with the patent-submission system. Specifically, engineers submit absurd patent ideas, such as proposing an app that scans urine to ascertain people's hydration situation. Occasionally, the patent ideas have a tone of resistance to them (e.g., a T-shirt for managers featuring the sentence "I can't remember any of your names"). Similarly, the Wizard team plays a game of adding ridiculous action items, in which engineers incorporate ludicrous action items, such as "having extirpated wisdom teeth," to make the software design or scrum planning meetings more fun.

Finally, countless spontaneous pranks can be spotted on the engineering floor. I have not categorized spontaneous pranks as dominant pranking games, as they are less systematic and more improvised. However, spontaneous pranks occupy a significant position in the field of games as they are played very frequently. Behemoth's spontaneous pranks are played to reduce fatigue, relieve boredom, and reinforce informal culture and group bonding, much like they are in any other workplace. I have listed two spontaneous pranks as examples, costume play and joking mentor-mentee relationship (Table 2.2, Appendix B). In Chapter 5, I devote a section to detailing the play of spontaneous pranks.

Concluding Remarks

In this chapter, I sketched a general image of engineers working at Behemoth and pointed out that gamer identity is located at the core of a majority of engineers' identities. I analyze gamer identity from various perspectives. First, I called attention to two types of gamer identity, implicit and explicit. Through analyzing why some engineers are willing to self-identify as gamers (i.e., explicit) while others are not (implicit), I bring social statuses, such as gender and race, to the fore and reveal that white male engineers are more likely to be identified as gamers. Not only does social status differentiate between implicit and explicit gamer identity; it also plays a primary role in shaping gamer identity in general. Finally, I wanted to unveil what gamer traits are defined as ideal traits at Behemoth. After all, only through interpellating these specific ideal gamer traits can Behemoth transform these gamers into productive gamers. Through a close examination of engineers' narratives, I distilled three major gamer traits that are highly valued: the tendency to blur gaming and programming passion, activities, and skills; modding attitudes and skills; and, finally, a heroic ethos.

As is shown in the following chapters, a field of games is an indispensable mechanism through which the tech firm transforms gamers into productive gamers. Before unpacking this transformation process, however, I devoted the second half of this chapter to offering a glimpse of the field of games. To illustrate the playing field, I categorized these games into four groups—simulation games, racing games, crowdsourcing games, and pranking games—and further divided each group into dominant and scattered games. This chapter sketched out a brief overview of these dominant and scattered games, including their basic playing rules, their embeddedness (if any) into specific labor processes, and their functions and outcomes.

Simulation Games and the Establishment of Gamified Governmentality

Introduction

The gamification of workplaces has been hailed as a novel development of the workplace. While labor scholars have previously examined the potential of labor games in making mundane workplace tasks more enjoyable, the emergence of video-game-oriented and technologically sophisticated gaming mechanisms in the workplace is a recent phenomenon (Burawoy 1979; Roy 1959; Sallaz 2009; Sharone 2002; Sherman 2007). Through advanced technologies such as data tracking, simulation, and virtualization, gamification mechanisms have become more relational, timely, and absorbing, thus enabling workplaces to transform into play spaces (Fleming 2005; Mollick and Rothbard 2014; Dyer-Witheford and de Peuter 2003).

These scholars fail to escape the mindset of conceptualizing gamification as a critical mechanism through which employers elicit workers' consent and establish hegemony in the workplace (Mollick and Rothbard 2014). However, Jennifer Whitson draws on governmentality studies to argue that gamification can also enroll individuals into self-governance by appealing to their highest aspirations and capacities (Foucault, 1991, 2010; Whitson 2013, 2014). Although gamification is believed to apply anywhere to achieve gamified governmentality in principle, it has its limits and can turn into bad applications in practice (Whitson 2013, 170).

Whitson examines a gamified workplace project proposed by Reeves and Read (2009), which overlays work practices in a British call center with the game Puzzle Pirates. Reeves and Read's analysis reveals that gamification can extend its function beyond simply eliciting consent by enhancing workers' self-governance. The project envisioned workers assuming the role of pirates, organizing into teams to quest for treasure. Pirates can check out their own and teammates' avatars to learn their work progress and can offer aids to their teammates once they notice they encounter blocks via the progress records. Ideally, if workers were absorbed into the game, they would have become active subjects choosing to inject the spirit of play into the otherwise monotonous work process and willing to conduct self-discipline and mutual surveillance to ensure everyone's subscription into the game.

However, Whitson's analysis of the project's failure highlights the clashing frames of call center work and play. The veneer of play was unable to mask the underlying reality of work, rendering the gamification ineffective (Whitson 2013, 173). Whitson's analysis inspires a discussion of the more radical function of gamification, drawing on Foucault's analytic frame. Whitson's identification of circumstances under which Foucauldian gamified design failed is reasonable. However, stories at Behemoth illustrate that in an uncertain engineering work environment, the gamification design of work may become a powerful tool for submitting engineers to a gamified governmentality.

Chapter 3 explores whether and how gamified governmentality is established in the scrum software development process. After laying down the foundation, the chapter moves on to managerial practices in further transforming the scrum process into simulation games. By transforming the scrum narratives into video-game-centered frames, managers construct a ludic gaming discourse in the workplace. The third section describes engineers' reactions to these simulation games. The investigations of engineering practices reveal that these simulation games effectively evoke these workers' gamer subjectivity. Engineers enthusiastically invest in these simulation games to enact their gaming selves, becoming subjugated and disempowered in the process.

Finally, the concluding section illustrates the consequence of transforming the scrum process into simulation games and analyzes the difference between gamified governmentality and hegemony. This analysis underscores the need to consider the potential limitations of gamification, which can become bad applications in practice. Overall, this discussion of gamification offers a sophisticated and inspiring analysis of the intersection of play, work, and power dynamics in the contemporary workplace.

Scrum Development Process: The Vessel of the Simulation Games

Simulation games are arguably the most prevalent games at Behemoth and infiltrate every stage of the software development process. These are designed to appeal to engineers' gaming predispositions, in part by structuring workers' active improvisation. Simulation games are developed directly from the core labor process of scrum development. A scrum is an agile software development framework first proposed by Takeuchi and Nonaka (1986). They claimed, "Companies are increasingly realizing that the old sequential approach to developing new productivity won't get the job done. Instead, companies in Japan and the United States are using a holistic method—as in rugby, the ball gets passed within the team as it moves as a unit up the field" (Takeuchi and Nonaka 1986, 137). Like rugby, scrum development adopts the concept of a *sprint*. For rugby, a sprint describes players' short bursts of speed when they run the ball down the field. In the software development world, a sprint refers to a task that is part of a larger project; these smaller tasks ("sprint goals") focus developer team efforts and motivate them to stretch and meet these interim goals at full tilt.

A scrum starts with sprint planning, which is led by a *scrum master*—the person responsible for acquiring resources and head counts for the project (usually the team manager)—and a project owner (often a senior engineer), who knows the project best and sets its priorities and direction. During sprint planning, a team typically identifies the most critical features and functionalities to be implemented in software products; these are called "product backlog items." Usually, the final list of backlog items is a result of an arduous negotiation process between client team representatives, managers, and engineers. Once the backlog list is made, the development team can figure out the best way to assemble all the features, establish a reasonable division of labor, and formulate a sprint plan that allows the team to divide the whole development process into several sprints and set the length of each sprint (generally from one to four weeks long).

After finishing the sprint planning, development teams push forward the projects sprint by sprint. This is also the process through which all functionalities and features are produced in the software coding process. In this process, responsibility for transforming agreed-upon software features into codes will be divided among engineers. Although engineers need solo time to code these features, they also need to consult each other frequently, so development teams use a task board to track the working process and ensure every team member is on the same page. The task board is divided into six columns that represent the six key steps of each sprint: "To Do (not started)," "Blocked," "In Progress/Implementation," "Code Review (CR)," "Release/Testing," and "Done." The team usually writes to-do tasks on Post-it notes to track their progress along the task board; for example, when a task has been started, a corresponding sticky note is written and placed under the "To Do" column. During the code-writing process, the sticker will move from the "To Do" column to "In Progress." When an engineer finishes writing the necessary code chunks for this task, they move the corresponding sticker to the "Code Review (CR)" column, which means the coding is ready for review. When the CR is completed, the sticker moves to the "Release/Testing" column, and after successful testing, the sticker lands in the "Done" column. If a team member cannot complete a task, a sticker is appended to the blocked column.

At the end of each sprint, the team holds a retrospective meeting to evaluate their successes and determine what they can improve in the future. Occasionally, the development team also conducts a "postmortem" to formally end the sprint. The next sprint cycle kicks off when the team organizes another sprint meeting and chooses another set of product backlog items.

The scrum development framework defines the core labor process in tech, through which engineers' design ideas are carried out in codes, transformed into software products (e.g., software features, functionality, and service), and then converted into profits. Connecting these dimensions, I consider how engineers create value and how informational capitalism appropriates engineers' value through scrum development.

Theoretically, the cost of an engineer's annual labor is approximately equal to the cost of buying 6,400 units of 16 gigabytes (GB) of random access memory (RAM)[1] and keeping them running over a year. The equation roughly looks like this: the cost of 1 engineer's labor time = the cost of 6,400 * 16GB RAM.[2] Of course, such an equation is based on the assumption that what the firm paid was precisely the labor that the engineer sold; however, as we all know, capitalist success stems from its extraction of workers' surplus value. Engineers' creativity is the most important productive force in the tech industry and the most invaluable place from which surplus value arises. Moreover, creativity defines the essence of scrum development; therefore, the scrum development process becomes fertile territory for capitalists to extract surplus. In other words, the more effectively and efficiently tech firms squeeze creativity out of engineers in the process of scrum development, the more surplus value the company can appropriate.

Let me illustrate the point, using an example from an engineer, Lei. As Lei explained, he was once responsible for iterating a feature (i.e., a web page link), which was listed as an important backlog item in the scrum sprint. While Lei browsed the original codes for the link operation, he figured out a "smarter" algorithm to replace the original one. So Lei spent about a week carrying out and finalizing his new idea—and his new algorithm resulted in reducing computational power usage by 43.5 terabytes (TB) over five years.[3] Lei's new algorithm was considered a significant achievement and placed on the scrum board as a "success story" during their team's sprint retrospective.

A simple calculation of Lei's success story reveals that innovative ideas render the most precious surplus value: Lei's one-week scrum sprint saved 43.5 TB of computational power for the company over five years, so the value that Lei created for the company within a week equaled 43.5 TB. According to the equation for engineers' yearly labor cost (the cost of 1 engineer's labor time = the cost of 6,400 * 16 GB RAM), an engineer's labor cost for a week was 2,178 GB (i.e., 6400 * 16/235 * 5).[4] 2,178 GB converts to 2.178 TB.[5] While the value Lei created for the company for a week was 43.5 TB, the value of his labor power was 2.178 TB. According to Marx's theory, then, the rate of surplus value (r.s.) from Lei's one-week design could easily reach 1897 percent.[6] Obviously, the surplus value that Lei created in one week was exceptional. Lei's further explanation implied that his algorithm innovation was the foundation for enormous surplus generation, in this case surplus computational power.

> When I actually started to carry out the idea through coding, it only took me a half day [to write them]. . . . The more difficult part was that you had to figure out . . . the new method, [which] took me about a week. . . . Even now when I think about it, I'm still proud of the idea. . . . The original algorithm [designed for running the web page link] is . . . To put it metaphorically, when it's asked to calculate the sum of the first one hundred numbers, it just simply added them up together, like $1 + 2 + 3 + 4$—that's the original algorithm's approach. What I wanted to do was find a quicker way to add them up, so I came up with a new formula . . . something like $n (n + 1) / 2$ . . . which took a shorter amount of time to add up the one hundred numbers, right? Of course, this is just a metaphor . . . but the logic is the same: using my new formula cost less time and fewer computational resources.

Inspired by Lei's case, we learn that the most efficient way to extract surplus value from engineers is not to appropriate labor time or output but to squeeze out creativity. On the one hand, the decreased consumption of computational resources was not necessarily associated with increased labor time, and indeed, engineers' actual labor time devoted to work was hard to measure. I learned later from my chitchat with Lei that during the first few days of that sprint week, while he was iterating the feature, he spent long hours lying on the bed and mulling over the algorithm. "But how can you calculate my work time?" he asked rhetorically. "You can barely find me in the [office] building those days." On the other hand, maximization of work output was not a good way to increase surplus extraction. It is common to think of engineers' work output in terms of codes—indeed, tech firms used various approaches to track the lines of code engineers composed. However, according to Lei, although the algorithm was eventually written in only a few dozen lines, it saved far more computational resources than the original algorithm, which took hundreds of lines of code.

Engineers' innovations often relied upon unconventional moves. Squeezing out engineers' creative capacity was informational capitalists' best shot to maximize their appropriation of surplus value; unfortunately, such flashes of genius were virtually impossible to plan, let alone control. This study found that organizing scrum development into a series of simulation games increased the extraction of engineers' creativity. As shown in this chapter, capitalists constituted a "subjection" type of control via simulation games, which directed engineers to explore their creative potential. By investing in the simulation games, engineers' experimental, adventurous, and imaginary abilities cultivated via video-game play efficiently transformed into the scarcest productive forces on the engineering floor—disruptive creativity—which could then be extracted.

Scrum development does not merely transform engineers' innovative ideas into software products; it also optimizes conditions for a seemingly endless cycle of innovation. The scrum development framework's secret for preserving creativity is its almost intolerant embrace of change and flexibility. Indeed, extreme flexibility is a feature of the scrum development framework. As mentioned in the introduction, major tech firms in the United States adopt an ethic of continual change—or, in other words, permanently beta—and promote an endless cycle of technological innovation. To keep up with the pace of innovation under informational capitalism, original product design can be completely abandoned to "pivot"[7] to new products during any sprint. This flexibility is why a complete development process is divided into different sprints: any new sprint can imply a change of developmental direction and an abandonment of previous sprints. Tireless changes of software development plans are achieved through the constant switch of sprint directions, and constant reorganization of development teams accompanies the continuous change of product direction. It is safe to say that the level of flexibility embodied by the scrum structure is beyond most flexible work structures in the post-Fordist era.

At any time, it seemed, a team might dissolve, recombine, or simply lose members. Take the Wizard team, for example. From 2013 to 2015, the Wizard team experienced four instances of development direction changes and reorganization when it developed an encryption software called the "safety deposit box" ("SD box"), which was used to safekeep a series of passwords (see Figure 3.1). Jack, as the only senior engineer in the team, assumed the responsibility of the project owner. After the first sprint of development, the Wizard team realized that they needed to enhance the product's scale. The Wizard team manager, Vikram, quickly assumed his responsibility as scrum master to acquire resources (i.e., head counts) and expanded the team from four engineers to seven. By the end of the fourth sprint (June 2013), the Wizard team realized they needed to split the product into two directions and

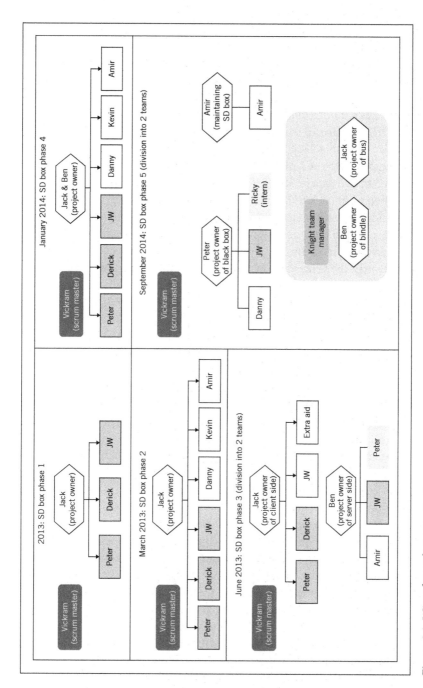

Figure 3.1 Wizard team's reorganization

separately developed the client side and the server side of the SD box. This decision, in turn, led to the division of the scrum team: Jack remained the project owner for the client-side SD box scrum team, who led three junior engineers and an extra aide transferred from the Assassin team. Ben, who originally belonged to the Knight team, transferred to the Wizard team to become the project owner for the server-side SD box team and led another three junior engineers.

In the middle stage of SD box development, the two scrum teams recombined as they needed to work together to resolve some vital technical difficulties. By September 2014, the two project owners for the SD box—Jack and Ben—transferred to the Knight team, as the Knight team's most crucial product pivoted to two new products ("Bindle" and "Bus"), and they needed extra help. So Ben went back to the Knight team to become the project owner for Bindle, and Jack became the project owner for Bus. In January 2015, at the final stage of the SD box development, the Wizard team realized they needed to upgrade their SD box product to a "black box" for better encryption. In other words, the Wizard team pivoted their development ideas from safekeeping a series of passwords (i.e., the SD box) to randomizing the sequence of passwords (i.e., the black box). Vikram divided the team again, promoting Peter to senior engineer and project owner to lead three junior engineers in developing the black box. For the SD box, Vikram promoted Amir, who became the project owner; Amir led another junior engineer and brought in an intern to perform maintenance and minor refinement tasks.

This kind of fluidity in the composition and recomposition of teams induced substantial anxiety. Specifically, the anxiety derived from three dimensions of the protean team experience. First, constant changes in direction and organization led to role ambiguity. Second, uncertainty about the final product included potential errors occurring due to systems changing, rotating, and pivoting. A third source of anxiety stemmed from the contradiction between the fluidity of teams and the perpetual need to maintain stable, working relationships among members.

As I show later, games constructed by managers and engineers have become the crucial mechanisms for addressing the issues of extreme flexibility, uncertainty, and anxiety. For example, managers' simulation of video- and board-game characters on the engineering floors is an important strategy for reducing engineers' panic resulting from their role ambiguity. Also, engineers' self-developed simulating strategies—manifesting as importing gaming relationships into the workplace and blurring the lines between battle teams in video games and scrum teams at work—became the critical factor in resolving the dilemma between the permanent-beta development ideology and the ongoing need for a trustworthy team relationship.

Throughout the scrum development process, the code review (CR) step plays a unique yet critical role in ensuring code consistency. Due to the encouragement of almost unbounded creativity, engineers' coding approaches reflect individual styles, which are challenging to standardize. Indeed, when asking three engineers to produce the same software functionality or feature, they will likely write segments of code that look entirely distinctive, using various algorithms, programming languages, and code structures. When engineers push the codes into deployment, however, these highly individualized segments must be joined together and function as though written by a single individual.

Given this code diversity, the CR step appears vital to the scrum process, as it ensures the consistency of functionalities and the smooth deployment of software. This step is used to allow scrum team members to review and examine each other's codes, reconcile styles, detect mistakes, and offer suggestions to code writers. Although the mutual reviewing process plays an essential role in harmonizing and standardizing the team's code, the CR process can trigger conflicts between code writers and code reviewers. When such disharmonious incidents occur during code exchange and review, however, various games developed by engineers can lubricate conflicts.

Simulating the Virtual World on the Engineering Floor: Managerial Construction of Simulation Games and Gaming Rhetoric

When I adopt the concept of gamification, I interpret it as something quite literal: the import (or transposition) into the workplace of a structure and culture of board and video games that workers have played for many years. I argue that managers adopted elements and narratives of these games to exercise control, surmount obstacles, and resolve dilemmas and conflicts that emerged in the scrum process, while also transforming engineers' creative potential into software products. The managerial importation of games on the engineering floor defines a new mode of production that interpellates and converts engineers' gamer experiences into a productive gamer subjectivity that ensures productivity and creativity by incorporating engineers' leisure time activities into the cycle of innovation, while suppressing potential forms of resistance against the capitalist approach to innovation and development (e.g., extreme flexibility, prioritization of profits over innovation). In general, managers draw on three key gaming elements to transform the workplace into a virtual gaming world. These elements widely exist within the gaming world: game roles, narratives, and artifacts. Game roles and narratives are usually applied simultaneously and are considered the most crucial gamification elements to adopt in the scrum process.

At Behemoth, engineers' individualist interest is believed to be a governmental problem and treated seriously by the management (Foucault 1991). This tendency is best shown from managerial efforts at reframing the scrum process from a sporty discourse into a video-gaming discourse to meet engineers' interests. Originally, Takeuchi and Nonaka's (1986) adoption of rugby metaphors to define the scrum process itself draws on the idea of a sports team to romanticize the software development process. However, the rugby scrum—a muddy, sweaty affair that evokes working-class masculinity—hardly elicits engineers' interests. After all, the majority of engineers are not regular visitors to the pitch. Instead, the virtual gaming world lends a more familiar context for eliciting engineers' interests. Targeting their employees' gaming subjectivity, Behemoth managers abandoned the rugby metaphor but strategically simulated video- and board-game characters and roles to infuse the software development process with the sense of adventure and fantasy conjured by games. Specifically, managers consistently drew a parallel between work roles and characters in video games (e.g., *World of Warcraft*), board games (e.g., Dungeons & Dragons), and fantasy novels (e.g., *Game of Thrones*) to lure their engineers into fantasizing that they are working in a gaming world. The reformation of the scrum narrative into a video-gaming metaphor reflects that managers well recognize the intertwined relationship between discourse and disciplinary power. In other words, it is not incidental that the video-gaming metaphor suppressed the sporty metaphor to become the most explicit and visible discourse in the engineering workplace. Instead, it shows that managers are very skillful to realize that the video-gaming knowledge resonates with engineers' subjectivity. By surfacing video-gaming knowledge, management enables the articulation of gamer subjectivity in scrum and provides space for engineers' to interpellate themselves in this gamified work process.

Many Behemoth managers have drawn parallels between the scrum process and the fantasy tabletop role-playing game Dungeons & Dragons (D&D), which is considered the precursor to computer games.

In an article shared by one team manager, Vikram, titled "A Dungeon Master's Guide to SCRUM," scrum team members are metaphorically referred to as a group of courageous adventurers with diverse skills, journeying through the vast plains of software development to reach the mystical Castle A in the cloud. With every sprint, the team moves closer to Castle A. Sometimes, the trip involves detours: for example, although the ideal plan is to travel straight toward the castle, the team might find that a bridge over a river is blocked, and they need to move south to find another bridge. Then, after going south, the "blind oracle" (i.e., the project owner) may decide that from where they stand, going to a new destination, Castle B, is more reasonable than going to Castle A (e.g., the Wizard team's decision to develop a black box instead of a SD box). The article has generated considerable discussion among Pipe Org members. Game discourse is further articulated in the D&D narrative. Such metaphors help to romanticize engineering work relationships and activities, imbuing engineers with heroic gaming characters and embedding them in narrative adventures.

Drawing on the D&D discourse, Pipe Org managers can cite the detour story to normalize the constant change in the labor process, reframing uncertainty into choice, freedom, and opportunity. The scrum development process is characterized by tireless sprints and the constant reorganization of development teams, leading to a high level of uncertainty. This uncertainty applies to unknowable, uncontrollable, and unpredictable situations, resulting in anxiety and a complete loss of information on the probability distribution of outcomes for choices (Knight 1921). However, managers can reframe uncertainty as an exciting adventure by parallelizing it with "detours."

Under managers' narratives, detours are imbued with a sense of adventurism and experimentalism. Indeed, in the world of tabletop role-playing games, detours are intentionally designed to offer players the freedom and opportunities to shape their paths and experiences in the games (Baerg 2009; Bogost 2007). The choices the players make in interaction with the game will likely result in a different experience every time the game is played. As described in the manual "A Dungeon Master's Guide to SCRUM," adventurers could freely change their paths from going to Castle A to going to Castle B when they found themselves blocked by a river on their way to Castle A. Such a framing offers engineers a choice-laden illusion, enticing them to interpellate a "responsive gaming self" to adventure the system to obtain a high level of freedom and pleasure.

Moreover, such a narrative allows Behemoth to frame uncertainty into "risk." Unlike uncertainty, risk applies to a given situation where people can hedge against it with knowledge of possible outcomes and manage it by calculating its odds. The reframing of uncertainty into risk, according to Neff (2012), was a vital process that helped to fuel the dot-com boom. Behemoth not only reframes uncertainty into risk but also implies that those willing to take risks are skillful and competent players. Risk-taking is a deeply held value within gaming culture. The narrative of "A Dungeon Master's Guide to SCRUM" implies that it has to be the "blind oracle" who has the competence to decide to make detours. Thus, reframing uncertainty and enrolling it in the D&D games are crucial processes of evoking engineers' gamer subjectivity.

Overall, the use of D&D discourse in the scrum development process not only helps to romanticize engineering work but also reframes uncertainty into choice, freedom, and opportunity. By parallelizing uncertainty with detours, managers can normalize constant changes and reframe uncertainty into a thrilling adventure. Additionally, reframing uncertainty into risk further entices engineers to interpellate a responsive gaming self to adventure the system, thus evoking their gamer subjectivity.

Not satisfied with merely using D&D game characters and storylines to fantasize about the scrum process, managers also harnessed artifacts to articulate further the gaming discourse embedded in the D&D narrative. For example, inspired by the article "A Dungeon Master's Guide to SCRUM," Morgan, the Assassin team's manager, fashioned paper hats in the sprint planning meetings to put on his scrum team members' heads based on the characters in the D&D game. Morgan put the Dungeon Master hat on the head of the scrum master and a Blind Oracle hat on the project owner's head—along with Warrior, Wizard, and Rogue hats for the team members' heads. This method was later adopted by the Wizard team during the phase in which they repeatedly reorganized their structure, and the project owner's hats were passed around to Ben, Jack, and Peter.

For their part, the D&D narrative assists team members in interpellating their gamer subjectivity. Engineers frequently drew on characters from D&D to give each other nicknames, and workers relied on their understanding of the D&D game and its characters to interpret their work and their roles. For example, when describing his tech lead experience in an interview,[8] WZH proactively offered an analogy to the role of Dungeon Master:

> I knew we could definitely finish designing the add-on of data store this sprint. But implementing it to replace the local backup might be too much. . . . It would be challenging. . . . Then I thought . . . Well, I'm the DM [Dungeon Master]. Just like the good DM who always needs to challenge players to make the game fun, I guess I'm also trying to find the right amount of challenge to inspire them to achieve their own feats of greatness.

The gaming discourse has become an important conceptual tool WZH uses to understand his work role. Like WZH, many engineers at Pipe Org would project gaming characters onto their work roles. Sometimes, workers complimented their project owners as the "best oracle" they have ever known; other times, a "wizard" would be admired for his mystic skill of finding a shortcut allowing his team to reach a milestone. Of course, if an engineer shouldered a huge reengineering task that couldn't be subdivided, he would undoubtedly be considered the team's bravest and toughest "warrior." Diverse images of gaming characters—some heroic, others visionary—were crystallized through repeated citations by managers and echoed by engineers. Thus, the often dull and sterile, though mentally challenging, work of coding was romanticized as heroic adventure, infused with the chivalric values of camaraderie and loyalty.

In WZH's case, I can tell that he applied the value system worshipped in the gaming world to make work decisions and evaluate work behaviors. Specifically, directed by a gaming discourse, skillful players can take on and benefit from risks and welcome them as an opportunity for a personal challenge. The underlying D&D gaming discourse creates a perception that risky endeavors could be evaluated as cool and avant-garde. This rhetoric directs WZH's choice of work direction. As WZH explained, the task of finishing the add-on feature was considered less risky and not challenging enough in comparison to the accomplishment of a complete replacement of the local backup. Self-interpellated as the DM (Dungeon Master), WZH thought he was not only responsible for himself but also for "mak[ing] the game fun" for his team members. Therefore, WZH led his team to pursue the risky and challenging approach to enact their "feats of greatness." The problem was that the labor intensity needed to finish a complete replacement product was far greater than that needed to design add-on product features within a given work period (i.e., sprint). That is, by internalizing the game characters and simulating the game value system, engineers, to some extent, chose to be self-motivated and self-exploited to enhance their labor intensity.

Another subtext remained hidden in WZH's narrative of weighing two tasks (i.e., accomplishing the partial design task or finishing the replacement task). The second task—the local backup replacement—was not only challenging; it connoted establishing a new product through crushing the old one. Such a bold move was, in fact, admired by most engineers, especially those who were game hobbyists. This build-anew attitude had long been cultivated in gamers via video-game play. Since the gaming world is fictional, it is easier for game players to destroy an established world and construct a new one; therefore, gamers' disruptive gaming approaches were more common and potentially more exciting. By bridging the gaming world with the software development world, players' disruptive gaming approach has smoothly transformed into the "disruptive innovation" found on the engineering floor. This disruptive innovation was significantly reflected in engineers' experimental and adventurous attitudes and their attempts to break established code systems or algorithmic rules to build something new. Of course, this kind of innovation can occasionally bring enormous surplus value to the tech firm.

Besides drawing parallels between board games and the scrum process, managers also simulate fantasy novels or fantasy television series storylines to heighten engineers' excitement for and commitment to their software development work. For example, Pipe Org managers borrowed themes from the popular television series *Game of Thrones*[9] to design posters that depicted

Pipe Org engineers carrying out sprints in service of the team's primary responsibility (addressing security vulnerabilities at Behemoth). These posters used a play on words from *Game of Thrones*—"in the Game of Security, we only play to win" or "maintaining security in a hostile world"—and portrayed security engineers as tough, brave, and loyal warriors marching in the world of ice and snow, ones never afraid to fight a (security) battle.

Engineers genuinely enjoyed these posters, so much so that they designed various ruses to steal them, charging these high jinks with the drama of epic battles. At one point, the Knight team "stole" one *Game of Thrones* poster from the hallway bulletin board, appropriating it as their team's poster and proudly displaying it on their team's wall. But the plunder incited jealousy among the other teams, and in fact, Knight's sister team made several attempts to snatch the poster, which forced the Knight team's tech lead to organize a "defensive battle" to protect their favorite team poster.

To provide a more realistic and 360-degree gaming experience, some managers even integrated more gaming artifacts, effectively "weaponizing" their teams by asking each team member to buy a toy gun to better imitate a warrior. Still other managers drew swamps on the office wall and labeled them with the names of various fishing technologies (software designed to dupe people into revealing such information as passwords) and security bugs (e.g., the Heartbleed Bug). They then warned their team members to "pay attention" and avoid these swamps.

Setting up these simulation games allowed managers to produce a kind of soft yet penetrated power. To some extent, the fantasization of the scrum is a process of "subjectification of workers." Subjectification is a concept developed by Foucauldian theorists to understand power as "not simply what we oppose but also, in a strong sense, what we depend on for our existence and what we harbor and preserve in the beings that we are" (Butler 1997, 2). For programmers, gaming worlds were the air they breathed throughout their youth. Importing key elements of this world into which they were immersed and socialized, managers also imported structures of control, camaraderie, and loyalty. This subjectification process works through implicit as well as explicit metaphorical statements, meaningful gamification processes, and gaming languages. By drawing the parallel between the scrum process and fantasy games or novels—and calling engineers Dungeon Masters, Blind Oracles, or Security Warriors—managers create the work subjects they need: highly motivated "adventurers" who are willing to accept any challenge, unleash their potential, and march together with each other to reach a destination. Consequently, gaming characters became a trope, a structure of meaning through which managers addressed engineers and around which they organized scrum development.

From the above illustration, simulated games are differentiated essentially from classic labor games documented in earlier scholars' analysis. If classic labor games organized on the shop floor primarily aim at establishing hegemony, then the simulated games constructed by Behemoth's managers strive for governmentality. Demonstrating the differentiated gaming result permits us to reflect further on the distinct nature of simulation games. To begin with, managers do not endeavor to design every element and rule of the game. Nor do they conduct close vertical supervision over these games. Instead, managers set up the discursive system for the simulation games (e.g., D&D metaphor) based on their comprehensive knowledge of their workers' gamer interests and subjectivity. Indeed, managers' technique of power is directly manifested in their comprehension of engineers' video-gaming interests. Due to their precise target of workers' gamer interests, these managers successfully draw engineers to internalize the power. In this sense, while classic labor games rely on gaming practices as the primary mechanism to obscure and secure exploitation, simulation games draw on gaming rhetoric as a medium to enact workers' gamer subjectivity. It was through workers' self-interpellation and self-submission that simulating games achieved discipline. Unlike the hegemonically oriented games that demand continuous negotiation between managers and workers to achieve a coordination of interests, simulation games are not concerned with coordinating interests between managers and workers. For simulation games, managers' interests, such as promoting the risk-taking path of innovation, permeate the gaming discourse and are so well internalized by workers that they can hardly even separate their interests from their managers'. In this sense, it is reasonable to speculate that the space of resistance in simulation games is more compressed than in hegemonically oriented games.

The following section moves the focus to the engineering side to further illustrate engineers' self-submission to gamified governmentality. For example, the next section details how engineers echoed the gaming rhetoric, even as they mobilized their gaming experiences and memories to formulate a productive gamer subjectivity. Engineers' self-recognition as productive gamers guaranteed their creation of rampant simulation games and their ensnarement in the gamified work system.

Entrapped in the Gaming World: Engineers' Self-Initiated Simulation Games

The scrum development process is often transformed into simulation games by managers, creating a space for engineers to express and fulfill their gamer subjectivity. This subjectivity is ultimately manifested through the software development process. The enthusiasm with which engineers participate in simulated games is evident in their adoption and improvisation of managers' rhetorical reconstruction of familiar game storylines during the scrum process.

For one thing, drawing on video-game heroes or fantasy novel characters to nickname each other emerged almost obsessively in engineers' daily conversation. For instance, "Jack the North" is the nickname for Jack, who is named after one character in *Game of Thrones*—the King of the North. The King of the North is portrayed as the symbol of a loyal warrior marching in the world of ice and snow, one who never shied away from fighting battles even if the chances of winning were slim. Similarly, everyone in the Pipe Org knew an engineer nicknamed "DKP," but very few knew DKP's real name. DKP was short for "Dragon Killing Point," a point-keeping system commonly used in many massively multiplayer online games. Since most engineers were familiar with this concept, memorizing this nickname was easy. Unsatisfied with merely nicknaming colleagues, engineers also renamed their software development projects: the Knight team engineers named their star project the "George Martin Project," revealing their aspiration to construct a masterpiece akin to the fantasy novel writer George Martin's *A Song of Ice and Fire*.

Through their nicknaming practices, engineers echo the gaming metaphors used by managers. From the perspective of Foucault's theory on technologies of the self, this development of metaphors aims at creating new relationships between knowledge, power, and the engineers' self-regulating abilities (Rose 1996b, 156). However, the new formation of knowledge could fail when the reality of work life does not live up to such metaphors. Nevertheless, the nicknaming practices demonstrate workers' willingness to invest in the metaphor, drawing on their gaming knowledge to further articulate the linkage between gaming narratives and the meaning of engineering work.

The nicknames that engineers give each other reflect the adventurous self, which is a vital dimension of the gaming self. The adventurous self is achieved through taking risks (reified as "marching at the impossible world"), conquering challenges, and overcoming dangers (reified as "killing the dragons"). The investment of engineers in producing the adventurous self further conceals the controlling power of the simulated games, making the narratives seem to refer to their inherent characteristics rather than external suggestions. The zealous nicknaming practices also make investing in the gaming self a requirement for self-fulfillment.

The engineers at Behemoth frequently utilized the improvisational development of simulation games, extending beyond simple nicknaming practices. For example, on the wall behind his desk, Amir drew a picture that consisted of two key figures: (1) a warrior with the words "I am totally 'Tier 1'" on his head, carrying a sword and a shield just outside the gate of a fortress, and (2) a monstrous stretch limousine with three skylights and at least seven or eight doors driving straight at the warrior. On the top of the limo, Amir wrote, "Q4 is coming." As discussed briefly in Chapter 2, Amir explained that he felt enormous pressure as the team pushed out a new feature at the conclusion of a fourth-quarter sprint; at that point, there is a high risk of a significant spike in errors, and Amir's job is to handle them all. Amir said that he drew the picture to give him the courage to face any possible rise in errors, fantasizing about himself as a heroic, well-weaponized warrior prepared to take on the onslaught. In Amir's story of self-addressing as a "tier 1 warrior," the productive gamer subject becomes visible.

Amir's self-fantasy is influenced by the managers' gaming language that reframes uncertainty into risks, opportunities, and choices. Engineers interpret this language as an opportunity to romanticize risks if the managers' discourse only aims to normalize risks. Amir reified risks, such as the high risk of an error spike, by drawing on his experience as a video gamer, depicting them as a monstrous stretch limousine. By connecting his work situation to the gaming world, Amir is able to parallel the crises he encounters at work with the virtual gaming world's common crises, such as battling monsters. Amir's portrayal of himself as a warrior provides the foundation for him to glorify his activities in solving crises. As a well-armed warrior, he is prepared to tackle any challenge that comes his way.

This type of self-fantasy is not unusual at Behemoth, where engineers frequently use video-game elements, characters, and storylines to romanticize their crisis-filled work. Engineers do not just envision themselves as warriors; they also portray themselves as "ninjas" and "adventurers." They imagine technical errors as "monsters" and algorithms as rafts built by codes to navigate across the river and defeat the "monsters" on the other side.

If simulation games interpellated the gaming self associated with experimentalism and adventurism, simulation games could also enact another side of the gaming self associated with crisis mentality. Unlike engineers' internalization of an adventurous gaming self that leads to their pursuit of disruptive innovation, as shown in WZH's Dungeon Master story, engineers register a gaming self that normalizes crisis mentality and forces them to accelerate work time (Wajcman 2014). Game hobbyists are well trained in tackling various types of crises in the virtual world and thus are more likely to tap into a calm yet focused state of mind when encountering real-life difficulties. Such a state of mind—sometimes described as being "in the zone" by gamers—was a popular topic on the engineering floor. This topic often came up when interviewees described their superb video-gaming performance, a subject I found to be an excellent icebreaker. Sometimes, they described their best battle performances as a product of entering "the zone." The colloquial expression of "in the zone" is academically defined as a "flow" mind state. The concept of flow was used to describe "the state in which people are so involved in an activity that nothing else seems to matter; the experience itself is so enjoyable that people will do it even at great costs, for the sheer sake of doing it" (Csikszentmihalyi 1990, 4). Scholars have already shown that gamers are more likely to enter a flow state of mind. Once gamers entered the flow state, their concentration level would vastly enhance as they lost a sense of time (Csikszentmihalyi 1990; Edery and Mollick 2008).

When recalling their flow state in gaming, even very shy interviewees waxed eloquent about their phenomenal powers of concentration during battle sequences as they completely lost track of time. Engineers employed similar narratives when recounting legendary stories of colleagues "so lucky" to "get in the zone" and to be "free of disruption" while conquering work crises. Amir himself had experienced the flow state of mind when he was busy guarding his team's new feature against being crushed by a "spike of error." According to the story, Amir encountered a very tricky issue while his team pushed the feature out. To handle this problem, Amir—the "tier 1 warrior"—stayed up in the office for about two nights, single-handedly killed the "pirates," and snatched the "ferry" to let his team navigate the difficult time. The highlight of his heroic fight was that he was so focused that he completely ignored any outside interruption, to the point that his sense of time became distorted. According to Charlie, Amir sent an afternoon email two days after he started tackling the problem, as if he had just started to solve it. In fact, many anecdotes were handed down about Amir's two-day "hack": some said that he had been wearing his headphones the whole time, while others said they saw him sleeping under his work desk. There were also discussions about Amir having consumed too many bottles of Red Bull, which made him "tremble like fuck" during those days. Despite the half-true gossip, one thing was true—a majority of engineers admiringly admitted that Amir was a real "tier 1 warrior" for fighting this work battle.

The concept of the flow state of mind is not a novel finding. Psychologists have extensively studied and documented it as a positive mentality (Csikszentmihalyi 1990). Meanwhile, several tech companies such as Apple, Facebook, Yahoo, Google, and Amazon have embraced this concept and attempted to stimulate the flow state through various mechanisms. Unfortunately, few sociologists have critically intervened or reflected on this concept. In light of this, I aim to draw on Behemoth's case study to contemplate the implications of the flow state of mind. From a sociological perspective, the promotion of the flow state implies a reconstructed perception of work time and a new mechanism of labor exploitation. As the British historian E. P. Thompson noted, the history of time is closely linked with the history of labor

(Thompson 1967). The Industrial Revolution transformed people's perception of time, which ultimately served the interests of capitalists. Similarly, the current change in the sense of time serves the interests of informational capitalists.

Amir's case highlights that when capitalists stimulate workers' flow of mind, they exponentially increase labor power in the given labor time due to workers' high concentration levels. The so-called distorted sense of time experienced by engineers like Amir implies their loss of control over time, especially regarding the termination of work time. Consequently, the flow state indicates engineers' voluntary increase in labor power intensity and extension of labor time. It is, therefore, unsurprising that tech capitalists are fixated on procuring the flow state. Companies such as Apple, Facebook, Yahoo, Google, and Amazon have attempted various mechanisms to facilitate the flow state, ranging from providing meditation courses to training employees to enter the zone more quickly, to assigning engineers expensive noise-canceling headphones to reduce external disruptions. However, this study reveals that the efforts adopted by informational capitalists were superficial. What was really at work was the engineers' self-interpellation of their gaming subjectivity, which awakened the crisis mentality borne of longtime gaming experience and thus triggered the mental flow state.

If the simulation games described previously were organized by managers from the top and echoed by workers, then the simulation games discussed next were workers' self-initiated games. The managerial use of gaming storylines, characters, and artifacts resulted in importing a gaming environment into the workplace; these efforts laid a solid foundation on which workers could further develop their simulation strategies. Building on the top-down support for blurring the lines between a fantasy world and working reality, workers imported the off-work relationship they constructed in the virtual video-game world to facilitate their workplace interactions and team collaborations.

The gaming environment nurtured by managers offered workers who described themselves as socially inept a familiar social structure that facilitated their ever-important collaboration. Engineers portrayed themselves as "shy" and "socially awkward" and admitted that they had difficulties smoothly interacting with coworkers to establish trustworthy, collaborative relationships. As one engineer explained,

A lot of the programming culture, a lot of the tech culture, stems from young people who are gamers . . . who are socially not so—they are not socially ready. . . . A lot of programmers don't know how to talk to properly . . . interact with coworkers . . . but they feel more comfortable when playing games with each other . . . because they grow up in an isolated kind of environment. Like me . . . I guess I had always played many video games as a kid. I guess this is kind of what I did—like I said, I kind of lived in a neighborhood without a lot of other kids. . . . All I can remember is playing Nintendo with my brothers and another friend.

The scrum development process, however, created a very high demand for collaboration: as development teams were continuously reorganized following the permanent-beta ideology, engineers needed to quickly establish trustworthy relationships with their new teammates. Facing such a dilemma, engineers again drew on their gaming skills and mentality to formulate solutions. As the interview excerpt illustrates, engineers' rich gaming history allowed them to feel comfortable enough to socialize with their teammates in the virtual gaming world. A majority of engineers in Pipe Org attempted to take advantage of such skills by retreating to the gaming world to build rapport through gaming relationships with their scrum team coworkers before extending such gaming relationships to the workplace.

For example, Danny, an engineer, shared that it took him three weeks to open his mouth to say "Hi" to "Little Zach," an engineer from another team. Eventually, he felt comfortable talking with Little Zach in real life after running into him on the Steam platform, and they played *Final Fantasy* together for several nights. Their first in-person conversations at Behemoth consisted of chatting about the game, only later broadening to include work topics.

Three key themes emerge from the discussion. Firstly, the strategy of utilizing video-gaming activities to socialize with colleagues represents a crucial aspect of gamer subjectivity. This implies that gaming is perceived as the ultimate solution to challenges encountered in the real world. Secondly, it is noteworthy that engineers predominantly resort to gaming as a means of enhancing collaboration. This entails that engineers have become the primary drivers of improving interactions and collaboration. Collaboration is the cornerstone of technological innovation, and therefore, improving collaboration should have been the primary responsibility of the tech firm. However, it has been transformed into the engineers' responsibility, a process referred to as "responsibilization," which is considered a standard technology of power in governmentality studies (Lemke 2001, 201). Finally, Behemoth establishes a norm of relying on virtual world activities to overcome real-life difficulties on the engineering floor by simulating the gaming world at work. Danny's social strategy may not be as celebrated in other work settings as it is in tech firms. In other sectors, such as finance or marketing, drawing on video-gaming interactions to compensate for a lack of social skills would be considered "nerdy," "geeky," and "socially awkward." This norm of retreating to the virtual world to socialize is aligned with the tech capitalist's goal of improving collaboration. As demonstrated by Danny, engineers' practices enable them to achieve this norm and affirm Behemoth's objective.

Using off-work gaming relationships to build scrum team rapport is not an individual strategy but an organization-wide practice. At Pipe Org, scrum teams coordinated video-game battle teams so that they faced off not only at work but on the "field of battle," as it were. The most popular games in which engineers organized battle teams included *World of Warcraft*, *Final Fantasy*, *Defense of the Ancients 2*, *Counter-Strike: Global Offensive*, and *League of Legends*.

For example, the Wizard team was famous for battling together in *Counter-Strike: Global Offensive (CS:GO)*. Some gamers from the Knight team occasionally joined the Wizards to play *CS:GO*; however, the Knights also had a gaming schedule for *League of Legends (LoL)*, and Danny from the Wizard team also occasionally joined the Knights for *LoL*. The Assassin team was really into two games—*World of Warcraft* and *Final Fantasy*—and gamers like Ben and Little Zach from the Knight team played those two games with the Assassin team. Although the Ranger team did not have a specific team game, members from the Rangers often played *CS:GO* with the Wizards.

Take the Wizards' gaming practices, for example. Game hobbyists like Danny, Matt, Old Jack, and Derick agreed that they would meet online every Wednesday and Thursday night to team up and play *CS:GO*. *CS:GO* is a multiplayer shooter game that pits two teams against one another; each team is tasked with completing a challenge and killing as many people as possible on the opposing team. The Wizard team formed a single *CS:GO* team that challenged various (often unknown) teams randomly formed online.

The Wizard team manager, Vikram, usually finished his team's weekly meeting early on Thursday (at 4:30 p.m.) to ensure the team could get back home early to start their game. Moreover, the Wizards' meeting room wall had a corner dedicated to tracking the team's *CS:GO* ranking. When the team's rank moved up drastically, Vikram included it as a "success story" in the weekly meeting or the sprint retrospective, blurring the lines between work and play. One thing that needs to be pointed out is that compared to managers' roles in implementing those rather "top-down" gaming elements (e.g., gaming characters, storylines, and artifacts), here, the managers had a supporting role. A critical feature of this "video-gaming social" was the high level of workers' autonomy. If managers completely controlled these practices, it could threaten workers' authenticity, and workers would very likely feel as if the work games were phony and not participate.

The engineers' effort to simulate the video-game battle team on the engineering floor was reflected in their routine socialization to increase rapport; it became a vital strategy for overcoming the contradiction embedded in scrum development. The inevitable contradiction within the scrum development process manifested as the tension between the instability associated with the permanent-beta development process and engineers' demand for stability to establish trustworthy, collaborative relationships. This contradiction intensified during periods when the development teams underwent constant reorganization: take the Wizard team's reorg, for example. As detailed in an earlier section (see Figure 3.1), the Wizards experienced four instances of team reorganization (e.g., expanding, splitting into two teams, merging with the Knights, and incubating a new sister team) from 2013 to 2015, when it developed an encryption software and attempted to pivot the development direction from producing a SD box to a black box. As discussed above, improvement of collaboration has become the engineers' responsibility due to the tech firm's responsibilization. As constant reorganization becomes a vital obstacle to collaboration, engineers naturally consider it their responsibility to solve this problem. Directed by their gamer subjectivity and mentality, simulating video-gaming relationships would be engineers' first choice for solving such a dilemma.

The best illustration of how engineers simulate video-gaming relationships to survive constant team reorganization is Ben's story. Recall that after dividing the original scrum team into two teams in phase 3, the Wizards' manager temporarily transferred a new project owner from the Knight team to take charge of the server-side box—Ben (see Figure 3.1). The project owner's success depends on his knowledge of his team and his interactions with them, so when Ben was assigned the project owner's role for the Wizard team, he sensed a pressing need to engage with his new team members. Knowing that almost all the Wizard team members played *CS:GO* together, Ben immediately opened a *CS:GO* account and asked to join the Wizards. Apparently, his "video-gaming social" strategy was a huge success: in a subsequent interview, Ben proudly shared that he was impressed that he could interact with the server-side team so well only one week into his assignment.

To be fair, Ben's video-gaming social approach could not have been as successful without the Wizard team manager's support. After learning that Ben had been playing with the server-side team for a while, Vikram invited him to the Wizard team area to check out their *CS:GO* scoreboard and asked him to join their team for lunch more often (lunchtime was when the scrum team discussed video games). By the end of the development process, Ben had become so popular in the Wizard team that he could even join their "stand-up" meetings—although it was a clear violation of protocol since stand-up meetings were typically limited to Wizard team members to discuss their internal logistics. However, both Vikram and the team believed that "he [Ben] is already one of us," so there was no reason to keep him out.

Ransacking Ben's story has revealed several important patterns that are pervasive in many simulation games organized on the engineering floor.

Firstly, the gaming capital possessed by engineers has been converted into the social capital vital for scrum team collaboration, with simulation games serving as the central route for this conversion. During this capital conversion process, engineers' productive gamer subjectivity is interpellated, as they are endowed with freedom and autonomy to strategize their practices and self-represent their understanding of an ideal work self and style.

Ben's practice provides a perfect illustration of how control operates through the technologies of the self. Engineers like Ben enjoy the freedom and autonomy to strategize their practices, enabling them to self-represent their understanding of an ideal work self and style. This, in turn, suggests that the productive gamer subjectivity is constituted among workers. For example, the Wizards accepted Ben as "one of us" on the server-side development team after they accepted his role on their *CS:GO* battle team. Interestingly, managers were largely absent from the scene, underscoring the notion that power had been exercised through interpellation and subjugation.

In simulation games, power is not something possessed and operated by the ruling class—managers (Foucault 2008; Gunn 2006). Instead, power is predominantly achieved through workers' self-discipline and mutual surveillance. Celebrating Ben's assimilation into the *CS:GO* game culture, the Wizard team disciplined Ben's choice of which gaming team he should join. The discipline, in Ben's case, was exercised positively through encouragement, support, and celebration. In other circumstances, discipline could be enforced negatively through shaming, repudiation, and punishment. Considering this, we can imagine that Ben's in-group membership might be repudiated once he showed less interest in, or even withdrew from, the *CS:GO* game under the Wizard team's watchful eye. Therefore, Ben has to keep investing in the *CS:GO* game continuously while under such surveillance. In other words, Ben's case perfectly exemplifies how the technology of power is exercised under an omniopticon—the many surveilling the many—on the engineering floor (Elwood and Leszczy 2010).

In Ben's case, his powerlessness is not only reflected in his incapacity to withdraw from the game under the omniopticon but also in his ineffectiveness in conducting resistance. In classic labor games, workers have the opportunity to negotiate and even resist managerial efforts to elicit their consent to invest in them. However, in simulation games, power is operated on workers' self-internalization of the gaming ethic, leaving engineers like Ben disarmed with the weapon of resistance. All these conditions contribute to Ben's eventual burnout, which hints at the disastrous outcome for engineers who are absorbed in the simulation games and its established gamified governmentality.

Brenda, a thirty-two-year-old Pipe Org engineer, shares Ben's tragic story and how the blurring between work and gaming teams, activities, relationships, time, and space contributed to his burnout. According to Brenda, the last time she talked with Ben was the day he quit his job. His resignation was a surprise to everyone, as he had just finished the server-side box project and was considered a rising star on the Knight team. When Brenda ran into Ben in the company's parking lot, he told her that he "couldn't do this anymore." Brenda explained that for a long time, Ben logged into the work system for about twenty hours every day, trying to answer all the questions his teammates sent him through the internal messenger tool. If his teammates could not find him via internal messenger, they could always find him on the Steam platform and pose their work questions there. Brenda told me she had repeatedly warned him, "It's just a job; don't go all in." At the end of our conversation about Ben, Brenda sighed and commented, "He always said that he was lucky that he could get paid for doing what he loved, get paid for hanging out with people he liked all the time . . . and get paid for having fun."

Another characteristic embodied in Ben's story is the blurring between work and gaming teams, activities, relationships, time, and space. Indeed, a majority of the simulation games at Behemoth are built on the simulation of video-gaming interactions and relationships in the scrum process. This blurring of the work and off-work boundary is a notable labor issue that has drawn attention from scholars, with mainstream discussion focusing on its consequences of enhancing overwork and destroying work-life balance (Bulut 2021; Fleming 2005; Gregg 2013). However, the mechanisms through which such blurring affects labor identity and facilitates labor control have received little attention. Therefore, investigating such mechanisms is significant as it can provide more nuanced insight into why work-life blurring becomes a prominent phenomenon in modern work settings. In the following section, I elaborate on how and why engineers maximally blur work and gaming activities in the simulation games.

To begin with, from the above documentation, one can tell that engineers were keen to extend their work relations to their gaming world, enhance rapport, and reimport the improved relationship back into the workplace. As a result of this simulation process, teammates became comrades in the video-gaming world. The romanticization of the working relationship into a comradeship reduced the engineers' work anxiety, which stemmed from the paradox between a permanent-beta instability and the workers' need for stable and trustworthy relationships.

Less obviously, the faded boundaries between game and work teams obscured the standards of evaluating a good scrum team member and a good video-game team player. The skills required in software development (e.g., quick reactions, teamwork spirit, multitasking, and reformulation of problem-solving templates) can overlap the abilities needed for playing fast-paced video games to a greater extent than those skills prized by other professions.

Indeed, gamers' abilities were constantly judged by their coworkers when playing video games together.

For example, when I interviewed Chuan from the Knight team, he told me he also played *CS:GO* with the Wizards but eventually quit because he realized that his less-competent performance in the game potentially discredited his work skills:

> I actually don't really like playing *CS:GO*. I am more into games like *WoW* (*World of Warcraft*). But Fei [Chuan's teammate] persuaded me that I needed to try to play with them for *CS:GO*. You know, to be more social. So, I just registered an account, and I told Mike. Mike is more like the lead. He seemed very satisfied and told me that I could just follow his lead. . . . So I played several nights . . . and always followed Mike's lead.
>
> But there was one night . . . I played poorly, you know. . . . I was so new to the game. And I [i.e., his game character] almost died, so Mike told me to crouch in the corner of the room to hide . . . and that's exactly what I did. But the thing is . . . I faced the wall of that corner. Then I heard Mike yell to me through the microphone, "Chuan, turn around! . . . What the hell are you doing there? Face to the enemy! . . . Shoot them!" Then I realized how stupid I was by facing the wall and leaving my back to the enemy. But the thing is . . . I don't think I am stupid or anything. It's just that I am new to the game and I am trying to get used to all the stuff . . . like the game setup . . . like how to use the shortcut key.
>
> The next day during lunch, Mike just broadcasted my mistake to almost half of Pipe Org in the public kitchen. He was like, "Can you guys believe it? Chuan just crouched there, facing the wall, like he needed to do some serious thinking about his mistake. . . . So funny." So I quit [the game] after that day. . . . It still bothers me a little bit whenever I remember Mike's cocky tone that day. . . . I have to admit it affects my relationship with Mike a little bit.

In Chuan's account of his participation in the *CS:GO* game, the critical role of subjectivity embedded in simulation games is made evident. Casual conversations among engineers about their teammates' gaming behaviors highlight the intertwined relationship between gaming and work identity, activity, and relationships. Firstly, the manifestation of gamer subjectivity as a clear, quick-minded team player willing to self-sacrifice for the team was reinforced through engineers' rejection of poor team players associated with opposite gaming traits (e.g., slow reactions and tangled minds). Secondly, this idealized gamer image denoted a player who can leverage their gaming capital to establish scrum team rapport at work. This constitution was reflected in both Chuan's narrative and Ben's story. All these features contribute to a particular image of a gamer at Behemoth that aligns its pursuit with the goal of engineering work, such as quick reaction to crises and building rapport. Thus, the gamer subjectivity constituted in the simulation games is a productive gamer subjectivity.

Moreover, Chuan's account of his decision to play *CS:GO* instead of his own favorite game, *League of Legends*, allows us to glimpse the normalized and disciplinary power of the productive gamer subjectivity. The discourse of simulating work into games designates an array of rules for the conduct of engineers' daily work life, such as regulating which game is considered appropriate. Autonomy is the foundation of engineers' interpellation process of gamer subjectivity: they take control of their undertakings, define their goals, and design strategies to achieve their goals and subjectivity. Engineers like Chuan subscribe to the gaming discourse and strategize their behaviors to approximate the ideal productive gamer subjectivity. What they strive to achieve is a normalized goal governed and enforced by all teammates in the team. In other words, through Chuan's narrative, we can clearly sense that he felt pressured to join the *CS:GO* game, which is considered the norm at the Wizard team, instead of playing *WoW* (*World of Warcraft*). It becomes apparent that his teammates' encouragement for him to participate in the *CS:GO* plays a disciplinary function in directing Chuan's choice.

More importantly, due to the overlap between gaming and working activities, the gaze of engineers' gaming subjectivity now extends beyond the private sphere and into the workplace, creating a panoptic environment where engineers are well aware that they could be permanently watched. This omnipresent gaze makes engineers more likely to inscribe productive gamer subjectivities. Engineers' willingness to subscribe to productive gamer subjectivity shapes their boundary-blurring practices between work and game time, space, skills, and personality, as illustrated below.

First, the temporal and spatial boundaries between work and game were primarily blurred. For Chuan, the point of playing *CS:GO* was to socialize with his work team; to some extent, playing games functioned like coworkers' happy hours. The problem, in this case, was that the happy hours had moved to the private sphere (i.e., home). The shift of happy hours back to workers' homes meant that their leisure time and space, which used to play a crucial role in facilitating workers' reproduction, was further compressed. Workers could hardly recognize that their reproductive time and space had been largely appropriated, however, as the appropriation was disguised by gamified discourse. Instead, many engineers expressed their gratitude for being able to find a job in which they got to "hang out" and "have fun" with a group of "like-minded" friends all the time, at work and at home.

Second, Chuan's narrative also illustrated that gamers' skills—as crucial elements of gaming capital—were enormously blurred with work skills and constantly judged by their coworkers. He talked at length about his mistake of squatting facing the wall during the CS:GO battle and how Mike broadcasted this mistake the next day at work, which made him become a target of team joking. Although the evaluations were made on the private sphere's gaming platform, they could (and were) quickly brought to the public sphere and enticed nonplaying workers to participate in judgment as well. Chuan attributed his chaotic reaction to his unfamiliarity with this game, but Mike attributed the response to Chuan's tangled mind, which created space for other engineers to use his gaming performance to explain work behaviors. More problematically, when engineers decided on whom they wanted to work with and which scrum team they wanted to join during a phase of scrum team establishment or reorganization, they could quickly draw on their observation of their colleague's gaming performance to choose scrum teammates.[10]

Finally, personal characteristics and dispositions (e.g., leadership quality, individualistic heroism, the spirit of self-sacrifice) displayed via video-game team battle, like skills and abilities, could be blurred with working characteristics and considered transferable to the scrum team. For example, engineers have continuously evaluated their teammates based on the idea of self-sacrifice as an essential personal quality in the team-based video game. Jammar's teammates on the Ranger team frequently discussed his "self-centeredness," evidenced by his preference for playing lead roles instead of supporting roles and willfully quitting midgame. Gradually, other players from the Ranger team excluded Jammar from their CS:GO game and secretly asked Ben, an engineer from another team, to replace him. The sanctions were not limited to the online world: when a manager accidentally left his computer unlocked, a Ranger team member used the manager's account to send a teasing email to all of Pipe Org, titled "Ranger is ready to trade Jammar with Ben." Although everyone claimed this was just a prank email, Jammar's unpopularity on the Ranger team was exposed to the whole organization, and ultimately, he was transferred to another Pipe Org team.

The interpellation of productive gamer subjectivity propelled engineers to create rampant simulation games that embodied their freedom, autonomy, and individuality. By embedding games into work, the scrum development process became an expression of workers' individuality, which aligned with the capitalist objective of maximizing creativity. However, specific development steps, like code review (CR), pursued the goal of standardization, repressing individuality. Indeed, as Barrett (2005) and other scholars have demonstrated, CR is a very typical control strategy many tech companies strive to adopt to standardize software development processes (Barrett 2005; Kraft 1977; Woodcock 2019). To overcome this, engineers mobilized self-governing capacities and organized minor games for the CR process to align their conduct and self-evaluation with the CR work process. The Code Review Roulette game invented by the Assassin team was an excellent example of how engineers drew on their freedom to design a CR game to standardize their coding behaviors. When engineers participated in this game, they went through their discipline, design, and act out their routines, becoming the best illustration of how simulation gaming practices are imbued with the technologies of the self.

As discussed at the beginning of this chapter, one key stage integrated into the scrum development cycle is the CR process, which was applied to let scrum team members review and examine each other's codes and offer suggestions before deployment of the software features or products. Not only were reviewers encouraged to find coders' mistakes, but they were also encouraged to provide detailed comments to the code writers. Commenting on teammates' codes played an essential role in ensuring coders from the same team shared a certain level of style consistency among their codes, thus standardizing the team's coding process. While some of the reviewers' comments just identified their teammates' "grammatical" inconsistency, other comments were more complex and tried to point out critical mistakes that might potentially crash a system. Like many high-tech giants in the United States, Behemoth designated CR as an obligatory requirement of scrum development teams; however, Behemoth allowed different development teams to independently determine how they divided up the CR tasks. Some teams asked their members to send codes to the whole group so that whoever was available could jump on the CRs. Other teams, such as those in Pipe Org, required code writers to send CR invitations to two teammates.

The CR process frequently elicited conflicts and resentment among engineers, since engineers' codes were viewed as an embodiment of their coding skills, coding competence, and even their personality. Too many mistakes and bugs identified by reviewers in the finished codes could be seen as a sign of the sender's suboptimal skills and technological incompetence. Many engineers complained that code authors were easily offended, and it took a lot of energy to convince them to revise their codes. As one interviewee, Howard, told me, "All programmers have egos. For the writer to insist his approach was right and my comments were wrong was very common. Sometimes I really didn't want to see something bad happen during release, so I had to point it out, which meant I had to fight hard over this. . . . Sometimes it's really exhausting."[11] Given the delicate nature of the process, it's not difficult to imagine that there were frequent obstacles to allocating CR tasks. Scrum team members had to solve these problems when the roadblocks were severe or conflicts were so intense that they even blocked development processes—but here again, games became the solutions that first crossed engineers' minds to overcome problems within the CR process.

Take, for example, the Assassin team's invention of the Code Review Roulette game. The Code Review Roulette game—inspired by Russian roulette—was invented to randomly designate an engineer to review Deron's (a fellow engineer) codes: while Deron's codes were vital for the feature's release, most engineers in the Assassin team tried to avoid accepting his CR invitation. According to the Assassin team's engineers, Deron's codes were "smart but messy," requiring reviewers to put substantial extra labor into their CR. One of Deron's teammates, Bob, offered a comprehensive analysis on why it was not easy to review Deron's code:

> Deron was really smart and his codes . . . all super complicated and weird, it's just like—you know, that's a real nightmare. . . . When he wrote . . . he can do really tricky stuff. But when you do CR for him, you kinda have to deal with the consequences of that. . . . When you do CR, you expect things to be, kinda, you know—laid out a certain way. . . . But if he starts to do really tricky stuff . . . things that aren't standard, that just makes it hard for you. I think he needs to learn that simplicity and readability are almost the most important [things].

Like Bob, many of Deron's teammates interpreted his code as "smart" and filled with "exciting new features normally not known by others," but at the same time, they criticized it for its "lack of consistency." Engineers commented that Deron's codes reflected that he showed no respect for "rules, standards, and formats." Besides, Deron's teammates in the Assassin team also mentioned that he did not like his code to be modified and could become irritable when his reviewers asked for code revisions. More problematically, when Deron was in a hacking-deadline mode, he tended to push his codes out to the pipeline for deployment without waiting for reviewers' feedback. These behaviors created potential risks for himself and his reviewer that needed to be mitigated, and these factors contributed to the Assassin team crisis: no one wanted to review Deron's chunks of codes, even though this sticking point would delay their software deployment.

Eventually, Deron's buddy Charlie solved his CR problem by inventing the Code Review Roulette game. The delivery of one team member's toy revolver gun gave Charlie a flash of insight. Like other Pipe Org teams, the Assassin team manager Logan encouraged his team members to be fully "weaponized." After WZH joined the team, he immediately adopted this "team tradition" and ordered a toy revolver gun. After the toy gun was delivered, every team member gathered around WZH and praised the gun for being well made—the chamber spun very smoothly and made a complete stop before locking in. Then, some members began discussing using the loaded revolver gun to play Russian roulette. Hearing the team's zealous discussion of Russian roulette, Charlie suggested that they could use this game to decide who was going to review Deron's code. Charlie's proposal immediately won support from his teammates, who started to write down basic rules for the game (i.e., Deron would not participate so that there would be six players for the six-chamber revolver).

In this context, as described in the introductory anecdote of the first chapter, the engineers of the Assassin team supported Charlie's proposal and started playing the "Code Review Roulette" game. This game involved each participant sequentially loading a bullet into a toy revolver, spinning the cylinder, and then pressing the muzzle against their temple before pulling the trigger. The engineers approached this game seriously, engaging in discussions about the probabilities associated with respinning or not. Consequently, a consensus was reached to modify the game's rules, specifically abolishing the option to respin the cylinder. The game continued until Charlie discharged the bullet, thereby assuming the Code Review (CR) task. Since then, Code Review Roulette has been institutionalized as a tradition within the Assassin team, with several members partaking in the game for the selection of code reviewers.

The core gaming mechanism embedded in Code Review Roulette was randomization. According to the engineers' narrative of the game's origins, it is obvious that this group of workers was very familiar with how the randomization mechanism operates, and their familiarity derived in part from their rich gaming history. Randomization is ubiquitous in various games, from fantasy games that use dice to randomize players' next move (e.g., Blood Bowl) to card games that require constant deck shuffling (e.g., Uno), to role-playing video games that adopt the randomization to ensure characters' every action has an equal chance to succeed or fail (e.g., *Diablo*).

Engineers' longtime immersion in the gaming world made them accustomed to drawing on game mechanics to solve work problems. In the Code Review Roulette instance, the randomization mechanism came to mind when faced with the difficulties of labor division; arbitrarily selected code reviewers symbolized a similar approach to many video games in which players must divide their roles or pick heroes at random. Once the mechanism was adopted on the engineering floor, it was harnessed to construct a relatively fair situation to ensure each engineer had the same odds of firing the bullet. Not only were engineers primed to rely on their gaming mentality to develop a gamified solution for a work puzzle; they also drew on their long-cultivated gaming skills to perfect that solution. The midplay discussion between Charlie and Peter showed that these game hobbyists were so well trained to calculate the odds in games that they could acutely recognize the potential unfairness embedded in the game's original design. Undoubtedly, such a quick reaction to the odds-changing issue was a result of these engineers' years-long dedication to playing games that constantly involved reshuffling and changing odds.

Again, it has to be recalled that gamer subjectivity played a critical role in stimulating the Assassin team to invent Code Review Roulette. First, these gamers strongly believed that they could resort to gaming skills, attitudes, and mechanics to conquer most work difficulties and that they were gifted in this regard. Once a gamer like Charlie drew on gaming mechanics to solve this work problem, other team members embraced his approach, and his gaming status was enhanced, which can be seen in the Assassin team members' zestful discussion of the game's rules. As gaming subjects, engineers were more likely to get excited by a new and unexpected game than other professional workers and more receptive to an initially tricky CR assignment when it was transformed into a fun game.[12]

Managers could confidently retreat behind the scenes due to workers' self-adaption of their gamer subjectivity and associated gaming traits. Indeed, in recollections of Code Review Roulette, the managerial role was limited to providing a precondition for the invention of the game—"weaponizing" the team and encouraging members to buy toy guns. Of course, the weapon (i.e., the toy revolver gun) was the critical instrument of the game, without which Charlie would not have come up with the idea. However, the weapon was nothing but an instrument: like the managers' role in the game, it was merely guidance that did not shape or determine any subsequent gaming practices. The absence of managers endowed enough freedom and space for engineers to self-mobilize their subjectivities and design their gaming actions.

Concluding Remarks

The scrum development process faces multiple sources of tension, such as the contradiction between the need for highly flexible development and stable development relations, the demand for both unrestrained creativity and code-writing consistency, and the difficulty in measuring, standardizing, evaluating, and squeezing out disruptive creativity, the most precious labor power in the software development process. To address this situation, a series of simulation games were introduced to the engineering floor. However, the question arises: How do simulation games facilitate capitalists' control over engineers?

According to Whitson's (2013, 2014) discussion on governmentality and gamification, gamification techniques may encounter difficulties in enrolling people into self-governance under certain circumstances, and workplaces could be challenging to construct such a governmentality. Drawing on the failed workplace game Puzzle Pirates envisioned by Reeves and Read, Whitson argues that workplaces could be perceived as challenging to construct such a governmentality.

Through the stories of Behemoth, engineering workplaces depict a specific work environment that makes fertile territory for forming governmentality. Via organizing simulation games, Behemoth has successfully established a gamified governmentality in the most central engineering labor process—scrum development. Three significant techniques contribute to establishing gamified governmentality, including gamifying the software development process, interpellating gamer subjectivity, and blurring gaming and working activities and relationships. Through these techniques, power is achieved by engineers' self-internalization of the gamified discourse and self-governing behaviors according to it, making technologies of self the central control mechanism in the scrum process.

Establishing gamified governmentality is primarily different from constructing hegemony, as capitalists usually introduce labor games and gamification techniques to the workplace to construct hegemony. However, the success of simulation games is destined to construct domination beyond hegemony, given engineers' strong individualistic expression of interests, skills, and creativity. The organization of simulation games to establish governmentality is the most efficient way of conducting control in these highly creative working groups. Therefore, gamified governmentality is achieved through the individualization of power and directing engineers to use their gaming capacity and imagination to constitute the self-expressed gamer subjectivities.

Unlike control formed under hegemonic regimes, control is not achieved through coordinating the interests between managers and engineers in gamified governmentality. As shown by a series of simulation games introduced in this chapter, none reveal a negotiated process between managers and engineers, and managers have primarily disappeared from any concrete operation of simulation games. They do nothing but promote the gaming discourse that workers are likely to internalize. By subscribing to and internalizing such gaming discourse, engineers' self-governing capacities can be mobilized, bringing out their ways of conducting and evaluating themselves in alignment with the capitalist's interests. In this way, the simulation games reflect a more severe labor control than hegemonic control, diluting any possible resistance that may remain under the hegemonic regime.

Of course, gamer subjectivity is an indispensable factor in the construction of governmentality. Simulation games are a prime example of engineers' investment in enacting various aspects of gamer subjectivity, such as their adventurous self, heroic traits, crisis mentality, and ability to integrate gaming and working relationships, skills, and characteristics. The gamer subjectivity that engineers formulate in their private lives is imported into the workplace and interpreted and reshaped through investment in simulation games, guided by the gaming rhetoric that is constructed on the engineering floor. In essence, workers' private lives are synthesized into labor time through the self-constitution of their gamer subjectivity. Their gaming capacity, including their gaming mentality and creativity, becomes the raw materials to be exploited. Hence, when productive gamer subjectivity is successfully established, engineers are subjugated to the production circle.

4

Hegemony or Not

A Comparison between the Collection and the Ticket Game

One noon, Danny and I planned to go out to eat together. Danny asked me what I wanted to eat. I told him, "Something easy to grab. Pizza, maybe?" Then he told me that he knew where we could grab pizza— the phone-testing event. The testing event was organized like a party: loud music filled the air; boxes of pizza, hot dogs, and beer buckets were scattered on several folding tables; engineers lined up in front of the testing booth to "get a taste of" the not-yet-launched phone; another booth was set up to draw engineers to join the "debug competition" to win water bottles; and if you wanted to share your thoughts about the phone (any thought) on the wall, you got a sticker as swag. However, none of these perks seemed to draw Danny's attention. After scanning his badge to get in, he went straight to the food table. It took Danny less than fifteen minutes to get in and out of the party.

When we sat on the stairs in front of the Whole Foods Market and ate pizzas that Danny got from the event, Danny took out his phone and scrolled down a page packed with colorful shapes. I moved close to Danny and asked, "What's this page used for?" He told me this was a page Behemoth used to document "icons" (i.e., colorful shapes) that engineers collected. I asked, "What are icons?" Danny told me they were awarded virtual icons to put on this icon page whenever they accomplish specific tasks (e.g., attend the phone-testing event). "OK, just like the game badges," I thought. Usually, virtual game badges listed on the game page were badges of honor for gamers obsessed with collecting all different kinds of badges. So I presumptuously thought Danny must be very passionate about collecting these badges and said, "Wow, congratulations on adding another one to your collection!" To my surprise, Danny sniffed airily and said, "It's just a corporate trick. I mean, you get nothing but the badge, right?"

Another encounter between Danny and me happened only a few days after the phone event, around Labor Day. That evening, when the Wizard team crowd had thinned out for the upcoming holiday, only Danny and I were left in the team area. Danny was waiting to pick up the relay baton of "ticket resolving" from his teammate Matthew. Tickets are notices of issues that require an engineer's attention; developers usually take turns manning "on-call" shifts to resolve tickets. While waiting, Danny logged onto the "trouble ticketing" board and soon found out a frustrating fact: their sister team, the Knight team, beat them in last week's on-call shifts, as they pulled out many more overtakes (when resolved tickets exceed unresolved ones) than the Wizard team. Danny pointed at the Knight team's two spikes of overtakes, telling me that he knew it was "Benji" (Ben's nickname) who did the "weekend ticket marathon" to pull out the overtake. Dan's eyes widened as he told me Ben's weekend marathon: "He is real hardcore. He worked forty-eight straight hours, sleeping on the bathroom floor." Then, Danny told me that he even wanted to hire some "rank boosters" to improve his team's shameful record.

Picking up on jargon like "rank boosters" and "weekend marathon" exclusively used by serious gamers, it dawned on me that some unique setup of the on-call process and the ticketing board must touch the gaming nerves of engineers like Ben and Danny. What was the unique setup? I became confused. After all, to an outsider like me, the ticketing board looked so formal that it could hardly trigger any association with the gaming world. Nevertheless, engineers leveraged their best gaming techniques (e.g., hours-long marathons) to beat "opponents." On the contrary, facing the badge-collecting board—where Behemoth went the extra mile to establish a gamelike feeling—engineers seemed very nonchalant. How could the "just-as-a-game" badge collecting attract gamers' minimum interest, while the seemingly "game-free" ticket resolving warranted gamers' enormous investment?

Construction of Hegemony in the Field of Games

While simulation games can lead to gaming governmentality, the two games discussed in this chapter are less penetrated and operate to establish a more traditional form of domination known as hegemony. Hegemonic power is a contested process in which the dominant class coordinates the interests of the subordinate class with its own. This involves making concessions and adapting strategies to gain the consent and subjection of the subordinate class. Two preconditions for the usefulness of hegemonic power are the ability of the dominant group to articulate the culture and interests of the sub-

ordinate group and their ability to coordinate interests and make concessions (Burawoy 1979; Gramsci 1971; Lee 1998; Thompson 1967).

It is under such a theoretical consideration, then, that this book argues that
gaming culture and subjectivity, as well as the coordinating practices, play
a crucial role in shaping the outcomes of the two games. By examining these
factors, this book aims to determine whether and how the different operations
of these variables contribute to the divergent game outcomes. Indeed, as shown
from the above anecdote, while the first game—the badge-collecting game—
seems to barely attract engineers' investment, the second game—organized
around ticket marathons and ranking boosters—apparently touches engineers' gaming nerves. Then, does that imply the second game is more efficient
in coordinating interests and mobilizing gaming culture than the first game?
If so, what are the particular mechanisms that facilitate these processes?

In fact, such speculation contributes to a core debate between the labor
game and gamification studies. The first game follows a more standardized
gamification setup, while the second game is a combination of gamification
and a classic labor game. Workplace gamification refers to employers adopting game mechanics, such as leveling up, data visualization, and badge collection, to reinforce their goals and interests, such as incentivizing workers'
engagement and enhancing productivity (Bogost 2007; Walz and Deterding
2014). Some scholars assert that gamification has adapted to the times and is
thus considered a more efficient labor control mechanism than labor games.
However, other scholars argue that gamification can only generate prescribed
and mandatory fun and is trivialized for its inability to attract workers' consent (Mollick and Rothbard 2014; Statler 2011; Trittin et al. 2018). This chapter aims to contribute to this debate by comparing the two types of games
and analyzing their outcomes.

In the following sections, I investigate and compare the two games by
outlining their gamification setup and examining whether they embody the
nature of classic labor games. I then examine the gaming culture and subjectivity, as well as the coordinating practices, of the two games and interpret
their operation from both the dominant and subordinate sides. The chapter
concludes with an analysis of the game outcomes and a comparison of the
two types of games. I hope that a comparative reading of these two games
sheds light on vital theoretical themes and helps solve puzzles proposed for
this chapter and the book in general.

Crowdsourcing Games: Task-Rabbiting the Workplace

The software development process is always in a state of permanent beta: instead of creating a perfect end product, development teams are encouraged
to deploy a minimum viable product (MVP) and then continuously improve

it through repetitive testing and optimizing. As a result, countless bricolage tasks are left unsolved while the development teams launch their MVP. As one engineer described, "There are thousands of unfinished tasks out there . . . but no one is really looking into it because they don't think it's worth looking into." In other words, there were hundreds of thousands of bricolage tasks scattered around the company. Optimizing these tasks is essential maintenance work for the company; however, it is less urgent than the routine maintenance work assigned to each team. Routine maintenance in the format of troubleshooting is far more pressing, as any problem can crash the system at any time. Optimizing maintenance is less urgent but usually more time-consuming.

Behemoth decided to crowdsource extra and segmented efforts from engineers all over the company to optimize maintenance. As frequently highlighted in this book, for these young engineers, hedonic and gamified experience usually works as a better incentive than other substantive benefits, such as monetary rewards and gifts. Therefore, Behemoth gamified this maintenance work as well, transforming it into a badge-collection game to motivate engineers' participation. The badges that engineers are encouraged to collect are called "phone-tool icons" at Behemoth. Phone-tool icons are pictures modeled after virtual-gaming badges displayed on an employee's phone-tool page.[1] They are designed by various teams at Behemoth that usually demand optimizing maintenance and given to employees who complete particular tasks or challenges. The use of these icons draws directly on the video-gaming environment, where virtual badges or similar status indicators (e.g., positions on a leaderboard) are used to encourage engagement. The collection game also integrates the second game element—the phone-tool page's display platform. The phone-tool page is designed to announce new badges and provide a visual overview of all badges that engineers collected, offering collectors extra bragging rights.

Specifically, there are three major types of phone icons at Behemoth: (1) icons used to reward participation in "bricolage tasks," such as testing products, finding bugs, and optimizing systems; (2) icons that encourage engineers to share extra "bricolage knowledge" beyond their job descriptions; and (3) icons given for fulfilling training or passing tests or quizzes.

The essential bricolage-tasks[2] badge type encourages engineers to devote labor to tasks that benefit Behemoth in general but are not tied to their own team's development responsibilities. For example, the I Played with the Behemoth Phone icons, proposed by the Behemoth Phone development teams, are given to engineers who participate in bug-bashing events to help them test out their beta-version product. Since testing for and finding bugs can be the most tedious part of engineering work, most engineers are reluctant testers, even for their own team's products. Thus, to entice other development team members to test the phone and to help them ensure that it was "bug-free," the Behemoth Phone development team organized several noontimes I Played with the Behemoth Phone bug-bash parties during lunch and created a phone icon to reward people who participated. Notably, as a lunchtime event sponsored by another team, those bug-bash parties were well beyond most Behemoth engineers' responsibilities.

As the second-most-important badge, the bricolage-knowledge[3] badge promotes knowledge sharing within the company. In the high-tech industry, where knowledge is constantly and quickly revised, the best way to keep up with new technical knowledge is by skimming other engineers' practical experience, not by book learning per se. The phone-tool platform functions as an internal knowledge-sharing site where engineers can continuously post about and learn new technologies from their colleagues—and be rewarded with bricolage knowledge icons. The Best Tipper icon is the best illustration of the second category of badges; Behemoth issued these icons to engineers who posted tips to the add-tip-of-the-day@behemoth.com website.

Finally, as an example of the third category (i.e., quiz- or training-based badges), Behemoth gives Customer Connection icons to engineers who participate in a workshop to train engineers in providing good customer service. In other words, these icons are a type of certificate that engineers receive after attending the training.

One can see that Behemoth adopted the gamification setup and converted these practices of crowdfunding skills, knowledge, and efforts into a badge-collecting game. More importantly, this collection game marks a divergence from labor games, such as simulation games, in that the collection game excessively depends on gamification techniques to modify workers' behaviors. As the Best Tipper badge demonstrates, encouraging engineers' "knowledge-sharing behavior" is the foundation of the game's structure (e.g., the structure of the phone-tool platform and the add-tip-of-the-day@behemoth.com website) as well as the game's elements and mechanics (e.g., badge tracking and leaderboard badge displays).

Such an overdependence on the gamification setup implies two things. First, this badge-collection game is doomed to rigidity due to its strict adherence to gamification mechanics. For example, instead of tying the Customer Connection icon to a general requirement, such as "always being patient with customers," the reward requirements are very strict and granular: participate in a workshop and receive at least one phone call from the customer/client team. In other words, the workers have minimal wiggle room.

Second, the game is designed by top management, so the badge-collection platform must be constructed at the corporate level—while middle-level managers (e.g., team and organization managers) play a minimal role in shaping the game or directing engineers' gaming behaviors. In addition to the game's top-down construction, the implementation of this gamification abandons the idea of consensus, which weakens the role of middle management. Instead of focusing on consent building to motivate engineers' commitment to extra labor, collection games bypass the persuasion step even as they directly try to "nudge" engineers' behaviors (Bogost 2007; Zuboff 2019).

Disappearance of Middle Management's Coordination

To some extent, the middle-management vacuum resulted in the failure of the badge-collection game, which can be seen in the different practices of the Wizard and Knight teams when it came to collecting the I Play with Hannah[4] icon. The teams' practices were made clear through my conversation with Old Jack, who transferred from the Wizard team to the Knights to help pivot the Knight team's core product. Old Jack told me that he noticed that he was the only one who put the company's beta-version e-speaker on his desk on his first day with the Knight team, which made him feel very awkward when he tried to test the product by speaking to it. The Knight team's disinterest in playing with the e-speaker formed a sharp contrast to the Wizard team, where there was an e-speaker on each engineer's desk. During lunch breaks and other lulls, Wizard team members would pepper a constant stream of questions to their speakers: "OK, Hannah, what time is it now?" "OK, Hannah, will it rain in the next three hours?" "Hannah, what's in the news?" "Hannah, give me a *Game of Thrones* quote." Old Jack had enthusiastically talked to the e-speaker as a Wizard but had to adjust to the Knight team's complete indifference to this game.

What contributed to the opposing attitudes between the two teams? To some extent, the Wizard team's enthusiasm for participating in e-speaker testing was prompted by their team manager, Vikram. Before the e-speaker was released to the market, Vikram brought a testing version of the smart-speaker back to his team and put it on his desk. The new product inspired a huge interest among the Wizard engineers, and when the team members gathered around Vikram's desk and asked him how he had obtained this not-yet-released model, he told them that he had participated in the I Play with Hannah testing parties to get the phone-tool icon. Additionally, during the testing event, he accepted the 5,000 Questions Challenge: participants willing to take the e-speaker home and ask it 5,000 questions would receive a limited-edition silver I Play with Hannah icon that they could list on their phone-tool icon page—and keep the e-speaker as a reward. Participants who were willing to ask the e-speaker 10,000 questions would receive a limited-edition golden icon and the e-speaker. As it happened, after Vikram brought his test e-speaker back to the team area, many members of the Wizard team went to the testing event and brought back their own e-speaker to participate in the 5,000 or 10,000

Questions Challenges. By the end of the week, every member of the Wizard team had signed up for the I Play with Hannah challenge. It was not long before Wizard team engineers became dissatisfied with asking the speaker basic questions about weather, news, sports, and the like. Instead, these engineers came up with funny and tricky questions to test the speakers: "OK, Hannah, when is the end of the world?", "Hannah, did you fart?", "Hannah, will you be my girlfriend?", "Hannah, are you smarter than me?"

Vikram, the middle manager, played a crucial role in connecting the badge-collection setup (I Play with Hannah icon) and the team practices (teasing questions toward the e-speaker). The gamification mechanics of the I Play with Hannah icon were inflexible, requiring engineers to register for the badge, complete the question-challenging task, and claim the badge. However, the Vikram team's play showed that engineers had autonomy in how they teased the e-speakers. They transformed the 5,000 Questions Challenge into a teasing game by asking ridiculous questions (e.g., asking the e-speaker questions like "did you fart?" and "will you be my girlfriend?"), making the game more appealing to the Wizard team. The engineers' participation was not motivated by the gamification setup but rather by the spontaneous development of the teasing game—a classic labor game.

Vikram's support and promotion were essential for launching the gamification setup on the ground and coordinating it with a locally developed labor game. To begin with, Vikram first brought the e-speaker back to his team, which gave a strong signal of his promotion of this badge's collection. While some managers might find the teasing game too rampant and unattractive to their team's software development tasks, Vikram showed his support for the teasing game.

Unfortunately, most middle managers were unlike Vikram. The badge-collecting system was designed to encourage engineers to volunteer for teams that requested extra help. The enthusiasm of engineers would have been triggered if the volunteering engineers' manager or the service-requesting team's manager had gone the extra mile to coordinate the company's interests with the engineers' interests. Vikram's story represented the critical role of volunteering engineers' team managers in eliciting engineers' consent to contribute to the e-speaker team.

The service-requesting team manager's recognition of badge collectors' volunteering efforts was equally important. When the powers that be set up the badge-collection games, they ensured all achievements would merely be symbolized as abstract badges. The creative sparks and concerted efforts dedicated to fixing problems were stripped away in the badge-counting system. Under such circumstances, if the service-requesting team managers had been more proactive and concretized volunteering engineers' efforts, it would have been very effective in coordinating the interests and stimulating subsequent volunteering efforts.

Peter's story illustrates this point. He was a security engineer but a huge fan of Behemoth's music platform, from which he purchased all his music. When the music platform team asked volunteers to optimize their service, Peter provided a revolutionizing method of charging for music. The team immediately adopted this music-charging idea as a part of their revision plan. So Peter attempted to transfer to the music team—but was rejected. Later, when we talked about his experience, Peter told me that what he wanted was to be in the driver's seat when his idea was carried out. "But that is just me, daydreaming," Peter complained. "What did I get? A badge." Apparently, the music team manager failed to recognize Peter's contribution or show support to assist his transformation into the music team. The only recognition Peter received was a badge, which sounded worthless in his narrative.

The lack of manager effort like Vikram's implied the failure of the combination of top-down gamification and bottom-up labor games, which resulted in exposing the rigidity and float of the badge-collecting game. The vacuum of the service-requesting team manager's recognition further unmasked the conflicting interests between management and workers. The core managerial interest was to crowdsource engineers' volunteering efforts via the badge game. However, engineers rarely received any recognition from the service-requesting team, resulting in minimal coordination of interests between the capitalist and the worker sides. In other words, the disappearance of middle management's support further exposed the unequal exchange between the two sides.

Failed Enactment of Gamer Subjectivity

If the disappearance of middle management's engagement dampened engineers' enthusiasm for playing the collection game, then the failure to mobilize engineers' gamer subjectivity decisively determined the game's collapse. If we suppose that the gamification mechanics had been set up properly and functioning well, then engineers would have been very vulnerable to being exploited by the icon-collection game. After all, engineers' gamer subjectivity, cultivated as it is in video-game play, should have been easily imported to interpret and participate in the collection game.

For example, one of the bricolage-knowledge badges—the Best Tipper icon—is one of the most popular phone-tool icons, with more than six thousand recipients. One reason for its popularity is that engineers get used to learning new knowledge through reading user tips, as they always skim through video-gaming forums to glean tricks and tips. Mike, a dedicated

World of Warcraft player for more than twenty years, accurately captured the parallels between sharing game tips and sharing work tips: "Like, I'm really interested in cryptography and security, so I'm checking out a lot of tips from the tipper website related to this . . . like every day . . . just kind of as a hobby. . . . I also do the same thing for video games. . . . I keep on top of things like this." Matt offered a similar comment, saying, "I like to spend twenty to thirty minutes every day reading tips from the tipper websites. . . . I always use lunchtime to skim through a subreddit for game tips. . . . It [the subreddit] gets a lot of different stuff. A lot of it isn't in-depth . . . but very practical." The popularity of the Best Tipper badge, then, partially stems from engineers' building a bridge between their experience exploring game forums and their experience on Behemoth's tips-and-tricks website. This bridge lets engineers draw on their gaming experience to recognize the benefits of tipper websites, which allow them to "keep on top of things" and quickly learn "practical"[5] playing strategies.

Despite the potential of the badge-collection game, its obstacles determined its inability to mobilize engineers' gamer subjectivity. To some extent, the game's obstacles are self-evident. One of the game's significant obstacles was its overreliance on gamification mechanics, which resulted in various issues. As discussed in Chapter 2, gamers tend to blur the lines between gaming and social communities due to their isolated childhoods. As a result, the virtual gaming community became a place for them to overcome social difficulties. Over time, this led to the erosion of boundaries between social and gaming relationships. It was precisely the blur of gaming and engineering teams/communities that drew engineers to invest in some simulation games, if we recall Ben's story on drawing on the *CS:GO* game to build rapport with the Wizard team.

However, the badge-collection game failed to provide a space for engineers to embed their social relations into work relations and blur the two. The game's core design logic was to strictly adopt gamification mechanics at the top management level, such as transparency of rules and quick feedback, while ignoring human connections and engagement. This made middle managers' maneuvers less effective, and engineers' volunteering efforts on other teams were only recognized virtually, creating frustration, as shown by Peter's narrative of his help with the music app.

The badge-collection game's failure to blur the lines between working and gaming relationships made it difficult to mobilize engineers' modder traits, which were embodied in many of them. For example, bricolage-task badges could have been popular, if the design of the bricolage-task badges had successfully mobilized engineers' modder traits. Modder traits enabled engineers to create, modify, and optimize game features. Deron, the engineer who tattooed his name in binary code on his arm and an enthusiastic *CS:GO* player, explained to me why he occasionally helped other teams modify or test their products, collecting bricolage-task badges in the process:

> Well, I guess it's like ... I just love tweaking around. ... I used to build [video-game] mods in my spare time as a hobby, for fun ... but now that I am at Behemoth, there's a lot of projects I can do. ... I might want to test out some new framework ... or just, I don't know—Behemoth is nice because there are so many problems to solve, and it provides enough tools and resources for me to play.

Deron naturally perceived his effort of helping other teams "test out new frameworks" as a form of his "hobby"—simply as an extension of play for "fun," like his previous video-game modding efforts. Deron's modding experience also allowed him to appreciate Behemoth for its provision of tools: game modding can require expensive software tools, the costs of which are usually shouldered by the modders themselves (Kücklich 2005).

Unlike Deron, most engineers do not like to invest in bricolage tasks. According to the record of badge collection, bricolage-task badges were awarded to fewer than 5,000 recipients. For a company that employed more than 90,000 workers, enticing less than 6 percent of its total workforce to collect these badges can hardly be counted as successful. Instead, the most popular badge was a quiz-based one named 100% Peculiar, which had attracted 35,231 participants by the time of my fieldwork. When I consulted gamers at Behemoth about this phenomenon, many told me that the rigid rules and setup of the badge-collecting platform runs counter to their pursuit of freedom, flexibility, and autonomy. As Phil, an engineer who self-identified as a modder, explained, "The key to modding is to create whatever I want and not have some manager telling you what to do."

Modders' desire for recognition from game companies was also crucial, as Peter's discussion on his optimization for the music app made clear. A mere badge was not enough for decent recognition. Game companies take an enormous amount of energy to support and vitalize the modding community and exchange modders' free labor for carefully designed recognition. These companies grant modders access to play with the source code and acknowledge modders as optimal future employees. Modding communities, essentially game companies' online cults, are the critical platform through which these game companies attract modders' loyalty and innovative ideas (Kücklich 2005, 4). However, the badge-collecting infrastructure's top-down setup failed to generate a robust gamer community, making it unable to trigger gamers' modder traits.

This observation provides a complementary perspective to many mainstream analyses of gamification in management studies. It is widely accepted in the field that gamification setups are more easily legitimized and accepted by employees who have a rich history of playing video games outside the workplace (Greenhaus and Powell 2006; Mollick and Rothbard 2014; Zichermann 2011). These employees are more likely to have accumulated gaming skills, perspectives, and affections outside of work, making them more aware of gamification elements. This awareness is directly related to their willingness to consent to gamification setups and to invest their gaming skills in workplace games.

However, I argue that this hypothesis misses a crucial link. Although employees with rich gaming histories may be more likely to recognize gamification setups, they do not necessarily consider them legitimate and may not be prepared to invest wholeheartedly in them. Only when their gamer subjectivity is fully mobilized will they consent to the game. Conversely, if the gamification setup fails to mobilize and even contradicts their gamer subjectivity, their rich gaming memories will make them more aware of the flaws in the gamification setup and may lead them to withdraw their consent to the games. Therefore, the preceding sections depict factors that may lead to an unsuccessful gamification setup (e.g., rigidity, top-down style, vacuum of middle-management efforts) and specific gamer traits that may fail to be mobilized (e.g., modder traits). The following sections illustrate how these gamers strategically withdraw their consent to the game.

Gamers' Indifference toward Collection Games

Engineers are generally indifferent toward collection games due to issues such as rigid gamification setup, disappearance of middle-management promotion, and failure to mobilize gamer subjectivity. Guided by this indifferent attitude, engineers developed three major coping strategies for the badge-collecting game: practical tactics, performance strategy, and perfunctory approach. Although I describe these three badge-collecting approaches as a formal typology of tactics, it must be emphasized that, in practice, engineers learn strategies not through explicit instruction but by word of mouth.

Firstly, workers' practical tactics involve investing minimum collecting time for maximum reward. To do this, engineers always browse the list of collectible badges and select those that are easiest to unlock. Some icons, such as the icons used to reward engineers who help other development teams to test their codes for bugs, require monotonous, mundane, and time-consuming debugging activities. It can cost engineers a whole day or even two to debug really tricky code; however, their reward for devoting ten to thirty hours to debugging activities is just a phone-tool icon, which has the same symbolic value as the Security Badge icon,[6] which takes engineers less than thirty minutes to obtain.

Engineers effortlessly discovered a secret—that is, the easiest-to-unlock badges are the quiz-based ones or the event-based badges from the bricolage-tasks category. The time needed to unlock these badges is very predictable, easy to calculate, and usually clocks fewer than two hours. I Play with the Behemoth Phone is a typical event-based badge. Although the company set up segments within the event to lure workers into devoting extra time to improve the phone (e.g., setting up the debugging table and testing booth), workers do not need to participate in these specific elements to obtain the badge. To collect event-based badges, workers can go to the product-release event, scan their ID card to register for the I Play with the Behemoth Phone badge, and then leave, which usually takes them less than an hour.

Consider the time when the Pipe Org Ranger team became legendary, as almost every team member suddenly doubled their badge numbers over a single weekend. Engineers from the Ranger's three sister teams poured into the Ranger team area to find out why, and it turned out that the Ranger team member Paulo accidentally found a post titled "Fastest way to grind 5000 badges" when he skimmed through the firm's internal video-gaming forum. This post was invaluable: it listed almost all the badges that took less than thirty minutes to get, and Paulo immediately shared the post with his teammates.

The second strategy, which I call "performance strategy," aimed to increase the visibility of collecting behaviors. Engineers adopt this strategy to value recognition gains by exposing themselves to the spotlight and choosing to collect highly visible icons. While they participate in this game, they attempt to attract more people to discuss or participate in their collection processes, thus making their collection a public event.

For example, as discussed before, the Wizard team engineers actively invested in the e-speaker game (I Play with Hannah badge), as promoted by their team manager Vikram. While the Wizard team invested in the game, they converted it into a public teasing game. Since investment in this game involved testing e-speakers publicly in the team area, the event was highly visible to the team. When engineers adopted a performance strategy to participate in this game, most of the Wizard team members participated in this collection game and accepted the 5,000 Questions Challenge, which led to hijinks.

While the Wizard team played the game, vigorous conversations around the e-speaker made the "playing with Hannah" scene further visible. One favorite topic of team discussion was how the e-speaker figured out answers for their testing questions. While some engineers' reactions to this puzzle involved serious discussions about the smartspeaker's AI design, others responded by ridiculing the smartspeaker design, assuming that there was no AI—only a group of "outsourced laborers" hired to hide in a cave and answer all of these questions. For example, Peter imitated an imagined "outsourced laborer" answering "What time is it now?" over and over again before reaching the end of his rope: "It's 2:30 P.M. . . . It's 2:31 P.M., my lord. . . . You have asked me this same question thirty times. . . . It's 2:32 P.M., you fucking idiot! Stop asking me the same question . . . question . . . question!" (Peter mimics a fading echo, as in a cave). Similarly, Jack the North personified the e-speaker but reclined and performed the e-speaker as an "exotic lady."[7]

The majority of engineers adopt the final strategy, the perfunctory approach. In other words, only a small fraction of engineers are passionate about probing practical tactics for collecting badges, and converting badge-collecting activities into public performance is an even more accidental phenomenon. Most engineers tend to follow the perfunctory approach and consider the badge-collection game too condescending to be played.

The perfunctory approach that engineers develop entails strategically maintaining a controllable distance from the game. As an engineer explained, "It's a typical corporation trick. Just make sure you collect some, like, ten or twenty; then you won't stand out for being a slacker." This statement reflects the typical perfunctory approach shared among most of the engineers, one that is completely directed by instrumental rationality and a cynical attitude. The longer I spent in Pipe Org, the more I became aware that this perfunctory approach was engineers' tactic of choice.

Engineers' perfunctory attitudes and strategies can occasionally heighten the tension between managers and workers. As discussed earlier, middle-level managers are largely absent from this collection game; consequently, barely any manager-worker alliance is formed when workers adopt the previous two strategies to play it. However, when engineers draw on perfunctory strategies to play certain games, managers tend to adopt a pretty straightforward, disapproving attitude toward those approaches.

For example, most quiz-based badges forced engineers to watch an hour-long tutorial video that relayed all the information they needed before taking the test. Watching the video, in fact, took much longer than taking the test. Engineers certainly did not want to waste time watching the video and thus found a way to muddle through this process, even though the video was carefully designed to prevent test takers from skipping it. Some engineers just muted the video and sent the tutorial window to the back of their screen while doing other coding tasks, waited until the tutorial ended, and then brought the quiz window forward and started the quiz.

These efforts, however, largely ran counter to Behemoth's original intent of setting up quiz- and training-based badges, which leverage the tutorial video's advantage in molding engineers' mentality and behaviors (e.g., cultivating engineers' sense of security, raising their awareness of clients' demands, normalizing their code-deploying behaviors). This corporate-level drive to shape behaviors could align with team managers' goals, so under such circumstances, the engineers' attempts to game the tutorial process would quickly be curtailed once spotted by managers. Take JW's cheating attempt: when he tried to mute the tutorial video that pictured thirteen security scenarios that engineers might encounter, Vikram, his manager, walked to JW's desk, pointed to his screen, and said, "Watch out! There is a test question there later on." JW was not the only one caught skipping the security training video, either. While I was in the Wizard team area, I heard Vikram remind several engineers to pay attention to the video—sometimes in a relatively soft tone, such as "Careful, here is a tricky question. They will ask you what you need to do when encountering a shooter in the quiz!" Other times, Vikram adopted a more threatening tone: "So you think you are so smart . . . you don't need to watch the video, right? Let's see how many you can get right." The tension between engineers and managers was vividly portrayed in many rounds of reminders.

As illustrated above, the incremental nature of the engineering work process means that bricolage knowledge is constantly in demand and bricolage tasks are hiding in every corner of the system. The collection game, therefore, is designed to entice engineers into contributing extra knowledge or effort to bricolage tasks that fall outside of their job description. While Behemoth adopts typical gamification mechanisms to package this work process as a badge-collecting game, the corporation's rigid gamification setup, middle-level managers' feeble promotion, and the half-hearted mobilization of gamer subjectivity, it is not difficult to imagine that this game would neither attract engineers nor achieve its goals.

The organization of the badge-collection game reflects a standardized application of gamification, which requires a predetermined game design archetype to pursue transparency in action and provide clear and efficient guidance (Carroll 2014). Scholars have highlighted that gamification design logic is widely used and appears effective in mobilizing productivity and innovation (Bogost 2014; Carroll 2014; Whitson 2014; Zuboff 2019). For instance, Mollick (2009) documented the Betal Game, designed by Microsoft's Windows Defect Prevention Team, to encourage engineers to test their new product, Windows Vista, voluntarily. The rules were simple, with engineers installing the beta version of the software to earn a B badge, voting on the version to earn an E badge, and running the software to earn a T badge, among others. Although the Betal Game was a minigame, it quadrupled participation in the Vista testing effort (Mollick 2008, 163).

However, caution is necessary when drawing conclusions from such observations, as exemplified by Behemoth's case, where the primary intention of implementing a badge-collection game was to extract extra productivity and creativity, which was only minimally achieved. The distribution of badges indicates this misfire. Bricolage-task badges, the most critical badges for

Behemoth to crowdsource engineers' voluntary labor, were awarded to fewer than 5,000 recipients and attracted only a few collectors. Conversely, collecting quiz-based badges typically takes engineers less than three hours on average and allows them to adopt a perfunctory approach, resulting in the most participants, ranging from 9,000 to 36,000. The most popular badge within the third category is 100% Peculiar, which, according to the phone-tool icon page, had attracted 35,231 participants at the end of my fieldwork.

Thus, the first half of this chapter reflects on why such a gamification implementation may not work as effectively as previous research predicts. The chapter notes that the gamified setup, characterized by a top-down and rigid pattern, laid the groundwork for failure. Such a setup largely compressed the space of middle managers' practices, which are crucial for coordinating workers' interests with the ruling class. The middle managers' role vacuum resulted in interest coordination failure. Additionally, the gamification nature of the badge-collection game, such as the rigid adoption of game rules and the superficial mimicry of video-game elements without touching authentic gaming culture, means that engineers' gamer traits can hardly be mobilized in this environment. On the contrary, their gamer traits allow them to more keenly recognize the phony nature of the badge game and push them to withdraw their consent further. As shown by engineers' coping strategies, the badge game hardly attracts their investment. Their gamer subjectivity is not mobilized, and gaming interests are not coordinated and embedded in their badge-collecting practices. In return, engineers barely yield any of their time, energy, and skills in the badge-collection games. Consequently, no concession was formulated between engineers and managers, and only a "mock hegemony" was established.

Game Over: Using Racing Games to Enhance On-Call Urgency

Resolving tickets—notifications of problems that require an engineer to address—is an essential routine maintenance task at Behemoth and is thus fertile territory for gamification. Ticket work is considered more vital and urgent than the volunteer maintenance tasks discussed earlier (e.g., helping with other teams' bricolage tasks). Addressing tickets is considered so important that developers usually take turns pulling on-call shifts in turn to perform this software maintenance. Behemoth's on-call shifts require developers to be available twenty-four hours a day for seven days, similar to—but longer than—on-call shifts for medical professionals. On-call engineers must clip pagers to their belts and keep a laptop next to them at all times, even while sleeping, and they usually avoid planning leisure activities during their shift.

In addition to handling new and urgent tickets, on-call programmers are responsible for closing out preexisting tickets left by other teammates. Typically, each team has anywhere from fifty to two hundred leftover tickets in the system, which are usually hard to resolve (and hence, "left over").

Urgency defines the core of the ticket-solving task. Especially when significant problems appear, engineers receive urgent tickets directing them to fix those issues in the shortest time possible, lest the systems crash and lead to what Behemoth called system "downtime." Pipe Org's senior manager, Jonathan, once explained in an email the need to minimize downtime: "We should be treating the unscheduled downtime of our services as a critical issue, and we should work quickly to resolve its impact on our customers. . . . Remember, there is no such thing as acceptable unscheduled downtime. . . . We should work to minimize the downtime for all of our services. . . . EVERY system we build should measure its downtime in seconds or minutes. Our customers expect Behemoth to always be up."

Jonathan's concern about downtime is not entirely misplaced. After all, for big tech firms like Behemoth, downtime is pricey. Some engineers told me that they learned a minute of downtime could cost $60,000. One manager, Anandit, talked about one of the retail department's more tragic downtimes—it was thirteen minutes long, and the price tag was $2,600,000. Anandit supplemented this story by emphasizing that to minimize downtime cost, on-call engineers needed to increase their stress tolerance. "It's the same as a hospital or a war zone; quickly look, assess the situation, and go help where you're going to have the most impact. . . . We shouldn't be putting people on call that are not ready to fix problems during a crisis."

Therefore, one purpose of designing the ticket-solving game involves speeding up engineers' ticket-resolving processes to minimize downtime. One method adopted by Behemoth is to gamify the process, for instance, by adding the "countdown bar," which pressures engineers to tackle the ticket within a specific time limit. Specifically, there were several countdowns within each ticket. The first timer (thirty minutes) appears on the screen right after people are paged, designed to trigger an engineer's action. At this stage, the on-call engineer only needs to change the ticket status within thirty minutes to notify the client team that the product (owner) team has received the ticket and is getting a handle on the problem. Before the thirty minutes elapse, the on-call engineer should get a preliminary understanding of the ticket and decide which category he wants to assign to the ticket. The first category, "work in progress," sets a four-hour countdown timer on the screen. If the on-call engineers cannot resolve the ticket within four hours, an alarm begins to ring in the final seconds, and the system automatically pages the team manager as time runs out. Alternatively, engineers file tickets under the "researching" category to get an eight-hour countdown clock. This classification implies the problem is more complicated, and they need more time to research and resolve it. The final category, "pending," places no time limit on the on-call engineers while telling the client team that they might not be able to handle the ticket immediately and will deal with it when time allows.

The leaderboard is another important gamification element that Behemoth incorporates in the ticket process. In the gaming world, the leaderboard displays the ranking of gamers in competitive video games; it is designed to get players to invest more time and energy to boost their ranks and thus drive engagement. In Behemoth's adaptation of the leaderboard design, the company displays the number of legacy tickets unresolved by each team, which remain on a dashboard. There is no fixed target for how many tickets each team should resolve; instead, the standard is that the fewer legacy tickets a team has, the higher it ranks on the dashboard. This setup introduces a high level of uncertainty to the development teams: they do not know *how many* legacy tickets they need to resolve to meet specific requirements; they only know that they need to resolve *more* outstanding tickets than *other teams*. Importantly, the ticket dashboard introduces a highly competitive framework in which teams need to beat other teams to move up on the leaderboard.

As demonstrated in the crowdsourcing game, the success of a gamified setup is not solely determined by the top-down approach. Instead, it depends largely on the participation of middle managers and the game's ability to instill a gaming culture and engage players on a personal level. Thus, before delving into the operation and function of the ticket game, it is crucial to examine these two dimensions.

Middle Management: Critical Role in
Shaping the Racing Game

Middle managers apparently are more actively involved in the ticket game compared to the badge game. Unlike badge-collection games that primarily serve other teams' interests, ticket solving is an essential task for these managers' own development teams. Moreover, the ticket queue can become a battleground for conflicting interests between managers and workers, leading to an increased motivation for managers to leverage the ticket games as a distraction from such conflicts.

Specifically, following Behemoth's permanent-beta ideology, managers tend to choose a riskier path when launching new products, even though they know the technology is flawed. As Anandit, a Level 6 manager, framed it, "None of our systems are perfect. They are all in varying states of being '100 percent available and perfect.' Some were built at a time when perfection was not a primary concern." The managers' choices are completely profit oriented: it is only by launching their products in the shortest time that their company can seize market share from other tech firms. This appeal to profit forces managers to aggressively develop new technology at the cost of its quality. As another manager, Josh, has confessed, "Of course, our systems have gaps. Some of them are deeply rooted in design. . . . It's not that we don't want to have 100 percent code coverage and stress test fleets—it's the fact that there are other concerns."

When Behemoth prioritizes launch speed over product quality, on-call work becomes a heavy engineering burden, and it is not uncommon to hear engineers complain about managers' nonstop delivery of new products. For example, one engineer complained about how the fast delivery approach led to intense maintenance by saying:

> Management is on the hook to deliver all these business things and features, and so what they'll do—or what they did a lot, for years at a time—is not put any time into operational stuff. And so, what happens is the operational burden increases or accumulates over time. . . . And, you know, it's just—it's a lot of prioritizations. I think what it also boils down to is that, you know, it depends on whether your management is like upward facing or downward facing. Meaning like, do they come in every day trying to make their boss happy or trying to make their employees happy.

According to this engineer's comment, he was dissatisfied with the manager's approach of prioritizing profit and delivering "all these business things and features" quickly. Such dissatisfaction implies conflicting interests between managers and engineers. While managers emphasize profit maximization through aggressively developing new technology, engineers tend to prioritize technology's perfection, regardless of how long it takes to make it flawless. Tickets are often caused by the excessive acceleration of software development. Therefore, discussion of ticket and ticket-solving burden became an outlet through which engineers expressed dissatisfaction with this conflict.

Managers use the ticket game's gamification setup to add more fun to this essential maintenance and distract engineers from their conflicting interests with management. One manager stated that he felt the need to make ticket handling more "exciting and sexy" by developing strategies that find the right balance for engineers:

> We get a lot of legacy code for maintenance, and maybe you know when you are doing maintenance, it's harder to get credit for [that]. You get more credit for building a new one than you get by maintaining much older [ones]. So, what you try to do is offer a balance . . . and good managers find the right balance for engineers. But sometimes,

it's just difficult, especially when you get a lot of legacy code to maintain. . . . So what you can do is make the maintenance exciting and sexy.

Then the question becomes, How can managers turn the ticket-resolving task into something "exciting and sexy"? One solution is to give the ticket game more symbolic meaning that engineers are likely to consent to. For example, the Wizard team manager, Vikram, compared the ticket game's countdown timer setup to *Super Mario*:

> You know . . . when you start *Super Mario*, a countdown time bar is activated on the screen, right? And you need to complete the level before the timer reaches zero, right? Otherwise, you are going to lose a life. So, the idea is the same here. . . . On the ticket page, the company sets up a countdown bar . . . to notify engineers of the time . . . and also add a sense of urgency. . . . Like, if you can't solve the ticket within four hours, you are out of the game. . . . The ticket will be sent to your manager.

From Vikram's explanation, it is clear that the deployment of the countdown bar blurred the boundaries between a video game, *Super Mario*, and the real-world challenges faced by the engineers who reported to him. In other words, it is Vikram who tries to connect the countdown timer setup with the video-gaming metaphor by parallelizing the situation of "timer reaches zero" with the gaming scenario of "losing a life." It is no coincidence that Vikram can draw such a parallel. At the very least, many middle-level managers like Vikram also have an engineering background and, thus, a rich gaming history. As discussed in Chapter 2, the sharing of gaming history between managers and engineers propels managers to "have a personal bias" to recruit gamers "who felt compelled to experiment and play and teach themselves the computer."

Managers keenly realize that most elements of the ticket game's setup mimic sports games and video games, such as *Super Mario Kart*. In addition, middle managers are familiar with their team members' gaming habits and can choose the most appropriate game to make such a connection. This is why the Knight team manager attempts to draw on *Midnight Club: Street Racing* to motivate their team engineers' interests, while the Wizard team manager attempts to draw on *Super Mario Kart*. Therefore, middle managers play an essential role in embedding the gamification setup of ticket games, such as countdown timers, in the routine maintenance work process.

Finally, it should be noted that middle managers expand not only the meaning of the ticket game but also the space to play with it. Managers leave enough space for their teammates to organize their games under the ticket game framework and open up enough space where their engineers and they can make concessions and negotiations around these games. Managers' efforts are vital for attracting engineers to participate and eliciting their consent. Engineers' strategies for making agreements with managers and investing in the game are discussed later in this chapter.

Mobilization of Gamer Subjectivity in Racing Games

The previous paragraphs describe how the setup of the countdown timer in ticket-solving tasks could be easily associated with video games and how the gamer subjectivity embodied by engineers makes them more attracted to the gamified setup. Seaborn and Fels (2015) state that the countdown timer is a typical game design mechanic. To gamers, when the countdown bar appears during gameplay, it implies that the game is approaching a do-or-die moment. Once engineers blur the critical moment of ticket solving with the "life-and-death" moment in the virtual gaming world, their gamer subjectivity would tell them to take on a heroic role to save their teams from crises. Gamers are well trained in mobilizing their "crisis mentality" to immediately become highly focused on dealing with the "crisis" situation (Seaborn and Fels 2015). After engineers' crisis mentality is mobilized, they are more willing to do whatever it takes to fix the problem and pull their team through a crisis, which always ensures a boost of productivity. The heroic spirit triggered by the countdown timer, emphasizing beating the clock to solve a crisis, can draw gamers' attention and induce engineers to be highly involved and absorbed in the ticket-solving activity. In other words, a mind flow is more likely to be generated when gamers' heroic self is triggered by the countdown bar (Csikszentmihalyi 1990).

This phenomenon was evident throughout conversations with engineers in the Pipe Org, who tended to associate their most impressive "killer moves" or "heroic actions" in ticket solving with a narrative of "losing a sense of time." One example of this was when the Knight team engineer Ben encountered a tricky ticket one Thursday afternoon that could have escalated quickly to SEVIS II[8] trouble, eventually affecting a wide range of teams' products. Ben decided to spare the whole afternoon tackling the ticket on Thursday. He cleared his schedule that afternoon, wearing his noise-canceling headphones and forcing himself into the zone quickly. Ben's team supported his behavior, as they all knew the ticket was a time bomb and could drag the whole team into crisis. To assist Ben in avoiding distraction, his manager helped Ben reserve an empty meeting room at the corner of their team's floor.

Then the story developed in an unexpected direction. According to Ben's teammate Philip, Ben was hiding in the meeting room for a full forty-eight hours, dealing with the ticket, and completely lost his sense of time. When he eventually solved the crisis, he thought it was still Friday afternoon, but it was already Saturday afternoon. Ben just sent his team an email and told them that he solved the crisis. Ben also said in the email that he wanted to ask for a work-from-home (WFH) day for the rest of the day, as he had already stayed in the meeting room for more than twenty-four hours and he really needed to take a shower. The reality was that nobody was at work at that moment since it was a Saturday. According to Philip, Ben's teammates on the one side sent their worshipful emails to praise his "bad-ass" move, on the other side, teasing Ben that he did not need to ask for a WFH day since it was the legitimate day for him to "stay at home." Later, when I talked with Ben about his "heroic save," he admitted that he enjoyed the state that he had been in for that forty-eight-hour period. That is, when Ben eradicated all other mental clutter and entirely concentrated on the ticket, he actually felt very energized. A similar story happened on the Assassin team as well. The Assassin team, according to legend, worked together one night to save their team from one tough ticket. And the team became so concentrated that they completely forgot about time. When the Assassin team eventually made substantive progress, they realized the dawn had already broken. So the whole team went to eat breakfast together. According to one Assassin engineer, WZH, it was a very fond memory that they ate breakfast together, as it made him remember a times in college when he and his roommates would stay up all night "opening the back door"[9] to play video games. "We usually ended the night with a big breakfast. It always made us feel a sense of satisfaction," WZH said.

This type of behavior is more likely to occur in engineers who possess gamer traits, as they are more sensitive to the countdown bars than nongamers and can successfully create a sense of urgency and get gamers' attention. The countdown bar can reframe the ticket solving as a "life-and-death" moment (Barnett 2007, 955), which can mobilize engineers' heroic traits and boost their concentration level. Once gamers are successfully mobilized to concentrate on beating the clock to resolve tickets, that focus could bring more fun to the work itself and thus make tickets more "exciting and sexy."

If the countdown timer setup functions well to enhance engineers' crisis mentality and heroic spirit, then the leaderboard is a de facto mechanism to mobilize engineers' competitive selves. Let's recall the leaderboard design. The key feature of the leaderboard is that there is no fixed target for how many tickets each team should resolve. The only ranking rule of the leaderboard is that the fewer legacy tickets a team has, the higher it ranks on the dashboard. As shown later, adopting this ranking mechanic turned out to be a big "success" in that it efficiently stimulates rivalry among engineers. And it transforms ticket tasks into a highly competitive game.

Engineers' gamer subjectivity again plays a fundamental role in ensuring their unreserved investment in the game: gamers are competitive creatures. In the gaming world, the leaderboard crystallizes and quantifies players' scores and provides an important service by allowing players to track their performance and compare their own with those of their opponents. Indeed, gamers are habituated to closely monitor every move up and down the leaderboard; their rankings embody their social and skill statuses within the game and are considered a notable aspect of their gaming identities.

Unsurprisingly, many engineers told me that they could not tolerate their rankings dropping too quickly in the games they played, and they developed all kinds of strategies to enhance their rankings. Some engineers told me that they would organize battle teams offline (they called these "premade" teams) and arrange a whole night or a weekend for intensive play ("marathons") to enhance rankings, while other engineers confessed that they were willing to adopt cheating strategies such as "account trading"[10] or hiring professional "boosters."[11] In fact, these kinds of gaming behaviors (e.g., monitoring or boosting rankings) smoothly fit into playing the ticket-resolving game. The following section specifies strategies gamers adopt to invest in the ticket game.

One can easily conclude that the badge-collection game should have provided a more hedonic experience—fun—to engineers than the ticket game. Indeed, the most pronounced experience in the ticket game should have been related to pressure, anxiety, and uncertainty. However, why do the ticket games attract more engineers' investment despite the anxious process? One can say that the successful mobilization of gamer subjectivity plays a vital role. By waking up the heroic spirit, engineers manifest more excitement and a sense of achievement from stressful working behaviors, such as beating the countdown timer and working around the clock. By mobilizing the competitive gaming self, engineers manifest more excitement from the leaderboard ranking than uncertainty.

Engineers' Reactions to the Ticket Game

If the scrum games discussed in Chapter 3 have successfully constructed themselves like role-playing games (RPGs), then the ticket-resolving game can be said to resemble racing games. Racing games, such as *Midnight Club: Street Racing* and *Super Mario Kart*, are cousins to sports games and mostly focus on stimulating players' competitiveness and aggressiveness. As we see in this section, engineers did in fact treat the ticket-resolving game like a racing game and adopted competitive techniques commonly seen at sports events to invest in the ticket games. These techniques can be roughly divided into two types. The first type can be called "defending strategies," as engineers concentrate on increasing their performance and scores to defend or even advance their teams' positions. The second type is "attacking strategies," which entail treating other teams as "imaginary opponents" and shaming them in public to boost their own team's pride.

As discussed above, the leaderboard setup successfully attracted engineers' interests, and engineers closely tracked their teams' ticket rankings. When engineers saw their rankings hit rock bottom on the dashboard, they adopted defending strategies to turn the tables, such as the "weekend ticket sprint/marathon." During a ticket sprint or marathon, an engineer worked incredibly long hours to resolve as many legacy tickets as possible. For example, Charles resolved sixty legacy tickets in one weekend, single-handedly clearing half of his team's total legacy tickets. Charles later recalled staying up all night Saturday and Sunday for his "ticket marathon weekend." On Sunday night, he began doing shots of alcohol while resolving as many tickets as possible. Finally, at around five o'clock Monday morning, he finished resolving all the tickets that he was able to handle and sent a very brief email to all of Pipe Org on behalf of his team: "[I] did a ticket marathon you jerks. Legacy tickets now down to 60." Then, he went to the bathroom to vomit and subsequently fell asleep on the floor until noon. This heroic behavior of self-organizing weekend sprints had been periodically occurring in almost every team within Pipe Org. Whenever someone pulled a weekend sprint, Pipe Org engineers recounted to each other what the marathoner had achieved and used heroic language in these accounts.

Ticket marathons are vital to reducing software risks. During weekdays, although on-call engineers contribute the majority of their time to resolving tickets, they are constantly interrupted by other work responsibilities, such as doing stand-up reports, participating in weekly meetings, answering emails, and holding office hours to answer sister teams' questions. Doing a weekend sprint implies a complete devotion to this task, which efficiently reduces the vulnerability of software and systems; after all, these legacy errors, first and foremost, increase the risk of deployment and system collapse. The problem is that once engineers try to prevent a crash, they cannot just target one particular ticket, since resolving one ticket usually triggers another one—hence, the "spike of errors." The engineers' adoption of the weekend ticket marathon strategy is beneficial for eradicating errors and eliminating potential risks once and for all.

Team managers' interests, of course, are well served by allowing engineers to organize weekend marathons/sprints. Managerial support for engineers' weekend marathons can be seen in their attitude toward the marathoners' absenteeism the next day. More often than not, marathoners ask for a WFH day after conducting a two-day weekend marathon, and it is a tacit understanding that such a WFH request implies that the sprinter will take the day off instead of working. Most team managers choose to be lenient and turn a blind eye toward this rule-bending behavior. Indeed, it is through such a compromise that managers coordinate their interests with engineers. Recall that I stated at the beginning of this part on racing games that there was, in fact, an embedded conflict between managers and engineers over whether to prioritize technology or profit. However, drawing on the leaderboard, the manager successfully mobilizes engineers' competitiveness and directs them to beat other teams in the ranking systems. By facilitating engineers' ticket marathons and tacitly permitting engineers' WFH days after an intense marathon, managers further articulate that they are in league with their teammates. Their real enemy is other development teams who might drag their ranking down. In this way, managers redirect the vertical conflicts between managers and engineers into horizontal ones between different development teams.

Managers' promotion of weekend marathons is also reflected by their highlighting of the parallel between ticket-resolving marathons and gaming marathons. As discussed above, managers know too well that eliciting similar feelings between gaming marathons and ticket marathons is the key to garnering engineers' interest in ticket resolving. This understanding can be seen in Zach's (an old manager in Pipe Org) narrative: "The [ticket] sprint is actually something they [engineers] come up with . . . but I find it very useful in making maintenance tasks more exciting. . . . You know, some guys told me that sometimes it's almost as exciting as doing a *Star Wars* marathon." Two interesting themes emerge from Zach's narrative. First, from his discussion, we can tell that the ticket sprint is actually a method created by engineers instead of managers. The manager's role in this game is that of a supporter, not an initiator. The second interesting thing appears at the end of Zach's narrative, where he cited his team members and drew a parallel between ticket sprints and a *Star Wars* marathon.

After consulting with my interviewees, I found that *Star Wars* marathons are a very popular weekend recreational activity among engineers. I talked with one engineer, Danny, about how he did it. He told me he had done this several times; sometimes, he would do it by himself, and other times he invited people to his apartment to watch together. According to Danny, he felt that he almost always lost a sense of time whenever he spent the whole weekend doing the *Star Wars* marathon.

To some extent, these gamers' lifestyles—typified by a disinterest in outdoor leisure activities, a lack of large social circles, and a habit of staying home to play games—make them willing and well suited to conduct the weekend ticket sprint. In fact, if they are not doing ticket sprints, they are likely to organize video-gaming or sci-fi–movie marathons, as Danny did. Another engineer's (Zhang's) wife once complained to me that her husband invited friends to their home every weekend to play *League of Legends*: "They just lock themselves in the corner room. They don't go outside to grab food or drinks . . . and they don't allow me to bring them food, for fear that I'll interrupt them." Weekend gaming was not unique to Zhang; many engineers liked to gather a group of friends over the weekend to form a "premade team" and play games—to "open the back door."[12]

When I later talked with more gamers, I found many overlaps between gaming and ticket marathons. Both activities involve doing one task for a long time without interruption, and sometimes the hours devoted to this single activity may result in a loss of sense of time. It seems like endurance is the key to surviving both types of activity. These engineers also told me that the feeling of accomplishment between gaming and ticket marathons was very similar—both involve seeing their team's scores boosted.

So the defense strategy is conditioned by engineers' lifestyle, their addiction to gaming marathons/sprints, and their habitual thinking to advance their positions in different types of competition by devoting more time or effort to them. However, engineers are not satisfied with just "defending" their positions and eager to beat their "competitors" in the ticket game, so they developed attacking strategies, which largely manifest in publicly shaming their imaginary opponents to boost their own team's pride. Trash-talking is a typical attack method. Yip, Schweitzer, and Nurmohamed (2016) defined *trash-talking* as an uncivil behavior in the form of boastful comments about oneself or insulting remarks about competitors, which can increase the psychological stakes of competition.

Naturally, heavy ticket loads have been a primary topic for these engineers' trash-talking practices. For example, Philip, an engineer from the Knight team, once accused the Ranger team of slacking off in participating in off-work video games organized by Pipe Org employees and related it to the Ranger team's heavy ticket load. Philip's theory was that the Rangers' ticket load made everyone on the team too tired to participate in off-work games. To support his theory, Philip hypothesized a linear correlation between the number of tickets and enthusiasm for off-work gaming: the more legacy tickets a team had, the less frequently those team members participated in off-work games.

Philip's hypothesis generated a heated discussion within the Knight team. Most of the Knights' engineers echoed Philip's theory and tried to provide more "data points" to strengthen the hypothesis. A few days later, the Knight team's theory passed to the Wizards. Peter, a very active member of the Wizard team, was not satisfied with contributing more data points to the Knight team's theory. Instead, he appealed to his teammates to find the "root cause" of the Ranger team's lackluster participation. Not long afterward, the Wizard team teased out a logic chain: the reason the Ranger team was slacking was their heavy ticket load, and that load in turn contributed to their poor software output—or, to use the Wizard engineers' turn of phrase, "Their software sucks." Thus, the Wizard team concluded, "their software sucks" was the root cause. Philip seemed very receptive to the Wizard team's refinement of his theory and updated it by hypothesizing a new linear correlation: teams with better products will participate in off-work gaming activities more frequently, and vice versa.

Why Are Two Games Poles Apart?
A Comparative Note

In the panorama of the maintenance work process painted throughout the chapter, we can discern two games embedded in that work—the crowdsourcing game and the racing game—and their divergent outcomes. In general, both the crowdsourcing game and the racing game aim to establish a hegemonic state in the terrain of maintenance work: their game designs target obscuring control, extracting surplus labor, and deflecting attention from conflicted interests between managers and workers (e.g., prioritizing maintenance or developing new software). However, the games' outcomes tend to veer between two poles—while the racing game achieves its goal and constructs a gamified hegemony, the minimal effect of the crowdsourcing game at best establishes a mock hegemony.

Specifically, the crowdsourcing game barely produces a hegemonic state. Managers fail to hide their attempts to extract surplus labor and receive a bare minimum of extra labor in return. The badge-collection game, representative of crowdsourcing games, shows the time engineers are willing to invest in collecting each badge to be under three to five hours. It is safe to say that minimum consent is manufactured through the badge-collection game, and the game establishes a mock hegemony. Compared with the crowdsourcing game, the racing game is far more successful at constructing a relatively stable hegemonic state in the maintenance work arena. Unlike the crowdsourcing game, the racing game does offer workers sufficient agency to organize gaming activities at will (e.g., weekend ticket marathons), and managers intentionally fade into the background in the series of engineers' self-organized games. Consequently, hierarchical control is replaced by engineers' self-management in a lateral direction. By investing in the racing games, workers' original resentment toward the capitalists' interests is diminished and converted into consent. Although Behemoth's engineers were initially dissatisfied with routine maintenance work and attributed their weighty ticket load to the company's permanent-beta development model, the game's setup distracts them and wins their consent. Ultimately, the engineers' consent to the game leads to their consent to the maintenance process's organizational patterns, so it is reasonable to conclude that the racing game achieves its goals and constructs a gamified hegemony in the routine maintenance work process.

What are the factors that lead to these very different outcomes? At first glance, one might think these two games should have had similar outcomes; after all, both games are engaged in the maintenance work process. Although the two maintenance tasks at the heart of these games emphasize different elements (one focuses on volunteer maintenance and another one on routine maintenance), these elements embodied a similar nature of maintenance work: low creativity, tedium, and a hefty time investment. On top of that, these two games follow similar gamification designs. They build a fundamental gaming infrastructure (e.g., the badge-displaying platform and the ticket leaderboard), adopt classical gamification logics (e.g., emphasize quantifying achievement and quick feedback or timely guidance), and draw on typical gamification elements (e.g., countdown timers and badges).

Both the nature of the work and the basic gamification setup are instances of material conditions and objective structures, which have always been the focus of gamification scholars. The highly overlapped material conditions between the two games do not contribute to the divergent outcomes. If that is the case, then what are some factors missing from mainstream gamification analysis that are vital to explaining the games' variance?

Table 4.1 reveals several critical factors that emerge from a comparative analysis of this chapter. In terms of gamification setup, the crowdsourcing game exhibits a stricter adherence to gamification mechanics than the racing game. This is manifested in its emphasis on step-by-step instructions and detailed quantification of achievements. In contrast, the racing game draws on gamification elements, such as countdown timers and leaderboards, but leaves more uncertainty and wiggle room for engineers. For example, the only rule for the leaderboard is that engineers must resolve more tickets than other teams. In other words, the leaderboard setup leaves enough uncertainty by not specifying the number of tickets to be solved, and engineers need to adopt particular strategies to solve them. From the perspectives of uncertainty and flexibility, the crowdsourcing game is closer to an original gamification operation, while the racing game is closer to a gamified labor game. The balance of uncertainty is a noteworthy feature of labor games, as repeatedly investigated by labor game scholars (Burawoy 1979; Sharone 2002). The divergent game setups, whether strict gamification or gamified labor game, provide critical foundations for the practices of various managers and engineers in the two games.

Concerning the involvement of middle-level managers, they are more motivated to participate in the racing game than the crowdsourcing game. This motivation is influenced by several preconditions. Racing games are

TABLE 4.1 COMPARATIVE TABLE BETWEEN CROWDSOURCING GAME AND RACING GAME

Features	Crowdsourcing game	Racing game
Basic setup	Total gamification – Rigid adoption – Top-down implication	Combination between gamification setup and elements of labor games – Countdown timer and leaderboard
Middle-management role	Disappearance of middle managers' role in – Embedding gamification elements in local team – Recognizing engineers' contribution – Articulating engineers' interests	Middle manager plays a key role in – Reinterpreting the racing game setup – Connecting it to video games – Distracting engineers' dissatisfaction – Coordinating engineers' interests
Enactment of gaming culture and subjectivity	Gamer subjectivity contradicts with the crowdsourcing gamification setup – Fails to mobilize gamer traits	Game subjectivity consistent with the racing games – Mobilizes heroic ethos, crisis mentality, and competitive self
Engineers' reaction to the game	Indifferent to the games, adopting – Practical tactics – Performance strategies – Perfunctory approaches	Actively invest in games, adopting – Defending strategies – Attacking strategies
Outcome	Mock hegemony	Gamified hegemony

more directly related to the routine maintenance work of development teams than crowdsourcing games, which are designed to offer prompt aid to other teams. The tension between management and engineers, reflected in the conflict between prioritizing profit or technology, is more prominent in routine maintenance than in volunteering maintenance tasks. In such circumstances, managers are undoubtedly more engaged in the racing game. As middle managers are more familiar with their own development teams, their intervention in the games can efficiently connect the gamification setup from top management to their local team environment and thus embed the game into the work process, as shown in Table 4.1. For example, Wizard team managers drew on their own team engineers' favorite video game (*Super Mario*) to interpret the countdown timer and add excitement to it. In contrast, without middle management facilitation, the crowdsourcing game is completely disembedded in the engineers' work environment and hardly articulates any of their real interests. Middle management plays an essential role in embedding games in the local environment and articulating workers' interests.

Regarding gamer subjectivity, it is evident that it plays a crucial role in shaping engineers' perception of and reaction to games. When gamification setup fails to mobilize gamer subjectivity, its legitimacy is easily challenged. As demonstrated by the crowdsourcing game, the rigid rules of badge-collection platforms clash with gamers' modder traits, which are built on their pursuit of freedom, flexibility, and autonomy. Consequently, gamers quickly recognize the crowdsourcing game's inauthenticity and feel disrespected, leading to perfunctory strategies in gameplay. However, if the game setup successfully triggers engineers' gamer traits, these traits become critical to ensuring their absorption and indulgence in games. For example, the countdown setup creates a "life-and-death" moment, which can effectively mobilize engineers' heroic spirit to save their team and turn the tables. After their heroic ethos is awakened, they will fight for their team and beat the clock without considering how much effort they have invested in the game.

Finally, the investments made by engineers provide validation for the distinct outcomes observed in crowdsourcing and racing games. As illustrated in Table 4.1, engineers have employed three primary playing strategies in the crowdsourcing game: practical tactics, performance strategies, and perfunctory approaches. These strategies signify that engineers give minimal consent to crowdsourcing games. When managers take measures to prevent engineers from adopting perfunctory approaches and cheating the badge system, it becomes evident that a consensus cannot be reached between managers and engineers. Therefore, it is reasonable to conclude that no true hegemony is established in the crowdsourcing game but only a semblance of it—hence, mock hegemony.

In contrast, engineers' playing strategies in racing games demonstrate their enthusiastic investment in the game, to the extent that they have transformed company-initiated games into self-organized ones, such as ticket sprint marathons. In fact, it is the engineers themselves who organize these marathons to outperform other teams, while managers play a facilitative role. Moreover, the tacit permission given by managers for engineers' absenteeism the day after these ticket marathons indicates that a concession has been made between managers and engineers. Therefore, it is evident that the hegemonic power has effectively worked through concessions in the racing game, and the interests of both dominant and subordinate sides are aligned through these games.

The Donut Email Game and the Construction of Chaotic Fun

On the engineering floor, I found my "outsider" status to be the most evident when engineers shared their memories of "funny" pranks. Mulling over this phenomenon, I gradually recognized why I felt my outsider status stood out: the engineers' pranks were usually heavily embedded in cultural codes that were rather exclusive to Behemoth. For example, when engineers recalled pranks like "the tinfoil welcome," they were in fact talking about a prank they pulled on their boss, in which they covered his entire office in aluminum foil to "welcome" him back from vacation. This kind of pranking rite was so taken for granted at Behemoth that no engineer would be confused by the joke or ask for more contextualization—therefore, no one bothered to ask for more elaboration but me.

I soon learned not to feel embarrassed about asking for more information. When these engineers shared a photo of an old-school green monochrome computer screen via their instant messaging tool and all "LOL'd" (laughed out loud) about it, I turned to my neighbor Mike and asked him what they were laughing at. He told me this was a prank they usually pulled on newcomers—they altered their computer screens to project a green monochrome display reminiscent of 1980s desktop computers. "But was that common? Why do you guys all find it amusing? What's the fun part of the prank?" I persistently probed, even though I knew it would further expose my outsider status. Then, it was Mike's turn to be stuck: he repeatedly expressed that it was just their way of having fun, and it was an accepted practice, so there was nothing to puzzle over. Later, others tried to help Mike by saying,

"Look, Tongyu, it's just Behemoth's thing" and "It's a typical Behemoth way of having fun." It soon became apparent that the expression "Behemoth's thing" was a popular one on the engineering floor, and it was frequently used when describing the company's culture. The company's culture, in turn, was so strong that it could imperceptibly guide its engineers' actions and identify outsiders (like me) who were not part of that culture.

This chapter shows that pranking games like those described above have become a critical channel through which Behemoth's culture is constructed, communicated, and reinforced. In the following sections, I look at two major types of pranks and how engineers organize and participate in them. The first are called "cultural pranks," and I elaborate on them in the second section. Cultural pranks, such as those meant to haze newcomers, serve to confirm workplace culture; they usually develop spontaneously and are mainly organized by the engineers themselves. The third section examines what I call "surveillance pranks," which managers systematically organize to monitor engineers' work behaviors. Engineers sometimes support managers' surveillance pranks and carry them forward to surveil each other; other times, especially when engineers' gamer subjectivity is mobilized, they are more likely to use a surveillance prank to express their resistance toward the company's surveillance.

Pranking Games and Chaotic Fun

So what is the Behemoth culture that the engineers inhabited? Those engineers who were invited to have more formal interviews with me were asked to fill out a demographic questionnaire after their interviews (see Appendix C). The form asked them to provide basic demographic information such as age, education, how long they had worked at Behemoth, salary range, and roles/positions. The second-to-last question, however, was demographically irrelevant: it asked them to "describe the corporate culture in three words." In the responses to this question, "fun" was the most popular theme, appearing in more than 30 percent of interviewees' descriptions or expressed by phrases like "work hard, have fun," or "tough but fun." The second-most-popular theme was "relaxed, casual, and free," which appeared in almost 20 percent of their responses, and youth culture terminology such as "cool," "lively," and "energetic" frequently appeared in engineers' descriptions. Of course, these most noteworthy themes aside, other terms like "flexible," "fast-paced," "passionate," and "intelligent" were regularly found in interviewees' answers.

Nonetheless, the three predominant themes—fun, casual, and young—sketched out the picture of Behemoth's corporate culture. Cultural pranks, as we'll see below, became a vital medium for dramatizing this culture and bringing it to life; this section details how these pranks were organized and what they meant to the tech workplace and its engineers.

Newcomers to the engineering floor were quickly informed of the organizational culture through pranks. Indeed, new members had to negotiate a series of humiliating initiation ceremonies—so-called newbie hazing pranks. The seemingly inconsequential routines of these hazing pranks constructed the cultural foundation within which engineers were expected to express and confirm sanctioned ways of interpreting and experiencing engineering life. Exposure to these pranks revealed the "fun and casual" culture to new employees and instructed them on acting and reacting in this culture.

At Pipe Org, the idea of the "welcome prank" was initiated by the Level 7 manager Anandit, who encouraged his teams (i.e., the Assassins and Wizards) to organize practical jokes as a welcome for newcomers. One Wizard team engineer, Peter, built on this idea and developed the "checklist prank." The checklist prank was designed to "tease and shock" the newbie—here, I use his initials, YR—by turning his idea of Pipe Org as a "fun and cool" workplace on its head and portraying the development team as a despotic, prison-like space with minimal freedom. Vicky, one of Peter's accomplices, helped me piece together how they designed a "checklist" that would leave YR with the impression that the company was a "total control freak":

> VICKY: You know YR, right? He joined the team three weeks after me. I remember that we had a weekly meeting the day before he came. So Anandit suggested that we should pull a prank on him. And Peter said, we can print a "checklist" and ask the newcomer to fill out the list whenever he leaves his desk. Like, if you want to go to the bathroom, you need to write down precisely what time you leave your desk and where you go. And when you come back, you must check the box next to this line.
>
> TW: Why?
>
> VICKY: Peter said it'd make him feel that this company is a total control freak.
>
> TW: So you actually carried out this prank?
>
> VICKY: Yes. So Peter printed out the checklist. Actually, he printed two copies. One was put on YR's desk and another copy on mine. So I needed to fill the form too. My desk is right next to YR . . . so me filling out the form would make the prank look more realistic. . . . And Mark, who was assigned to be YR's mentor at that time, helped with the prank too. I heard that . . . when Mark introduced the daily routines to YR, he emphasized that it's important for YR to use the checklist and track his daily activities. Mark

also added that our manager would do a random inspection to ensure YR did use the list.

TW: So . . . did your manager do anything to help you with the prank?

VICKY: He didn't do much . . . but I remember he was there, nodding his head to Mark when Mark explained the checklist to YR. . . . So he was, like, offering an authoritative confirmation. . . . Months later, when I became close to YR, he told me that it was exactly Mark's warning that Vikram would inspect his checklist that made him feel this was very serious. He told me he actually felt very anxious about it.

TW: When did he find out this was a prank?

VICKY: It took him a whole day, actually. . . . He called his Chinese friend working at the cloud [organization] that night and asked him about this checklist. . . . I guess that's when the guy told him there's no such thing. So he figured it out.

The checklist highlighted the "freedom" that engineers enjoyed at Behemoth by completely overturning it in the prank. Indeed, the checklist portrayed a very typical despotic labor regime that had been used to control blue-collar workers under Fordism—control that primarily relied on time discipline. The core of time discipline is to divide time into calculable units (e.g., work time, toilet time) and underline how each use of time would be documented and monitored. However, newcomers like YR would soon learn that their workplace was precisely the opposite of what the checklist prank portrayed. Therefore, the game these senior engineers created—the checklist—mocked Fordism's rigorous time discipline.

Engineers were reminded that they enjoyed enormous freedom to determine their schedule and activities through the prank: if they wanted, they could ask to work from home for three or four days to work on their projects. While in the team areas at work, as well, they had very high-level autonomy to determine their schedule. For example, some engineers on the Wizard team were morning people, and they chose to come to work at 6:00 A.M. and left at 3:00 P.M., while night owls could come to work around 11:30 A.M. but not leave until 7:00 or 8:00 P.M. Similarly, instead of being asked to record their bathroom time on a checklist, engineers' absences from team spaces were rarely tracked by managers, whether they left for work activities like meetings or private activities like walking dogs or taking naps. The Wizard engineers' design of this prank showed that they were familiar with an organizational culture characterized by freedom and flexibility and demonstrated their willingness to promote that culture.

One thing that needs to be pointed out is that this study by no means intends to imply that we should celebrate such a work culture. On the contrary, we need to be vigilant: such a work atmosphere can increase workers' self-exploitation. This disastrous consequence came through loud and clear in Gregg's (2013) analysis. In her book *Work's Intimacy*, Gregg unveiled that promoting a highly flexible work schedule—for example, when workers are told they can work from home whenever they feel it necessary—brought new challenges. When people worked at home, for instance, Gregg found that they were inclined to make themselves reachable at all times. In other words, when workers were endowed with the freedom to work from home, they also relinquished the right to preserve their off-work hours and their home as utterly intimate spheres separated from work.

In addition, Vicky's narrative showed that the checklist prank was very well planned and organized by the Wizards. As he explained, the newcomer's mentor, Mark, naturally played the role of instructing YR about the importance of filling the out form. Vicky, for his part, served as an accomplice by filling out a checklist with YR, modeling this behavior and thus making the prank seem more real. According to Vicky's narrative, the two managers' roles in this prank were crucial but subtle. Anandit, the senior manager who supervised the Wizard and Assassin teams, initiated this prank. In other words, Peter's implementation of the prank was a direct response to Anandit's call to pull a prank on the newcomer. Unlike Anandit, Vikram did not initiate the prank but supported it by providing an authoritative backup for Mark's claim that the "manager would do a random inspection to make sure YR used the list." Moreover, from Vicky's narrative, Vikram's confirmation of Mark's claim (through nodding) played a crucial role in intimidating YR and reinforced his belief that the checklist was real.

Newcomers like YR were not just socialized in the engineers' culture through a single prank. Instead, they were grilled by a series of welcome pranks before being accepted as members of the engineering community, such as the phone-tool prank. If the checklist represented the kind of pranks organized at the team level, then the phone-tool prank embodied those that were more systematically organized throughout the whole company.

The idea behind the phone-tool prank was simple: when new engineers came to work their first day, managers told them that they needed to update their basic information (e.g., the university they graduated from, the team they belong to, their start-work date) on their own phone-tool page (the personal web page where engineers list their basic information). However, they could not update this information themselves; instead, they needed to join the "phone-tool page email list," and people responsible for this mailing list would update their information for them. When newcomers sent emails to this phone-tool page email list and asked to join, they received a reply asking them to take an enrollment test—and only after passing the test could they be added to the email list. Newcomers were told that if they failed the test, they would not be able to update their personal information on the phone-tool page. This consequence was threatening for most newbies, as it implied that they would not be accepted as members of the Behemoth online community.

The enrollment test was a prank. Typically, the test questions were ridiculous: one oft-used question was to ask applicants to take a typing-speed test, in which they needed to type as fast as possible to meet the minimum, and these newcomers were told they would not be added to the Behemoth online community if they failed the test. After receiving this question, many would dive into the question as quickly as possible.

Even after newcomers saw that this email list was a prank, they would still automatically subscribe to the "phone-tool page email list." However, the actual function of the list is not to assist engineers in updating their personal information on their web page; instead, it collects new "test questions" (a.k.a. phone-tool prank ideas) from the list members. Of course, engineers have the freedom to unsubscribe from the list and refuse to help design future newcomer pranks, but if these new employees choose to stay on the email list, this implies their willingness to participate in future pranks by contributing their ideas and observing how their pranks work on later newcomers. It suggests that they have decided to claim their membership in this online pranking community.

Who was willing to continue their subscription to this list? It turned out that white engineers were more enthusiastic about joining this group and becoming pranksters. For example, in my interviews with Peter, Philip, and Charles, each one mentioned how they enjoyed joining the email list and designing test questions to tease newbies. As Charles commented, "OK, sometimes I just use the test question [that] they tricked me with into tricking others . . . you know, the most famous 'typing speed question.' . . . I saw through it easily. . . . Now I give it to [those newcomers]. . . . It's like . . . OK, you can see through it. . . . OK, you're cool. . . . You're at least as smart as I am . . . so welcome aboard." Participating in the phone-tool prank list offered these engineers another opportunity to make sense of Behemoth's culture. Some people, like Charles, preferred to use "classic" test questions (e.g., the typing speed question) to continue the tradition, which manifested as "cyber satire." Others attempted to invent new test questions to illuminate other aspects of Behemoth's culture. Pranksters' participation in list conversations about what test questions to adopt and what types of culture those questions manifested allowed the engineers to reflect on and reaffirm Behemoth's culture.

The phone-tool page is a space where engineers communicate with one another and form a virtual community, and cross-team collaborations often happened in that community rather than within the physical workspace. Valorization of the virtual community is an indispensable dimension of Behemoth's culture—thus, accepting and familiarizing themselves with their membership in that community was an inevitable task for Behemoth newcomers. To some extent, the phone-tool prank became a key mechanism for transforming the abstract virtual community into a lived experience. Phone-tool games not only gave newcomers a sense of their membership in the online work community but also emphasized the "fun and amusing" culture of that space.

There are differences worth considering when comparing this phone-tool prank with the newcomer welcome prank (i.e., the checklist prank). While the checklist prank is team based, the phone-tool prank operates at the organizational and company level. In other words, the number of participants for the checklist prank was rather small, while those who took part in the phone-tool list prank were spread throughout the organization (and a bigger number overall). Thus, the cultural norms that guide the design of the phone-tool prank are shared by a wider audience. For the most part, engineers who subscribe to the phone-tool list as either pranksters or observers also share that larger group membership, even if their connection to and investment in those pranks are weaker than those for team-based pranks.

Having said that, the similarities of these two hazing pranks are apparent, as both are set up to present a fun culture to the newcomers. In addition, the kind of fun generated by the newcomer pranks is authored by the engineers: they are the primary actors in designing, organizing, and operating the pranks. Managers are only "silent partners," in that all they need to do is support and occasionally facilitate the pranksters. Another similarity between these hazing pranks reflects the particular version of fun they produced: it is not fun possessed "by" engineering work per se but fun "around" work, which takes form at a ritualistic level. This difference creates a sharp contrast between these pranks and the games analyzed in the previous chapter.

Specifically, simulated games generated fun *in* the software development process, such as parallelizing the fun of conquering technical difficulties with the fun of beating a monster in the virtual video-game world. Of course, finding the video-gaming fun within engineering work makes high demands of engineers' ability to self-mobilize their gamer subjectivities, and it directly resulted in enhancing productivity and creativity in engineering work. On the contrary, the fun generated in hazing pranks is about work in a general sense, in that it does not aim to enhance productivity in the work process so much as it serves to remind engineers of the company's highly liberating, flexible, and informal culture. The source materials of this type of fun are not closely related to video-game activities or mindsets, which implies that engineers do not need to mobilize their gamer subjectivities to interpret and participate in this fun.

The hazing pranks described above were necessary processes of welcoming new members, which unfolded in predictable stages and had a clear purpose of socializing newcomers to facets of Behemoth's culture. Having graduated through a series of welcoming pranks, these new colleagues would be accepted as "one of us" who knew the tech culture in this organization well and were able to participate fully in teams' engineering culture. The pranks I discuss later, in comparison, can be labeled "spontaneous," since they are less systematic and more improvised. Welcoming pranks contained certain institutionalized aspects of the fun culture and were orchestrated through some key events (e.g., one's first day of work) or mandatory procedures (e.g., updating one's phone-tool page), but spontaneous pranks were carried out with far less calculation and staging.

Among all the spontaneous pranks organized by engineers, one—the "Friday suit-up" prank—was widely celebrated. Engineers enforced the "casual and dress-down" culture highly prized in tech workplaces through the cynical design of a formal Friday suit-up prank. The Wizards collectively designed the Friday suit-up caper to trick an engineer named Amir into wearing a suit to work after he had returned from Pakistan for a three-week vacation. His colleagues conjured Suit-Up Friday, convincing him that all employees would be wearing suits on Friday. To make this prank seem more realistic, Vikram sent an email to the whole team announcing the start of the Wizards' Suit-Up Friday. Of course, everyone on the team who planned the scheme knew that this email was bait written for Amir to swallow, and during Amir's first week back at work, every engineer on his team tried to ensure that he had already checked out their manager's Suit-Up Friday announcement. In their interviews, all shared the good cheer that came from their collective planning of the prank's every detail—the setup, the assignment of roles, the hidden agenda, and the backstabbing. To some extent, there even appeared to be good comradeship that emerged from organizing this prank.

Despite slight skepticism, Amir wore his suit to work that Friday. The moment he entered the team area, he realized that he'd been had—no one else had worn a suit, and everyone on the team was readying their phones to take a picture of him. Afterward, this episode was referred to many times through stories related to the team's new intern, other teams' engineers, and me.

A month later, when the prank had almost disappeared as a conversation topic, Amir was caught not locking his computer. Seizing the opportunity, one guy on the Wizard team used Amir's computer to send out an email titled "I'm the Sharpest Developer at Behemoth," along with his suit-up picture. Peter replied to this email first and provided a vivid description of Amir's suit-up day for those who were not in attendance:

> Amir was wearing a Karagar jacket, tie by Calvin Klein, shirt by Blue
> Harbor, and a pair of distinguished designer dress shoes by Lark &

Finch. Complemented with a sharp pair of Gucci glasses, a contemporary yet traditional hair style (product by American Crew) and an attitude that says "Let Me Code," this developer is sure to turn heads come Q4. His look may be copied by many this fall season, but this trendsetter won't settle for uninspired redundancy. Amir only accepts the highest fashion and the latest looks.

Following Peter's lead, many engineers contributed to this conversation. Engineers from other teams thanked the sender for sharing this picture so that they could "get a chance to see Amir 2.0 launch." An engineer from Amir's team replied to the email by saying, "Amir would be more than happy to give you fashion advice!" These mocking emails enforced the dress-down culture through the detailed ridiculing of Amir's formal dress, showing how collective support for the cultural framework of "fun and informal" was bolstered by the team's organization of the Suit-Up Friday.

Jonathan (a Pipe Org senior manager) saw Amir's suit-up picture and read one of the response emails to Peter's initial post, which joked that Amir wore the suit for an interview with another tech corporation. Jonathan, however, took it seriously, went to the Wizard team, and blamed Vikram's incompetence for their inability to attract and retain talented engineers. Jonathan also jokingly threatened Amir that if he chose to become a "traitor" to Pipe Org, he would lose his trust forever and never be able to work at Behemoth again. The Wizard team laughed and explained the whole suit-up prank to Jonathan. Despite his attempt to use humor, Jonathan's sudden appearance in the Wizard team area brought unanticipated tension.

Amir's failure to receive the message that "Suit-Up Friday is a prank" marks his temporary outsider status. The primary reason he believed in this new Suit-Up Friday tradition was that he was absent for a vacation when the whole group discussed this trick; in other words, the selection of Amir as the prank's target was his "temporary outsider" status, preconditioned on his three-week vacation. Pranks conducted toward these "temporary outsiders" are so popular at Behemoth that they have become rituals to celebrate vacationers' returns. To put it another way, pranks have become an important "rite of passage" to transform colleagues' identities from vacationers back to team players (Van Gennep 2019).

At another level, Amir's failure to see through this prank marks his status as a cultural outsider. Jokes always play an essential role in reinforcing group culture by temporarily suspending the culture. Some cultural elements that are so common that they risk being taken as unconscious routine can only be highlighted when they are suspended and overturned. Therefore, by designing a prank that overturned the engineers' tradition of dressing down and made a ritual of dressing up, these pranksters presented their awareness of their community's dressing-down culture. In the same vein, if the target sees through this prank, they show their shared insider status within the engineering communities.

To a certain extent, the Suit-Up Friday prank was a mockery of the "casual Friday" trend adopted by the mainstream business world. For engineers, their casual dress code was their way to demonstrate their individualist values that went against the values of control and being serious or formal. Many white engineers I interviewed mentioned Mikey Dickerson, a former Google employer whom the White House hired, and how he kept dressing casually even after joining the White House staff. Others told me that they took pride in having no dress codes laid out by their managers.

However, when discussing the issue of dress codes, I realized that while the casual dress code demonstrated great symbolic value to the white engineers, it brought consternation to their Asian counterparts. Few of the Asian engineers knew the stories about the White House guy and his dressing-casual action. Many of them expressed that they struggled over how to dress on different occasions. After joining Behemoth and observing what their colleagues wore, Asian engineers knew they could just wear T-shirts and jeans on a daily basis. But what should they wear when they had an interview with other companies? What was the dress code for conferences? And were there different dress codes between junior and senior engineers or between managers and engineers? These kinds of quandaries partially contributed to Amir's failure to recognize Suit-Up Friday as a prank. In general, the lack of cultural knowledge can trap Asian immigrants like Amir in an awkward situation when they fail to figure out what is considered a joke/prank and why, thus contributing to Asian workers' outsider status.

Both newcomer welcome pranks (e.g., the checklist) and the daily spontaneous pranks (e.g., Suit-Up Friday) resembled those stages of ritual that Turner (1969) refers to as "liminal," as shown in his ethnographic work on tribal societies, as occasions for role reversals and for the dramatized exchange between up and down or strong and weak. Turner emphasized that the liminal phases of ritual played a critical role in presenting the specific dimension of culture through the role-reversal process. Of course, for these pranks, the liminal process has a different flavor from the rituals of Turner's tribal societies: what reversed were not participants' roles but the rules, values, and commonsense understandings held by predecessors about the company's culture. Thus, the majority of these pranks consist of articulations and enactment of cultural norms valorized at Behemoth (e.g., the importance of freedom and autonomy, the centrality of communication in the virtual space, the relaxed and informal environment) and the engineers' valued attitudes and feelings (e.g., fun, exciting, cool, togetherness, and commitment).

Surveillance Is a Joke: The Donut Email Prank
and Its Supporters and Challengers

Donut email pranks are considered the most typical and systematically or-ganized email pranks at Behemoth. The original rule for the game is straight-forward: when engineers fail to lock their computers upon leaving their desks, colleagues hijack their email and send embarrassing email messages organization-wide. As a penalty, the guilty party has to purchase donuts for his colleagues. Although disguised with a humorous tone, donut email pranks have a punitive nature, in that a violation of the rules (i.e., forgetting to lock one's computer screen) is penalized. In this case, the penalty evolved from docking wages to asking the guilty party to bring donuts for sharing. The punishment also became a space for engineers to assert their creativity; for example, when a guilty party was caught making a more serious mistake, their colleagues could ask them to bring "nicer" pastries. Donuts not only defined the punishment format but also constituted the script for the donut email prank. Through longtime practice, workers developed a scripted sub-ject line for these donut emails (e.g., "I love donuts"). This email subject line can effectively mark the donut email as a prank among other work-related emails. Of course, the title itself also signifies a very distinct cyber satire (Tay-lor and Bain 2003).

When confronted by donut email pranks, engineers are divided into two camps: while the game's supporters extended the donut emails' function be-yond the surveillance of locking computers, the game's challengers questioned the donut pranks' surveilling intention. To depict two groups' divergent reac-tions to the game, this section starts with supporters' playing strategies and then follows with those of the challengers.

To be clear, supporters are the majority among engineers. When par-ticipating in donut email pranks, supporters have never been satisfied with using donut emails to merely expose their teammates' lack of security con-sciousness. Via these donut emails, supporters mock coworkers' code qual-ity and absence from work, expose coworkers' absence from work, and laugh at other teams' slack in participating in donut games, their slowness in meet-ing deadlines, their newly added features full of loopholes, and their barely functioning service. These engineers converted the prank into an all-around "whistleblower" game, transforming the donut email platform into a forum for conducting panoptic surveillance and using the donut email system to drive their fellow engineers to work hard to surpass them—or at least match them.

Among all the whistleblower email themes within the donut email sys-tem, exposing other teams' slowness at meeting deadlines is one of the more popular. Delivering software before a deadline is the most important standard high-tech firms use to evaluate development teams' performance. Moreover, team competitions focused on delivering products before the deadline are critical instruments deployed by managers to increase productivity (Ó Riain 2001; Perlow 1998). Of course, development teams attend to other teams' deadlines not only because they intend to compete but also because of their interdependence on each other's accomplishments being on schedule (Barrett 2005), so laughing at other teams' inabilities to meet deadlines is a common joking theme in this surveillance game. However, when engineers incorporate the topic of deadlines into their joking content, they achieve self-discipline on behalf of their managers.

The following field note excerpt among Jack the North (white, male) and Dinesh (Hispanic, male) serves as a typical example of how programmers' donut emails work:

> Jack the North approached Dinesh's unlocked screen and criticized a team that had recently been widely congratulated for finishing a major project, writing: "Finally, you [the Knight team] got the feature. You guys should have done this a long time ago!" Upon return, Dinesh reported to the recipients that his message was a prank, and proceeded to congratulate the team. The culprit, Jack the North, continued to chide Dinesh, suggesting his success at intimidating his coworker by sending another email to the team: "Dinesh, you haven't left your desk in two hours . . . —Jack the North."

Jack's prank effectively converted the workplace into a hypercompetitive space charged with hatred. Indeed, Jack's "torture" of Dinesh illustrated his cruelty toward coworkers; in this case, his determination to construct Dinesh's "bad guy" image led him to go toe-to-toe with Dinesh's protestations of innocence. By claiming "Dinesh, you haven't left your desk in two hours," Jack eloquently asserted three things: (1) Dinesh lied about leaving his desk; (2) no one else could use Dinesh's account to send the email while he was at his desk; and thus, (3) it had to be Dinesh who attacked the Knight team.

More importantly, the prank email's content suggesting the Knights had delayed a product completion was, in fact, a serious accusation. In the tech world, a development process for one project might range anywhere from six or seven months to one or two years. On-deadline project delivery held the possibility of promotion for junior as well as senior engineers; on the other hand, if the development team failed to deliver the project on time, consequences could be severe, including the possible dissolution of the entire team. Sadly, Jack the North—a member of the Wizard team—had a lot of weight behind this assertion of the Knights' slowness. The Knight team developed encryption software, which is used to encrypt the data transmission software designed by the Wizards. In other words, Wizard members could speak authoritatively about the Knights' progress on the encryption software, as these two teams were working as sister teams on this project.

From this anecdote, one can tell that the donut email game provides a channel through which the managers' responsibility for controlling deadlines has been placed on the engineers' shoulders. In donut email pranks, engineers can perform managerial roles of reviewing their colleagues' work time and assessing the development team's productivity. By stating, "Finally, you [Knight team] got the feature. You guys should have done this a long time ago!" Jack the North supervised the Knight team's progress, shamed the Knights for their launch delay in front of other teams on the donut email platform, and potentially intensified the Knights' stress as a whole. Hierarchical control becomes unnecessary when different development teams are busy leveraging mutual disdain against each other's slowness.

Jack's prank is not an accidental phenomenon; mutual surveillance across development teams is a common theme in so demanding a work environment. Sometimes surveillance attends to deadlines, while at other times it applies to code quality, system vulnerability, and errors. Mutual surveillance derives from team interdependencies, since one team's assigned work is contingent upon completed work done by other teams. As shown from Jack's case, the Knights' falling behind schedule could result in the Wizard team's failing to deliver their feature on time. Indeed, software development always involves different teams closely working together, frequently consulting with each other, and carefully tracking one another's functionality design, coding style, quality, and progress to maintain a certain level of consistency; therefore, it is engineers themselves who organized the donut game to coordinate the development process across teams. Those teams that were behind, like the Knight team—for whatever reason—might quickly feel the wrath of their sister teams in several rounds of donut emails. In other words, donut emails constituted a type of disciplinary force in this seemingly laid-back workplace, ensuring that the apparent anarchy at the surface covered a foundation of good order.

As shown above, the supporters' investment in donut email expands the prank's function from mere security-procedure monitoring to that of a Foucauldian panoptic supervision system. For instance, in addition to monitoring work progress across teams, donut emails can involve mutual monitoring over abnormal or inappropriate behaviors between colleagues as well.

For example, Peter once snapped a picture of Kevin taking a nap in the conference room and used Kevin's unlocked computer to send out a donut email titled "this is how [an] engineer works" to snitch on Kevin's sleeping on the job. Kevin was one of the typical engineers among my informants who emphasized a passion for engineering work. While I chatted with him, Kevin revealed that the major factors propelling him to join the tech industry were his interests in gaming, programming, and computing in general. And he did not mind displaying his passion, sometimes even in a rather excessive way. For example, when he was assigned some projects that he felt were not challenging enough, he would aggressively display slacking off on the job site—publicly watching Twitch gaming streams on his screen or taking a brief absence from the workplace for a nap. In the meantime, Kevin also heavily promoted the freedom and autonomy of the engineering work in terms of choosing his favorite working schedule: he preferred to stay up late working at home and thus became very sleepy during the day.

His team manager, Vikram, seemed to understand that a brief nap could make night owls work more productively in the afternoon, so he always turned a blind eye toward such behavior. However, Kevin's teammate Danny recently learned that even though Kevin always stayed up late, he was not always working. Instead, he spent the whole night playing video games, and all his gaming hours were visible to his teammates through Steam, a gaming platform. Several days later, after learning about Kevin's sham from Danny, Peter sent out a donut email that contained Kevin's nap picture and made his sabotage known to all of the Pipe Org teams. After Kevin's nap picture went out, Vikram told Kevin that if he really needed to take a nap from now on, he had to write a "one-pager" to justify his reasons/behaviors—and everyone on the Wizard team knew that Vikram's asking someone to write a one-pager was his way of saying that they had done something really inappropriate. By requesting the document, Vikram deployed an indirect disciplinary tool that appears to offer engineers the space to choose a course of action as long as they can justify their reasoning.

Similarly, another type of individual-to-individual shaming email exposes engineers' misconduct during their on-call shift. As discussed in Chapter 4, developers usually take turns fielding on-call shifts to resolve tickets; each on-call shift typically lasts one week. During their on-call week, engineers remained on duty when they left the workplace, and they seemed to agree as a whole that they should avoid making too many plans for off-work leisure activities during their on-call shift. As a result, once some engineers went too far in violating this implicit agreement and were caught, their misbehaviors could be exposed via donut emails.

For example, one Monday, everyone on the Ranger team received a short donut email sent from Charles's account by an unidentified assailant with the subject line "I will bring donuts for the team tomorrow" and a single line in the email body: "because I was drunk when solving tickets." Here is how Charles's drunken ticket solving happened: During the weekend when he was on call, Charles went to a keg party organized by some other Pipe Org engineers. He was completely drunk when his pager annoyingly beeped to inform him of an urgent ticket. Upon seeing this email and learning about what Charles did, his teammates reached an agreement that Charles needed to get the team a better grade of pastries (nicer than donuts) since being "drunk on call" was a grave misdeed. Charles brought scones to his team the following day and replied to the donut email, "Homemade cranberry scones (out of the oven an hour ago) on Nick's old desk. Hope you can taste the spite in every bite (Haha just kidding)."

In Charles's story, the donut email functioned to expose and punish an engineer's on-call misbehavior. However, unlike a factory's disciplinary regime in which punishments rely on docking wages and how much to be docked is fixed in writing in the handbook, high-tech firms' punishments (in this case, pastry requisitions) can be adjusted based on engineers' decisions, which seem more humane on the surface but in substance are more challenging to be resented. More importantly, the donut email clearly stated a latent standard about what engineers should and should not do during on-call shifts. Although there were no formal regulations regarding what engineers could or could not do when they were on call, a majority of engineers consented to an unwritten rule about keeping a low profile on their on-call week's leisure activities. This shared unspoken rule became explicit in this donut email prank when Charles was reprimanded for violating this assumed expectation (i.e., partying and getting drunk while on call). The statement "because I was drunk when solving tickets"—written by the whistleblower and confessed to by the engineer—explicated one of the consensual, if unwritten, on-call work norms. Furthermore, engineers' fear of being humiliated and punished via donut email ensured their self-policing of this on-call norm, even when no colleagues were watching.

Managers also actively invest in engineers' whistleblower games. Through their teasing with engineers, managers demonstrate they are approachable and less intimidating, making the workplace seem more meritocratic. For example, Peter is well known for being keen to tease Jonathan, a senior manager of Pipe Org. One day, after someone used Principal Manager Josh's account to send out a donut email, Josh began chatting with engineers to figure out who sent the email. Seeing this, Peter replied to Josh's donut email conversation, saying, "Make sure you thank Jonathan for teaching you about security." Jonathan's response went head-to-head with Peter: "I don't know why you're blaming me. This is a libelous insult to my character!" Ignoring Jonathan's self-defense, Josh replied directly to Peter, saying, "Yeah, helpful of him." To a certain extent, the conversation showed Peter's explicit resistance to authority as manifested through written disdain toward a senior manager. By successfully fitting in donut pranks, managers can reshape the resistance-laden joking practices that intensify antagonism between managers and workers into a practice that builds solidarity between the two groups.

Occasionally, donut emails encounter resistance among engineers. The actors who fight against this game belong to a subgroup within the engineering community: the hackers, who are guided in resistance by their own culture. Hacker culture is an indispensable subculture in the tech world, and one fundamental value prized by hackers is technological freedom, particularly the freedom to access cutting-edge technology without any restriction or surveillance (Castells 2002; Turkle 2005). Therefore, the Foucauldian panoptical surveillance constructed via donut emails must be a burning shame to those identifying as hackers. Sometimes, hackers idealize themselves as the "rebel enemy of establishment" (Turkle 1994, 667) and insist that rules are meant to be broken (McDonald 2013; Thomas 2012; Turkle 1994). Unlike other engineers who use donut emails to conduct surveillance, hackers use donut emails to invoke rebellion against it; most hackers' investment in donut email pranks entails interrupting the emails' surveillance function.

Hackers adopt several strategies to mess with the surveillance system. For example, one popular strategy invented by hackers involves "creating a false alarm." Part of the donut email's authority lies in its accurate identifications of rule violators, so to challenge the emails' authority, hackers frequently drew on their technological skills to deliberately interfere with this email system and cause it to make wrongful accusations. On one occasion, a hacker, Mike, used his advanced programming ability to break into another engineer's terminal remotely and rewrite a portion of its core operating system code. This altered code tied a routine command used in coding to the terminal's email account so that whenever the engineer entered this specific code (in this case, the LS code to generate a list of files) in the course of their regular work, a bulk email similar to the donut pranking email would inadvertently be sent to the entire team, thereby sounding a false alarm and embarrassing the engineer whose terminal had been hacked.

Mike's terminal hack deconstructed the surveillance system in several ways. In particular, the hack questioned the surveillance email's accusational authority. Additionally, by offering an alternative version of the prank's rules (e.g., sending donut emails not to tell someone off but to mess with others' terminals), Mike also reinforced the "youth mayhem" embodied by these donut pranks. Mike's approach is a typical one that most hackers would use to engage with donut emails; most pranks that hackers initiate involve invading the target system and inserting or modifying command lines, such as the "md command hack," "ipconfig command hack," and "netuser command hack." Of course, hacker culture, which emphasizes outlaw nature and technological determinism, becomes the critical resource that motivates hackers to participate in donut emails in this specific way.

The "fake screen saver" trick, which was considered one of Danny's donut-prank masterpieces, also reflected hackers' rebellious orientation and their focus on creating false alarms. The trick was simple: Danny took a screenshot of his desktop at a moment when his email account was visible and then set it as the desktop's wallpaper. When Danny left his seat, everyone found that Danny "forgot" to lock his screen since they could clearly see the email list on Danny's screen. Matthew, who took the bait, went to take Danny's seat and prepared to use his computer to send out the donut email—but he immediately realized that Danny's screen had frozen. As Matt sat futilely clicking Danny's mouse, Danny himself went back to the team area. Seeing this scene, Danny laughed and told us the secret of his screen saver. After hearing about this prank, everyone on the Assassin team tried to change their screen saver by taking a screenshot of their current desktop screens. All of a sudden, Danny had become the master of the prank; he strolled around the team area with an exaggerated swagger and constantly offered guidance to those teammates who tried to copy his trick.

Danny's fake unlocked-screen prank also showed that hackers tried to use the donut email as a way to express resistance to the surveillance rules. One fundamental rule of the donut game was that whistleblowers would never be identified; as discussed above, this rule created a rather panoptical environment and perpetual surveillance, enforced by the programmers themselves. This panoptical control begged hackers, whose cultural foundations rested on rebellion against convention and rules, to dismantle it. So, by tricking Matthew into accessing his "unlocked" screen and exposing him as the whistleblower, Danny broke the secrecy rule and destabilized the panoptic, placing attention on the would-be prankster.

Although these challengers' hacks indicated a potential for resistance against the donut email games, they only happened occasionally and could hardly transform into collective resistance. For example, although Mike and Danny's colleagues openly worshipped their hacks, their praise focused on their enviable hacking strategies and the technical competence embodied in these hacks, not on the motivations behind them (i.e., their resentment toward the donut emails' surveillance). Indeed, when I chatted with Danny's teammates about his fake screen saver pranks, they all praised Danny for being a "smartass"—but no collective interests were mobilized to problematize the donut emails' surveillance tendencies. Also, challengers' donut hacks happened far less often than supporters' donut emails: while supporters sent donut emails every two or three days, donut hacks occurred fewer than a dozen times in my thirteen months of ethnographic work. In short, although such donut hacks did signal a hint of resistance, such resistance was highly individualized and occasional and can hardly be said to have captured the sympathies of the majority of engineers, to say nothing of motivating them to collective action.

Even those challengers who instinctively resented the donut emails' surveillance elements perceived the prank as a little "annoying" but admitted the donut game, in general, was "fun," "funny," and "cool." In other words, even these transgressive, challenger-driven episodes did not emphasize the surveillance nature of the donut email per se or contest the game's legitimacy overall. After all, participation in the donut emails also brought challengers enormous social status (e.g., the admiration of hackers like Mike and Danny for their technological competence and smartness). Therefore, when developing donut hacks, challengers were more likely to focus on the technical details needed to carry out the pranks than to consider their symbolic gesture of resistance. In other words, although challengers tried to problematize the surveillance nature of donut games, they did not completely withdraw their consent or their investment in the game; nor did they challenge the games' entire setup.

In general, donut emails are an excellent illustration of how the original purpose of a game can be largely distorted once the game playing is beyond control. The donut emails' initial designed goal is very straightforward and only centers on disciplining engineers' security consciousness. After engineers' creative modifications of the game's rules, however, donut emails have transformed into a whistleblower game in which engineers mutually conduct panoptical surveillance to serve their interests (e.g., completing work on schedule, coordinating code quality and style). Managers largely tolerate engineers' rule bending in this case, as this strategy benefits their interests by obscuring their control and transforming the vertical conflicts between managers and workers into lateral conflicts between development teams (e.g., surveilling sister teams' progress). However, once the teasing gets out of hand, engineers developed aggressive attacking strategies (e.g., the humiliation of their sister teams) and aggressive resisting strategies (e.g., creating false alarms). Such playing strategies, when allowed to run rampant, increase hostility among workers or between teams, create a culture of hatred in the workplace, and entirely distort the original purpose of surveillance games.

To some extent, the execution of donut email pranks displays a tug-of-war between control and resistance, with the emergence of "occasional hegemonic states." According to the supporters' participation in the donut emails, one can tell that surveillance, including but not limited to security consciousness, is achieved through engineers' internalized discipline. Supporters of the game gave their consent to this surveillance-oriented game but only on the condition that they could push the game in the direction they were interested in (e.g., nudging it from a simple security game to a whistleblower game). In other words, the sustainability of the donut game can be attributed to the engineers' ability to extract concessions from the managers and, in turn, the managers' capacity for exchanging concessions for consent. However, as we all know, hegemonic domination is always a contested process—and hackers' resistance, as counterhegemonic culture, arises every now and then. Although the hackers' resistance is rather marginal most of the time, it demonstrates that pranking games are subject to challenge and that hegemonic and counterhegemonic states can coexist in the "chaotic fun" culture built out by these games.

Concluding Remarks

Unlike other games, pranking games are largely separate from the core engineering mode of production. One might claim that other games described in this book must be embedded in the engineering work process—racing games are best for on-call shifts, and simulation games are only suited for scrums. However, pranking games can be found in every kind of office: the fun generated through hazing newcomers is not "engineering fun" per se but "bantering fun," which can be found on the shop floor as well. Similarly, the mutual surveillance sugarcoated by pranks is a common scene in other working contexts as well (see Collinson 1988).

In a general work context, pranking games are the most ordinary type of game; however, they are the most special type of game in engineering. These pranking games have been dislodged from an engineering context to the point that they barely mobilize engineers' gamer subjectivity. Indeed, the pranking fun can be generated without establishing a video-gaming world, gamified environment, or gamification techniques (e.g., badges or score tracking), which implies that engineers do not need to mobilize their gaming mindset to invest in pranking games. Instead, pranking games are closer to classic working-class games: sometimes, they are organized to establish seniority in front of newcomers, in the same way as perpetrators played rough with apprentices on shop floors (see Collinson 1988). Other times, pranking games are organized to express a mild level of resistance and antagonism to control (e.g., donut hacks), just like the blue-collar horseplay found in every factory.

Even so, pranking games occupy an irreplaceable position in the array of games played on the engineering floor. On the surface, pranking games, like those hazing newcomers or the donut emails, contribute another layer of chaos to Behemoth. However, these pranking games are the hidden order amid this anarchy. The corporate culture—manifested as "fun, young, and causal"—is articulated through these culture games and becomes the key force that guides workers' behaviors, like work scheduling, participating in the virtual community, and how they dress. Similarly, donut emails become a strong disciplinary force to maintain order in many aspects (e.g., sabotage, deadlines, sense of security) in this seemingly anarchic workplace.

Also, pranking games are indispensable in the gaming field to ensure the permeation of hegemony. Indeed, while racing games ensure hegemony in maintenance work and simulation games establish hegemony in software development, pranking games guarantee hegemony in engineers' daily interactions. For example, through the distribution of Kevin's picture, a consensus was formed around when slacking on the job could be interpreted as appropriate (e.g., when staying up late working) and when it is understood as sabotage. However, unlike racing games or simulation games that can produce a relatively stable hegemonic state in the engineering work process, pranking games can only form occasional hegemonic states. Under some circumstances, managers' and workers' interests coordinate, such as when pranks conduct mutual surveillance, reduce fatigue, and valorizes the organization's flat structure. Under other circumstances, however, managers' and workers' divergent interests emerge, reflected by hackers' resentment against specific pranking rules.

6

Out of the Game

Peasant Coders' Suffering under
Behemoth's Gamification

Asian Engineers' "Peasant Coder"
(*Ma Nong*) Subjectivity

Since 2010, first-generation Asian engineers have become the majority in the U.S. high-tech industry (Equal Employment Opportunity Commission [EEOC] 2016).[1] The percentage of Silicon Valley's tech workforce who are of Asian origin grew from 39 percent in 2000 to more than 50 percent according to the 2010 U.S. census, and subsequent analyses of EEOC data indicated a further increase by 2018 (Kim, Peck, and Gee 2020; Scott et al. 2018).[2] This trend manifested at Behemoth as well; take my field site, Pipe Org, as an example. First-generation Asian engineers compose 24 percent of the total engineering population and represented a large share of the Pipe Org workforce at the time I was conducting my fieldwork. In terms of status, however, Asian engineers remained "outsiders" for most games organized on the engineering floor. Why were Asian engineers considered outsiders when it came to workplace gameplay? Moreover, how did they cope with this hypergamified workplace and respond to their white counterparts' heavy investment in games? This chapter attempts to address these questions.

The subjectivity of first-generation Asian immigrant engineers plays a critical role in differentiating their gaming behaviors from those of white engineers. I adopt the term "peasant coder" to portray Asian engineers' subjectivity; it is a term invoked by Chinese engineers themselves to draw a parallel between "peasant migrant workers," who left their farms for urban centers to sell low-skilled labor, and "professional migrant workers," who left developing countries to sell their coding skills in developed countries.

How can we perceive peasant coder subjectivity? The first commonality that connects peasant migrant workers and peasant coders is migrant status. By drawing the parallel, peasant coders underline their precarious working experience in the United States and associate it with their status as temporary workers. The sense of insecurity is rooted at the core of these workers' self-identification, which directly results in their interpretation of work as a path to maintaining legal migrant status. Second, many of my interviewees used the term "peasant coders" together with "moving bricks" (*ban zhuan*). Asian engineers told me that writing code resembles moving bricks: they move chunks of code from one project to another, the same way that construction workers move bricks from one place to another on the job site. Although "moving bricks" is a self-deprecating expression, it does reflect peasant coders' interpretation of their job; the key to performing good coding work is hard work, which is the same thing needed to excel at construction work. In other words, peasant coders deemphasize the coding jobs' traits—creativity, concentration, and a crisis mentality—and approximate their work to low-skilled construction work. Finally, the concept of a "providing self" is embedded in the peasant coder's subjectivity. As documented by previous research, this self-conceptualization as a provider reflects as an overriding commitment for peasant migrant workers to send remittance to their families back in the countryside (Hochschild 2002; Lee 1998; Rodriguez 2010). Being a valuable provider for their families sometimes defines the core meaning of peasant migrants' work. Peasant coders, for their part, resemble peasant migrant workers in their commitment to being important providers for their families.

With this outline of peasant coder subjectivity in mind, we can now turn to a few more questions. How is peasant coder subjectivity formulated? To what extent does this subjectivity differentiate from white engineers' gamer subjectivity? How can such a distinct subjectivity direct Asian workers' gaming behaviors and status at Behemoth? The following sections of this chapter explore these questions.

Peasant Coders as the Precarious Immigrant

We know that immigrant status is the foundation of peasant coder subjectivity. Some peasant coders expressed straightforwardly to me that the primary reason they chose to enter the tech industry was for relatively stable migrant status. In the United States, the H1-B visa endows professional workers with relatively long-term migrant status, and the high-tech industry's labor shortage leads companies to aggressively recruit foreign talent and actively sponsor their applications for H1-B visas. In 2017, tech companies assisted 900,000 to 1 million foreign-born tech workers in applying for H1-B visas (Wakabayashi and Schwartz 2017).[3] Tech work is the most viable means for peasant coders to settle in the United States.

This calculation was clearly reflected in my conversation with Jammar, an Indian worker. During our interview, he insisted that I should change my major from sociology to social work or try to double major. Seeing I was unconvinced, he went a step further: "You know you can easily find a job in some NGO organizations [sic] if you have a social work degree. I know the pay might not be pretty. I know the work probably won't be exciting. But the point is you get the H1-B! . . . Pay is less important, and occupation is secondary. Getting the H1-B is the most important, right? And you know there are no limits on H1-Bs for social workers. That's the point!" Jammar's statement was loud and clear—and representative of many peasant coders' concerns. For peasant coders, their most fundamental insecurity comes from the fact that they may not be able to obtain legal status to put down roots and build a life in the United States; this insecurity forces them to view the essential purpose of a job as to gain legal immigrant status, which takes precedence over all other considerations (e.g., whether the job has "pretty payment" or the occupation is "exciting").

Of course, landing a job in the tech industry does not completely eliminate peasant coders' insecurity. A long-lasting sense of precarity comes from the employer-bonded H1-B visa system. If a foreign worker on an H1-B visa is dismissed by their sponsoring employer, they need to find another sponsoring employer within sixty days to keep the visa—or leave the United States to avoid an illegal overstay.

The precarious status of peasant coders profoundly separates them from their white colleagues. For one thing, peasant coders are far more hesitant to invest in games that encourage disruptive ideas and behaviors (e.g., simulation games) or those with boundaries that can be stretched to elicit rebellion (e.g., pranking games). After all, an investment in these games can increase their instability and put their legal status at risk. A second consideration follows: peasant coders do not need gamification to increase their willingness to engage in high-intensity engineering work for long hours. Previous research demonstrates that the vulnerability of immigrant workers' legal status ensures they are always more likely to consent to harsher punishment, overtime work, and lower pay than domestic workers (Bank Muñoz 2011; McKay 2006).

However, it is dangerous to underestimate peasant coders' agency in their encounters with the insatiable, insecure, and precarious nature of their immigrant status. Immersing myself in the peasant coders' community made me realize that they are a very enterprising group capable of turning the disadvantage of instability to their advantage. As Yang, one Chinese engineer who was forced to hop to another company in Vancouver due to the expiration of his H1-B, told me, "If they didn't close the door for me, I would be too settled to open another window." Indeed, among peasant coders, instability is likely to be reinterpreted as opportunity and mobility.

Peasant coders confessed that they were more mobile than their white counterparts, which was confirmed by the statistical record from my fieldwork. By the time I finished my fieldwork, the average length of time that Asian engineers stuck with the same company was 1.22 years, compared with an average of 2.38 for white engineers. As a result, peasant coders felt less committed to Behemoth's corporate culture and much less attached to the game-rich work environment. To be fair, the increasingly high flexibility of the tech industry has largely destroyed the idea of core employees—once considered central to the business, salaried with bonuses and stock options, provided with career ladders, and contrasted with contractors at the "periphery"—who were targets of the corporations' cultural engineering and commitment building (Kunda and Van Maanen 1999). Compared to core employees, peasant coders are much more mobile and much less committed to certain corporate cultures than white engineers.

Take Danny and JW's divergent career paths, for example. By the end of 2015, when one of the Wizard team's major projects came to an end, two engineers who were responsible for this project—Danny and JW—began thinking about changing career directions. Danny, for his part, decided to stay at Behemoth but transferred to another team. When we talked about his decision, he said he felt like Behemoth's "whole system," which was designed to encourage the "work hard, have fun" ethic, just worked for him. Then Danny blushed to admit that somehow he felt so "attached" to Behemoth that it was as if he had "no life"—he went on Behemoth's internal forum to check for new phone-tool pranks or new badges even while on vacation and during a trip to Europe. He absolutely would not leave Behemoth; he just planned to transfer to another team to seek "sexier" projects. JW's decision, however, was a completely different story. He offered a frank commentary on Danny's choice: "Look, I don't support internal transfer. It's not a wise investment. I honestly don't understand why he [Danny] did this. Like, if you hop to a different company, you probably will be promoted like a half level. At least, your pay will be raised. But if you just transfer within the company, you get nothing." Apparently, for JW job hopping is a very rational calculation; it should be treated as an investment. The purpose of changing jobs is to achieve upward mobility, both administratively and economically. The factors that influenced Danny's decision—Behemoth's culture and work environment—were not part of JW's calculations.

Peasant Workers as the Hardworking Student

If immigrant worker status drives peasant coders' embodiment of the "precarious self," their cultural, educational, and national backgrounds shape their "hardworking self." Indian and Chinese engineers choose to study computer science out of a pragmatic consideration—to find a job. In Chapter 2, I discussed Guang's case in detail; here, I briefly summarize his story, which serves as a good illustration of Asian engineers' educational choices. Guang was a twenty-seven-year-old Chinese engineer who worked at Behemoth. When we first met, he told me he actually preferred humanities to science:

> I wanted to choose the humanities track [*xuan wen ke*] for Gaokao [the National College Entrance Examination] back then . . . but my parents told me, "You are a guy. . . . You need to be a manly man. . . . No real man studied the humanities. . . . There is no future in studying humanities." And they warned me that it would be very difficult to get a job if I studied humanities . . . so I chose to go the science track for Gaokao. . . . After that, I majored in math and then computer science. . . . Then everything after that seemed very natural.

Throughout our conversation, Guang said repeatedly that he still considered humanities to be his hobby, while emphasizing that programming was "just a job." Then, the topic switched to his white colleagues. Guang expressed his admiration for these white engineers who could treat programming as a hobby and not just a job:

> They did see programming as a hobby. . . . Whenever they started talking about coding, their eyes gleamed and danced [*mei fei se wu*]. . . . They took all different types of programming courses, not for credits, just for fun. . . . I mean, you need to really adopt it as a hobby to be willing to devote such a lot of time and energy to dig into it. . . . They just naturally found interest in it. . . . They don't need other people to tell them that they should learn it.

Guang's choice weighing humanities versus science is not uncommon among Chinese engineers. Chinese students do not need to individually select courses until the eleventh grade, right before the Chinese National College Entrance Examination (Gaokao), and then the selection is only between two tracks: sciences or humanities. The majority of Chinese students choose the science track for Gaokao and then go on to have STEM majors in college. More often than not, Chinese students' choices are highly influenced by their parents or schoolteachers, just like Guang's was—and his parents' choices are very representative. By saying "it would be very difficult to get a job if [he] studied humanities," Guang's parents expressed a common sensibility shared by many in Chinese society: the pragmatic belief that the ultimate goal of a college education is to find a job. Such a practical take poses a sharp contrast to the American idealistic understanding of college education, which foregrounds self-exploration, the discovery of personal interests, and the pursuit of individual passion. This contrast was made clear when Guang discussed his American counterparts' college experience—their passionate pursuit of programming courses and adoption of programming as one of their hobbies. At a more fundamental level, claiming that "there is no future in studying humanities" suggests Guang's parents were also influenced by a long-standing national discourse in China that valorizes the study of science. The Communist Party promotes a discourse modeled after the former Soviet Union, one that prioritizes STEM fields with an eye toward industrialization and modernization: "Mastering math, physics, and chemistry, one is fearless in the world" (Ma 2020).

Coincidentally, Indian engineers' paths to entering STEM fields were similar to those of their Chinese colleagues. For example, both Naji and Hasini followed their parents' suggestions and chose to major in computer science. Naji was the family's oldest son, and his parents thought it important for the eldest son to enter the "most rewarding industry." So Naji applied to all of the top computer science programs in the United States and eventually did his postgraduate study at Columbia University. Hasini was the second daughter; after her oldest brother became a doctor and her big sister pursued biology, her parents allowed her to major in computer science, as they thought "studying CS [computer science] now has become a 'hip thing' in India." Similar to Guang, personal interests were not a concern in Naji's or Hasini's narratives about their decisions to enter a STEM field. Instead, choosing CS were familial decisions influenced by an Indian national discourse that portrayed the tech industry as "rewarding" and entering this field as a "hip thing." Indeed, the valorization of computer science has been linked to the Indian development discourse that has arisen since 2005, which emphasizes that industries like information technology can help India "leapfrog" other nations in the race for social and economic development (Radhakrishnan 2011).

So just as it is for Chinese engineers, higher education for Indian engineers is a way to realize familial and even national development prospects but not an avenue for pursuing individual hobbies. This point is made even more explicit in Umish's story. Umish's interest is in language learning, and he is proficient in English, Japanese, and German. However, when he reached the year in which he needed to decide on a college major, he felt a strong sense of urgency to make his education "useful"—so he chose to study computer science. When I asked him whether he liked studying computer science, he told me it was definitely not his first interest but immediately added, "It's a good investment, though. It gets me a good-paying job, like, really fast." For Umish, studying computer science had nothing to do with his passions or interests: it was an economic investment calculation. Umish's straightforward investment logic is not unique; in fact, many Chinese engineers made similar calculations. Ah Hao, for example, told me that his parents had spent so much money on his two-year postgraduate study that he felt obligated to find a good-paying job to pay them back quickly. So, when he had many tech companies' offers in hand, he did not hesitate to choose Behemoth, as Behemoth's decent pay allowed him to repay his parents within a year and a half.

Working Hard, "Eating Bitter," and Being Professional

Coming from a differentiated background from white engineers, peasant coders draw on a distinct value set when interpreting the meaning of their work. Naji's story offers an excellent example of peasant coders' working attitude. Naji, in his thirties, comes from India. He works on a database service team that is considered one of Behemoth's most critical teams; as such, it is known for its high work-related pressures. The day I met him, I brought another friend, Jay, a Chinese engineer close to Naji. We met in front of Naji's apartment building on First Avenue. When Naji came downstairs, he asked us whether we had trouble finding his building. I told him that it was easy to find his place, as I often went to the art museum across the street. Naji immediately replied, "The art museum's 'hardworking man' sculpture is one reason why I rent this apartment!" The actual name of the "hardworking man" sculpture is *Hammering Man*. Stretching forty-eight feet into the air and weighing in at 26,000 pounds, *Hammering Man* portrays a working-class man using the tremendous might of his metallic left arm to pound his hammer around the clock throughout the day. Naji told me half jokingly that he wanted to use the sculpture to remind himself to work hard; if he did not work hard enough, he said, "This hammering guy will smash my apartment." This icebreaker on the art installation made our conversation atmosphere very pleasant. To keep the conversation light and humorous, Naji told us more "fun facts" about the hammering man: "You know, he works really hard. . . . He pounds like all day long except for from one A.M. to five A.M., and of course, he took a break on Labor Day." We all laughed and Naji continued, "Well, in that sense, I work harder than him. I went to the office during the long [Labor Day] weekend!" Now it was Jay's turn to be surprised. "Why did you go to the office on Labor Day?" Naji told us that he agreed to cover one of his colleagues' on-call shifts, so his colleague could take his family on vacation. Jay popped out a series of questions: "But why did you go to the office? You can totally work from home. Was the office even open on Labor Day?" Naji replied proudly:

"Of course it's open! But I am pretty sure that there was only the doorman and me in the building that day."

Indeed, hard work plays a prominent role in shaping peasant coders' working attitudes. When questioned about the keys to workplace success, peasant coders always mention traits associated with hard work: keep forging ahead, persistently update programming skills, strive as an individual, and "eat bitterness."[4] In other words, peasant coders with a hardworking mindset believe that success should be driven by long-term perseverance and continuous skill perfection, not reliance on creative ideas that come with an adrenaline rush. After all, no matter whether these peasant coders come from India or China, they have been selectively screened from their peers, first in higher education and later in the job market, based on their personal striving, resilience, and hard work, not their passing interests or spur-of-the-moment decisions.

Peasant coders' denigration of creativity in tech work is well demonstrated by their comparisons of coding to construction work. As discussed above, many Chinese engineers told me that writing code resembled "moving bricks" in that they move chunks of code from one place to another, just like construction workers. A very similar self-deprecating expression was brought up by Indian interviewees as well. Take Manjuf, for example. Manjuf is a thirty-one-year-old engineer who was just promoted to Level 5 on the Scable team. When Manjuf learned over dinner that I also took graduate-level statistics courses, he suggested I change my major to computer science. When I told him that I neither liked math nor had talent in that field, he immediately interrupted, "Who needs to be good at this? You think we have to be good at math to do coding? A monkey can code! This job does not require you to be good at math or smart or creative or whatever.... What you need is to endure the boredom ... the boredom of endlessly finding bugs." Manjuf's comments are representative of a common interpretation shared among my Chinese and Indian engineers: a hardworking attitude and endurance are more important than talent, creativity, and passion.

Drawing on their valorization of hard work, peasant coders denounce their white colleagues' "disruptive creativity" and equalize it with "moodiness," "instability," or "unprofessionalism." During interviews, peasant coders often criticized their white counterparts as having unreasonable "egos" and only contributing their flash of genius when assigned projects they find sufficiently interesting. This kind of denunciation is well illustrated by Fang, a twenty-seven-year-old Chinese male engineer who worked as a Level 4 engineer at Behemoth. Fang was contemptuous of white engineers who "only wanted to be assigned the most creative task":

> I felt like white guys were more like when they loved what they did, they devoted 100 percent or 150 percent of their energy to work. They

worked during the weekend.... They did not sleep. But once they were in a bad mood, they asked for OOTO[5] straight for two days. You see the problem here?... Their productivity relied on their mood... but I just treated it professionally.... I consider myself a craftsman [*shou yi ren*].... I sell my craftsmanship to earn bread and feed my family... so I do what I am assigned, do my share, and do the best... but they [white guys] thought themselves as masters.... They only wanted to be assigned the most creative task.

In this response, Fang identified and then promptly dismissed what he thought white engineers were doing—treating work as a medium for expressing their creative freedom and their technological mastery. Fang drew a sharp contrast between himself and the white engineers: while he represented "professionalism," white workers represented "moodiness," and whereas he self-identified as a "craftsman," white engineers were branded as "masters." The craftsmanship Fang referred to is heavily embedded in China's traditional Confucian social structure (Elman 1989).[6] Usually, craftsmen would possess a particular skill (e.g., carpentry). Craftsmen's skills are not difficult to acquire and require a minimum level of creativity and abstract knowledge; however, mastering those skills requires long stretches of hard work and repetitive practice. Self-labeling as a craftsman is not merely a way for Chinese engineers to express their modesty; they adopt the morality code shared within craftsmanship to regulate themselves, which can be reflected in Fang's emphasis on hard work and self-discipline.

On the contrary, to Fang, white engineers' obsession with the most creative projects was a factor that could affect productivity—once white engineers lost interest in their project, they slacked off and "asked for OOTO straight for two days." The problem is that white engineers' valorization of their creativity and passion sometimes helps them legitimize their opportunities to work on more creative projects, whereas Chinese engineers' lack of emphasis in requesting creative projects increases their likelihood of being assigned to more peripheral tasks. To use Bulut's (2020) expression, when white engineers' passion and "love" toward engineering work are largely legitimized in the workplace, the tech workplace actually manufactures an invisible gatekeeping mechanism that shapes the engineering work.

Fang describes what preoccupies most of the peasant coders I talked with—being responsible, self-disciplined, and a good craftsman. Indeed, Chinese and Indian engineers take pride in their self-discipline. Take Jie, a twenty-five-year-old Chinese male engineer who graduated from Cornell University and worked on the Portal team. Jie forced himself to be at work before 9:00 A.M. and leave no earlier than 6:00 P.M., even though Behemoth had no fixed work schedule, and he told me he would like to make himself have a more disciplined schedule because it is "healthy." Jie regulated himself to work over eight hours a day because he knew his productivity was low in the hour after lunch—such that he hardly counted it as an hour's work. Also, Jie felt a little annoyed working with some white engineers, "who won't show up to the office until 11:00 A.M.," as the later arrival vastly shortened their overlapping working hours and made cooperation difficult. Similarly, Jai, a twenty-six-year-old Indian female engineer who got her master's from Northeastern University and worked in the digital book department, was confused by why her department always needed to arrange drinking parties every Thursday afternoon. She told me that her white colleagues were "so into it." She complained, "I don't understand how you can still concentrate and work after you have a couple of drinks." To Jai, "drinking on the job" is a sign of a lacking work ethic.

The "fun" established in the workplace severely contradicts with peasant coders' valuation of "seriousness" and "professionalism" at work. To peasant coders, qualities such as being hardworking and professional are important sources of dignity and self-respect. The value embodied in white engineers' behavior (e.g., treating work as a way of having fun and as an expression of gaming habits) erodes peasant coders' working self. Therefore, one can say that the different national, cultural, and educational systems cultivated peasant coders' interpretation of the meaning of work, which became an essential precondition for Asians to withdraw from workplace games.

Peasant Coders: A Married Man and the "Providing Self"

"Boss Lei" introduced me to Liang Yuan. Lei told me that I had to talk to Liang and listen to his story of chasing his "math dream"—and with this impression in my mind, I met Liang. He is in his early thirties and works as a Level 5 engineer on Behemoth's Credit team. After a brief chitchat, I got straight to the point and asked about his math dream. It is quite a story: After Liang obtained a master's degree in computer science from Columbia University, he worked at an investment bank in New York. The longer Liang worked there, however, the more bored he felt. According to Liang, the bank was a "stuffy," "formal," and "white" workplace. His manager, who once majored in math at Cambridge University and was an absolute "math nerd," was the job's only silver lining. Working with his manager made Liang realize that his real passion was being a mathematician, so he gave up his bank job and began preparing to get a doctorate in math.

Liang commented on his decision: "It was a bold decision, I admit. But I was still young then. If I did not give it a try, I felt I would regret it when I grew old." He did make substantive sacrifices; he quit his job and his life in New York altogether and went to his wife, Dujuan, in St. Louis, where she was pursuing her social work PhD at Washington University. Liang recalled their lives in St. Louis: "It was a tough time. We lived on my wife's TA [teaching assistant] salary." Even so, Liang went all out for his math dream. However, after about a year, when Liang was close to getting into a math PhD program (e.g., after taking the GRE mathematics test, collecting recommendation letters, and drafting statements of purpose), his wife became pregnant—and all of a sudden, everything changed. With a baby on the way, Liang had more expenses to think about. Could they raise a baby on two TA salaries? Being accepted into a PhD program and becoming a TA was, in fact, the best-case scenario. What if he didn't get in? He was not allowed to work on a spouse visa.

Liang told me that it did not take him long to make a decision—he had to return to the industry and get a job. "It was very clear at that moment that taking care of my family conflicted with my personal interests. I felt duty bound to support the family." Soon enough, Liang took the offer from Behemoth and moved his family to the West Coast. In a flash, he was making the down payment for his four-bedroom house, which he thought was "spacious" enough for his newborn baby. Hearing the end of his story, I asked, with somewhat of a palpitating heart, "Do you regret giving up your plan to get a math PhD?" He replied promptly, "Not really. You know, at a certain age, as a man, you have to learn to make the sacrifice." Then he took the initiative to lighten the tone and told me something he thought was fun—he named his newborn baby "Nash." "Do you know which Nash I referred to?" he asked, and I shook my head. "It was John Nash," he told me, "the mathematician who invented the Nash equilibrium and won the Nobel Prize in Economics."

Later, I became closer with Liang's wife and was invited to their house to hang out. The moment I entered their yard, I saw a typical family-life scene that can be spotted in every Chinese immigrant engineer's household: Inside the house, Dujuan was busy taking care of their newborn baby. Outside, Liang was building a fence. Seeing that I showed great interest in Liang's fence building, Dujuan told me Liang developed this new hobby very recently. Dujuan continued, "This is much better than his old hobby—video games. He used to invite Lei and Jialin [two Chinese colleagues from Liang's team] to play video games on the weekends, and it was very unhealthy. Now he likes doing stuff for the family, like building the fence, assembling porch chairs, or mowing the lawn. I don't expect him to take it too seriously. But it's a good hobby, at least, dragging him to go outside."

For Liang, the turning point in his life trajectory was his wife's pregnancy; before then, Liang planned to sacrifice his family's financial condition to his passion for math. After Dujuan became pregnant, Liang's pursuit of a math PhD and the fulfillment of his family's financial needs were just incompatible tasks, and eventually, he chose to put his family above his passion for math. As Liang said, "At a certain age, as a man, you have to learn to make the sacrifice."

Indeed, age played a prominent role in differentiating Asian engineers' identities and behaviors from those of their white counterparts. A majority of the Asian engineers were older than the white engineers. Among my interviewees, the median age for Asian engineers was 27, while the median age for the white engineers was 26.5. One reason for the age difference is the different degrees Asian and white engineers earned: among sixty-six interviewees, more than 94 percent of Asian engineers had obtained master's degrees, while only 38 percent of white engineers held master's degrees. It is plausible that the age difference between peasant coders and white engineers could result in very disparate life experiences, friend circles, and maturity levels between these two groups.

As exemplified by Liang, most Asian engineers had reached the age of getting married and raising children and thus had more at stake than their younger white colleagues. Even for people like Liang who were determined to pursue their passion, passion must give way to familial responsibilities at a certain age. On top of that, these life milestones also change peasant coders' leisure time activities. As Liang's story illustrated, he used to be preoccupied with video-game playing with friends in his spare time, which is a typical way for young men to have fun. After the baby, he spent his free time doing household-centered activities like yardwork.

Among peasant coders, leisure pursuits are normally family oriented. Hasini, a thirty-year-old Indian engineer, once chatted with me about her Memorial Day trip to Portland and self-deprecatingly said that she had felt enormous pressure to get married afterward: "Among all nine of us who went on the trip, I was the only person [who is] single. You can imagine how awkward I was. Seeing them eat and play in pairs, I had an impulse to marry whomever I met the next day." Hearing her story, I teased Hasini that she probably would never travel with so many couples again. She denied it right away. "Not really. You know, it's wonderful traveling with four couples. They are so organized and considerate. Like, they will book the house; they will filter out the best places that we should visit. They are so considerate that they even brought an extra blanket for me."

The problem is that when peasant coders move on to the next life stage, they are more likely to interpret gaming activities that their white colleagues continue to indulge in as "immature." For example, the interview excerpt below illustrates how Umish, the Indian engineer, interprets white engineers' gaming strategies in the simulation games (i.e., those that blur the boundaries of the gaming-working relationship) as childish and a sign of white engineers' "low emotional quotient":

Most engineers here are kids. . . . They are smart . . . have a high IQ . . . but they don't have high EQ . . . so they don't know how to interact with each other . . . but they know that people working on the same projects should know each other better. What would normal people do to build relationships? Go out to eat or drink together, right? But those kids . . . they use video games to do this. . . . They played games together. . . . It's really childish. . . . Like, I once brought one of my friends visiting our team. . . . He worked in finance . . . and after he saw the *World of Warcraft* posters hanging everywhere in my team and board game boxes scattered [around] . . . he teased me, like, "Are you working for a high-tech firm or just babysitting kindergarten kids?"

Umish's comments are very representative of peasant coders' denunciations of white engineers' "immaturity," "childishness," and "naivete." While peasant coders rarely expressed these sentiments publicly, some of them did tell me that organizing the workplace like a playground was considered condescending; several Asian engineers felt that the "kindergarten" environment gave management a somewhat paternalistic flavor.

From Liang's story of abandoning his pursuit of a math doctorate, one can tell that he put his provider role as his top responsibility. Liang, however, is not the exception. Let's recall Fang, the engineer who was contemptuous of white engineers' moody pursuit of most creative projects and portrayed himself as "a craftsman" who only "sells craftsmanship to earn bread and feed my family." Fang's description reflected his pride in sacrificing his pursuit of creative tasks in the name of familial responsibility. This understanding was widely shared among peasant coders; to these engineers, the essential meaning of their work was to fulfill their role as breadwinners.

If one draws on a masculinity framework, white gamers and peasant coders are not thought to possess traditionally macho masculinity, which in the American context can be characterized as tough, dominating, aggressive, and sexually attractive (Connell 2005). White gamers choose to draw on technological obsession to compensate for their lack of masculinity. Peasant coders, however, try to draw on their provider role to enhance their masculine status. Analyzing through the gender lens, one can see that the "field of games" then becomes an invaluable terrain where gamers can display their technological skills, passion, and mentality, thus enacting their technological masculinity. For example, when we discussed how gamers developed "self-defense" strategies to boost their teams' ranking on the metric ticket board, they would undoubtedly be admired by their white colleagues. The long hours that these gamers invest into winning the game demonstrate their technological commitment and obsession and can be interpreted as a "heroic" masculine behavior.

In contrast, if we recall peasant coders' comments on what it means to be a "real man," it is clear that they draw on the masculine standards that valorize responsibility, professionalism, and the breadwinner role. Steeped in these masculine values, it was difficult for peasant coders to recognize gamers' heavy investment in the "field of games" as an appropriate way of displaying masculinity. Instead, peasant coders were more likely to interpret gamers as an unmanly and childish group who had not yet learned how to be responsible adults. As a result, peasant coders' disagreement with white gamers' enactment of technological masculinity directly shaped their differentiated gaming strategies, which is discussed in detail in the following sections.

Getting Marooned on the Field of Games

Stop Face-Losing: Reducing Risks in the Pranking Games

As discussed in Chapter 5, pranking games—hazing games, donut emails, and other spontaneous pranks—are organized and operated to confirm Behemoth's workplace culture. Through embedding pranking games into routine work activities (e.g., newcomer trainings, meetings, email communications), Behemoth conveys a clear cultural message to its employees: "chaotic fun" is highly valued in this workplace. A majority of the white engineers devotedly organize pranking games to support this celebration of fun.

Guided by their peasant coder subjectivity, however, Asian engineers hesitate to participate in pranking games. The "precarious self" embodied by peasant coders directs them to be more mobile and less committed to a specific corporate culture; therefore, to peasant coders, cracking Behemoth's cultural code via pranking games is both a time-consuming and unworthy practice. In addition, the occasional rebellious tone underlying white engineers' pranks worries peasant coders enormously. After all, their precarious migrant status makes them unwilling to challenge managerial authority and disrupt the workplace order via pranks. Furthermore, after moving to the next life stage and becoming a provider, peasant coders generally lose their student temperament and begin to find pranking games condescending, childish, and immature. Of course, such a denunciation of pranking games' condescending nature is also closely associated with Asian engineers' initial understanding of work, which is that it should be taken professionally and seriously and not be treated as a joke. Finally, since pranking games are used to enhance corporate culture, they are filled with cultural symbols that peasant coders are not familiar with, which can easily expose Asian workers' cultural naivete in a Western context; this fear of exposing cultural naivete further alienates peasant coders from pranking games.

So the message is clear: peasant coders strive to distance themselves from pranking games. This leads to more questions. How do these peasant coders successfully maintain their distance? What are the consequences of peasant coders' withdrawal from pranking games, to the company and the peasant coders alike?

Most peasant coders frankly described pranking games as "counterproductive" and "time-consuming." When asked about why they thought pranks were "counterproductive," many offered me very vivid examples. One Indian female engineer, Jai, told me about one of her awkward moments: Her team had a tradition of naming each sprint with a "funny" name. When she first joined the team, the team decided to name the sprint after the worst movie. Jai soon found it difficult to join the email threads discussing potential names, as she "basically has no knowledge about American movies." She spent a lot of time searching movie lists on IMBD and even made an Excel form to rank movie scores. However, when Jai felt she was ready for this game, the team switched the game up and decided to use "fictional prison names" instead. Eventually, Jai gave up; she found it "very time-consuming" to participate in this type of game. Nevertheless, Jai made it clear that this did not mean she completely withdrew from her teams' pranks, which would make her look like a "willful girl."

Jai's struggle was very representative among peasant coders. Although peasant coders expressed their resentment for pranks, they admitted that they always felt pressured to invest in these games. Peasant coders who were determined to withdraw from these games risked being stigmatized as "disloyal employees" who failed to appreciate the "gameful" culture and did not try to fit into the work environment. At the team level, peasant coders encountered a subtle form of group pressure to participate: gaming interactions were considered an essential mechanism to increase mutual trust, bonding, and rapport between teammates, so peasant coders risked being labeled "bad team players" if they did not strive for their team's victory in various games. Consequently, peasant coders were compelled to display a certain level of interest in participating.

To balance the danger of being labeled as bad teammates with the downside of "time-consuming" games, peasant coders developed what I call an "investment strategy." The trick to this strategy is to participate in a limited number of pranks that require a minimum input (e.g., the time needed to design, organize, and participate) but produce maximum output (e.g., exposure within the team, proof of workability or achievement). Lei is one such engineer who adopted this investment strategy to show his team spirit in pranks. As Lei recalled, as of late he had narrowed his potential investments to two pranks organized by his team—one prank asked team members to hack into colleagues' email accounts and replace their profile pictures with funny cat pictures, and the other prank asked team members to find the oldest codes in their team projects and add funny comments to these codes. Lei explained why these two pranks made his final list: these games required minimum cultural knowledge, which would save him enormous "wiki" time. Then, Lei introduced the pranks' favorables: "Both games are rather 'technical,' which is good . . . as it should be my strength." Lei eventually gave up changing colleagues' profile pictures, as it was "a little bit too 'technical' and probably needs more researching time."

Lei's calculations were widely shared among peasant coders. While discussing their prank participation, I constantly heard them judge and weigh different pranks' advantages and disadvantages. Time-consuming pranks were the least popular, and pranks filled with cultural codes were very likely to be screened out. Pranks that relied on verbal humor were not favorable investments. Pranks related to work content or that demanded objective skills, however, were much more likely to see peasant coder participation. Many peasant coders have a vague investment quota for pranks: some, like Lei, feel they need to select one or two to participate in each week, while others think they would prefer to not spend more than an hour per day on pranks.

When facing email pranks, peasant coders develop a very distinct play strategy from their white colleagues. As shown in Chapter 5, engineers who organize phone-tool-page pranks rely on the email system to send newcomers ridiculous "tests" to "pass" in order to be enrolled into Behemoth's online communities (i.e., the phone-tool page). Similarly, donut email pranks are organized to encourage engineers to hijack their colleagues' email accounts to send out embarrassing email when those coworkers fail to lock their screens. Of course, in addition to these systematically organized email pranks, there are countless email threads that involve spontaneous horseplay, mutual ridicule, and cyberhumor.

While white engineers enthusiastically participate, organize, and patrol email pranks, a majority of the peasant coders I spoke to considered pulling pranks on public email platforms as "humiliating," "embarrassing," and "inappropriate." During my interview with Umish, an Indian engineer, he told me how he was publicly humiliated via email: Umish once emailed the team and told them that he would bring pastries the next day. By the end of the email, he added a sentence saying that he would bring vanilla-flavored pastries, as vanilla is his favorite flavor. His teammates promptly replied to his email and told him that he basically liked "beavers' butt scent," since the vanilla flavor was distilled from anal secretions used by beavers to mark their territories. Umish told me that he did not respond to the teasing; he thought it was "low taste," "improper," and "a little bit humiliating" to discuss this matter in a workplace email system. Similarly, Chinese engineers also interpreted involvement in email pranks as very "face-losing." Here, *face-losing* can be roughly translated as "being ashamed or humiliated."

When peasant coders feel obliged to participate in email pranks and show team spirit, they usually adopt a strategy of "minimizing humiliation." Normally, peasant coders send out teasing emails to the email list with the fewest recipients to reduce humiliation. Or in the Chinese engineers' language, this strategy is used to "save face" for the victims of these pranks. For example, Qifan, a Chinese male engineer on the Tablet Application team, told me he always sent his donut emails to the smallest U.S.-based team's email list, which only included eight engineers:

> When I sent out the donut emails, I always chose to send them to the central@ list. . . . The central@list only included eight members. . . . It's all people working in the US. But the "team email list" included two additional Indian teams. . . . They are the tech support teams that helped us handle maintenance tasks. . . . So when I send donut emails, I usually just send to the central@list. . . . After all, getting caught by donut email is still a quite *diu lian* [losing face] thing . . . so I always try to *liu mianzi* [save some face] for others when I do this . . . so if they caught me, they would also save some face [*mianzi*] for me.

When Qifan said that "getting caught by donut email is still a quite *diu lian* [losing face] thing," he illustrated his acute sense of the nature of this game, which concentrates on shaming people. Once peasant coders like Qifan chose to invest in the donut emails, they were prepared to cooperate with the shaming practices. Damage (i.e., shaming) had to be done on the caught engineers; this feature was not negotiable. However, the degree of shaming could be modified: by sending to smaller groups, peasant coders managed to minimize the level of shaming, which is an act of *liu mianzi* [saving some face] in Qifan's narrative.

It is worth noting that the moral code of reciprocity was embedded in Qifan's donut-email play: if he saved someone else some face this time, then that person would reciprocate by saving Qifan some face next time, when he himself was caught. This understanding was widely presented to me by many interviewees, and it was not limited to donut pranks; it was adopted for most email pranks. Another Chinese engineer, Tao, used an old saying to express his understanding of why they always wanted to restrict their prank emails to the smallest email circles: "Saving some room [for your enemy] today while you are the winner, [just in case] you encounter them again tomorrow when you are the loser" (今日留一物, 他日好相见).

The problem is that when peasant coders tried to reduce the amount of humiliation in pranking games, they potentially engendered a certain level of resistance. As unpacked in Chapter 5, one essential function of donut emails or email pranks in general is the promotion of mutual surveillance among peers. Many email pranks are sent out to expose colleagues' misbehaviors and embarrass them (e.g., taking naps on the job or being drunk during an on-call shift). For this kind of work-related misbehavior, the more publicly it is displayed, the more humiliating the prank. Therefore, when peasant coders attempt to minimize exposure and only send their prank emails to the smallest circle, they dampen the disciplinary function of these games and reduce their coworkers' punishment, which would not be a popular strategy in the eyes of managers.

Another peasant coder rule of thumb is to never tease colleagues who are higher on the corporate ladder. If we recall the discussion on white engineers' participation in pranking games, they actually love to tease managers: to these engineers, challenging or even reversing the power relationship between themselves and managers is an inseparable, fun part of pranking games. Moreover, white engineers display their fearlessness, rebellion, and disruptive character through teasing people higher in the ranks. To Asian engineers, however, higher-ranking colleagues or managers have never been considered prank targets. This self-imposed rule reflects the persistence of a traditional value in most Asian societies that involves respect for senior people and hierarchy (Hibbins 2005). A Chinese male engineer, Little Hao, offered a very detailed explanation of how he started to notice this self-regulation:

> During the first few weeks I worked here, I learned about this donut email. . . . At first, I thought those catches [of unlocked computers] were just random . . . but later, I realized there was an authority thing going on among these donut emails. . . . Like when a Level 6 manager got caught, only the Level 6 or Level 7 managers dared to reply to his donut email . . . and all Level 4 or Level 5 [engineers] were quiet. It's pretty obvious . . . not everyone dares reply to them . . . so I figured there is at least one rule. . . . It's that [I should] not pull donut email pranks on managers. . . . Later, I felt it might be safer for me to not pull donut pranks with anyone having a higher rank than me.

Only if an individual possesses an "authoritarian" mind can he or she intuitively interpret other people's behavior from an authoritarian perspective. Indeed, Asian programmers' years of immersion in authoritarian systems resulted in their unconscious interpretation that "there was an authority thing going on among all these donut emails." For Asian engineers, managers, as authoritative figures on the team or in the organization, should be respected and not challenged. This understanding results in Little Hao's inference that he "should not pull donut email pranks on managers."

Indeed, the fear of challenging authority is shared by most peasant coders. My Indian informants self-imposed an equally strict rule of respecting upstream power figures. Growing up in a caste system, Indian engineers know that members of higher castes have higher social status, privilege, and power than those of lower castes. In fact, some Indian interviewees were more likely to have a short period of work experience in the outsourcing tech company back in India before migrating to the United States. According to their description, tech corporations in India pose a sharp contrast to U.S. tech companies: while U.S. companies emphasize flexibility and a flattened hierarchy, Indian tech companies are rigidly hierarchical. As my Indian interviewees explained, in the Indian tech firms where they worked before migrating, employees have to "obey" managers and address their manager as "sir." Cultivated in such an environment, Indian engineers are even less willing to challenge managers or people in authority in pranking games.

Problematically, peasant coders' self-imposed gaming rule—avoiding ridiculing authoritative figures via pranks—contradicts Behemoth's primary intention. Implicitly, Behemoth attempts to use pranks to demonstrate that it is a meritocratic workplace. As stated in Chapter 5, managers are very actively invested in white gamers' games to illustrate their approachability and open-mindedness. Daily email communications involve the frequent ritual exchanges of insults between gamers and managers; frequent interactions via pranks enhance the bonding between white engineers and managers and create the illusion of a work environment where there is open contempt for authority. More importantly, there is a wide belief that innovation vitality in the high-tech industry starts with this contempt for authority—in other words, innovation is built upon the courage to break the rules, challenge authority within the field, and explore the field in a new way. In this sense, peasant coders' consciousness of hierarchy and respect for power is considered a pivotal resistance to innovation potential. That is why several of my interviewees admitted that there would be no Edward Snowdens, Mark Zuckerbergs, or Aaron Swartzes in Asian societies. One of my Chinese informants, Vicky, even joked that if Snowden were in China, he would not have been able to leak any information from the National Security Agency (NSA), because he would have been too young and too junior to access any high-level classified information at all.

One final thing that should be pointed out is that although peasant coders can develop coping strategies for pranking games, they cannot prevent themselves from becoming prank targets. In fact, as cultural outsiders, peasant coders are more likely to be victimized in pranking games than their white counterparts. As illustrated in Chapter 5, one "legendary" prank organized collectively by the Wizard team was the "suit-up prank," designed to trick Amir into wearing a suit to work after his three-week vacation to Pakistan. Amir was a better target for the prank, as he was less likely to see through the ruse than his white colleagues—he was less familiar with the North American tech industry's "dress-down" culture. White engineers, however, would be hard to trick with this prank, as they knew very well about dress-down culture and the cultural symbols underneath (e.g., dressing down as a way to celebrate freedom and go against the values of being serious or formal).

Treat the Job Professionally: Don't Romanticize Collection and Racing Games

As discussed in Chapter 4, Behemoth designed crowdsourcing games for crowdfunding engineers' extra skills, knowledge, and labor. The most systematically constructed crowdsourcing game is the badge-collection game; the badges that engineers are encouraged to collect are called phone-tool icons at Behemoth. Phone-tool icons are pictures modeled after virtual-gaming badges that are displayed on an employee's phone-tool page, and each icon represents a specific type of task (e.g., testing, debugging, training). Whenever engineers fulfill a task, they are rewarded with a virtual badge that they can display on their personal phone-tool page. However, the badge-collection game is so rigidly designed that it leaves little room for engineer discretion; thus white engineers are generally indifferent toward this game and cope by using a practical tactic, a performance strategy, or a perfunctory approach.

Peasant coders followed white engineers and adopted a perfunctory approach to badge-collection games, but their perfunctory approach was far more consistently applied (in peasant coders' eyes) than that of their white counterparts. In my conversations with peasant coders, they identified certain "moments" and "situations" in which white engineers became absorbed by badge collection. Scarce badges, for instance, have always been a lure to white engineers. Wei, a male Chinese engineer who has been working at Behemoth for four years, told me he found that his white colleagues become excited when they collect "plated badges," "limited edition badges," or "rare badges." They would display these badges at the front of their badge queue to earn them more bragging rights. But what white engineers ignored, according to Wei, was that they have to invest exponentially increasing amounts of time in collecting rare badges.

Wei offered me an example about his colleague Ben, who helped a subscription team optimize products to earn badges. The subscription team made various badges: a bronze badge was given to engineers who submitted one hundred lines of codes for their optimization task, a silver badge for five hundred lines of code, and a gold badge for one thousand lines. Wei explained, "You know it's not like . . . you just spend ten times longer writing one thousand lines [than one hundred lines]. For a one-thousand-line project, sometimes it can be a big project. And you need to think through every element of the code chunk. I knew Ben was like, once you reach the silver badge, you just don't want to stop, and you want the rare gold badge. But I just don't think it's worth it." Wei was right. Many peasant coders explained to me that they would rather avoid rare badges, such as the Patent Puzzle badge that rewarded engineers who proposed patent ideas and some badges that demanded intense "brainwork" to automate specific development procedures. Rare badges usually require enormous effort. As some engineers explained, "You just cannot estimate the time that you need to invest into it—it's difficult for you to pull yourself out once you start."

Guided by this attitude, peasant coders firmly carry out the perfunctory approach. I was allowed to skim through many of my Asian interviewees' phone-tool pages and found that quiz-based and event-based badges were the most popular ones for peasant coders. As discussed before, the time needed to unlock these kinds of badges can be precisely estimated and usually clock in at less than two hours. The badges that a majority of peasant coders collected usually took less than one hour. For example, almost every peasant coder I interviewed collected the Customer Connection badge and the 100% Peculiar badge. Earning the Customer Connection badge collection took under an hour, since it only required participation in a customer service workshop.

Similarly, to collect the 100% Peculiar badge, peasant coders would spend less than thirty minutes taking the "peculiar quiz," designed to test whether engineers know about the corporate "principles." Also, by observing the peasant coders' badge display lists, one can see that peasant coders strictly follow the perfunctory principle—"Just make sure you collect some, like ten or twenty; then you won't stand out for being a slacker." I rarely saw a peasant coder with a list of badges obviously longer than that of others; additionally, peasant coders' badge lists were very standardized. Badges like Customer Connection, 100% Peculiar, Making Great Hiring Decisions, 100% Peculiarups were must-haves, while badges such as Patent Puzzle, Continuous Deployment, and Meowtstanding Achievement were avoided at all costs. To push the perfunctory approach one step further, peasant coders sometimes perform "collecting behavior" but avoid devoting substantive time and labor to the badge. For example, some badges encourage engineers to participate in specific interest groups (e.g., coding or researching groups), gaming groups (e.g., Thursday night board game groups), or alumni groups. Many peasant coders earned badges for joining these groups—but after enrolling, they mut-ed the discussions, conversations, or notifications from these groups and never attended any of the group events.

Racing games, however, are embedded in maintenance work. Usually, Behemoth engineers take on-call shifts to monitor their software products and ensure the products operate smoothly. Whenever errors occur in the system, the on-call engineer receives a ticket notifying them of the problem. Managers incorporate gamification techniques (e.g., leaderboard ranking systems and countdown timers) into the ticket-solving workflow to stimu-late engineers' gamer subjectivity (e.g., competitiveness and crisis mentality). As discussed in Chapter 4, white engineers consent to the gamification of maintenance work without reservation. After being interpellated with their gamer subjectivity, engineers develop various gaming strategies to race against the machine, fix problems, and boost their team's leaderboard rankings.

Incorporating the gamification mechanic of the leaderboard has success-fully mobilized white engineers' student temperament, which is character-ized by high competitiveness. Behemoth adapted the leaderboard design for the work setting by displaying the number of each team's unresolved legacy tickets on the dashboard and ranking teams' ticket-resolving performance accordingly. As a result, this ranking system efficiently stimulates rivalry among white engineers. These engineers generally adopted two approaches to protect their teams' maintenance-work reputations. The defensive strat-egy entails organizing ticket sprints or weekend ticket marathons to devote concentrated time and energy to resolving as many tickets as possible in one go. The offensive strategy largely manifests in engineers' attempts to shame their imaginary opponents and their ticket-resolving performance.

White engineers' defensive strategies, which usually involve romanticiz-ing ticket resolving and transforming the work into fun gaming events (e.g., ticket sprint parties, weekend marathons), are considered "childish" and "unhealthy" by peasant coders. Ah Hao, a Cantonese engineer in his early thirties who worked on the machine learning team, told me that he was once invited to a ticket sprint party and said, "They called it a party. But it's just a bunch of guys getting together to solve tickets. . . . To make it like a party, they just threw on loud music. And they asked everyone who came to the party to only bring drinks. So, it's like we stayed up really late, restlessly doing tickets, eating nothing, and only drinking. So like, after gulping down the second can of Red Bull, my hands trembled so violently. And I'm thinking, 'OK, enough, I am too old for this childish game. I don't want to kill myself, and I will never go to any party like this again.'" From Ah Hao's narrative, one can sense that age played an important role in preventing peasant cod-ers from organizing ticket sprint parties; as discussed previously, peasant coders have passed the stage of life in which "partying" is most enticing. Once they entered their early thirties, peasant coders started to see things differently. Like Ah Hao illustrated, to peasant coders, the continuous consumption of alcohol and energy drinks while staying up late to resolve tickets is not exciting or fun but thought of as a way to "kill themselves."

To be clear, peasant coders voluntarily set aside blocks of time to resolve tickets. I remembered there was one time when I met ZH the day after he worked for sixteen hours straight, and he explained what happened: He came to work at 10:30 A.M. as usual but was prepared to work overtime to deal with a tricky SEVIS II ticket. After 6:00 P.M., when most of his colleagues had left and the office grew quiet, ZH started to work on the ticket. However, the ticket was far more complicated than ZH had thought. He spent about three hours trying to find a solution, but no luck. Around 9:00 P.M., he felt he had no choice but to "ping" David, a white senior-level engineer who was considered a "ticket guru" on the Knight team and seemed to be available for ticket questions at all hours. David and ZH had a phone call that lasted an hour and a half. Afterward, ZH had a preliminary idea of how to resolve the ticket, and although it was very late, he did not want to wait until the next day to test his solution—and thus continued to work another four hours. By the time ZH resolved the ticket, it was 2:30 A.M., and he had worked for sixteen hours straight.

Like ZH, many peasant coders have spent long hours or stayed up late when they were on call. Peasant coders, however, emphasize that such behaviors are not driven by competitiveness and refuse to interpret them as defending teams' rankings and pride. Instead, these coders stress that their primary consideration is whether the problems represented by the outstanding tickets will make their products increasingly fragile. This understanding can be seen by ZH's explanation about why he chose to work sixteen hours on the ticket:

So for the whole month last month, we had been adding new codes to update our product. And we planned to launch the product in a day or two. The ticket notified us that a serious mistake was buried in those new codes. So what I was doing was trying to resolve the ticket before we launched the product so that it wouldn't crash the system. That's why I kind of pushed myself to get it done yesterday. And it did get a little bit annoying, as I had to "roll back" to the time before any new codes were added and figure out where the error came from, bit by bit. And also, I had no clue when I started. So it did take a really long time. But look, let's not make a big deal out of it. I mean, *some people* might think . . . that this type of *heroic action* saves the team's product from being crushed. But I just figured that if I didn't resolve it before launching, the error would still be there, which would cut me another SEVIS II ticket. And I still need to solve it.

ZH's narrative clearly showed the two factors that motivated his overwork: first, as that week's on-call engineer, it would always be ZH who had to solve the ticket, either before or after the launch. In this case, fixing the problem prior to product launch would cause less damage and avoid crushing the system—so ZH decided to stay up late until the ticket was resolved. Apparently, ZH did not want to romanticize his behavior and make a "big deal out of it." Second, ZH was guided by the peasant coder subjectivity associated with "professionalism" and took his on-call work seriously; he considered it his responsibility to try hard to minimize system risk. Then, ZH drew a comparison to white engineers—or in his words, "some people"—who might interpret these behaviors as "heroic action." To ZH, it was unnecessary to endow a ticket-resolving responsibility with heroics.

Although peasant coders disagree with white engineers' "defensive strategies" and their efforts to heroize maintenance work, they still devote blocks of time to resolving tickets. However, peasant coders show an entirely different attitude toward white engineers' "offensive strategies." To peasant coders, offensive strategies in which white engineers attack other teams for their heavy ticket loads and poor ticket-resolution rates are not just "childish" but downright "hostile." Challenging other teams' managers and engineers and creating hostility would be the last thing peasant coders would want; they possessed a rather precarious work identity, and such hostility could only increase but in no way reduce the vulnerability of their work status.

In addition to the anxiety of hostility, peasant coders also fundamentally resent methods used by white engineers when they go on offense. "Annoying," "exhausting," and "a waste of time" are typical comments made by peasant coders when they discussed white engineers' attacks. Jammar, an Indian engineer who joined Behemoth in 2014, told me that his white colleagues once drew a regression graph on their wall to illustrate the relationship between their sister team's "unhappiness" and their "heavy on-call burden." Jammar commented, "I understand that they feel this is a fun part of the work. But I find it disturbing, especially when they always do it in the team area. So I always go downstairs to find a meeting room to work on my own project. It's quiet there, and I can concentrate." Here, Jammar identified the potential problem with this behavior. While white engineers perceived their behavior as "working," peasant coders like Jammar were not convinced that such trash-talking was work per se. Quite the opposite: these practices were so disturbing that Jammar needed to distance himself from them to focus on work. Several peasant coders expressed a similar willingness to excuse themselves from these "dog-eat-dog" games to avoid wasting time and ensure that they would not need to work until 7:00 P.M., 8:00 P.M., or even midnight. In general, peasant coders' loathing of white engineers' aggressive and hostile attacks resulted in their complete absence from leaderboard offensive strategies.

Struggling to Fit In: Being Victimized in the Simulation Games

As discussed in Chapter 3, workplace simulation games—battle simulations, adventure simulations, and crisis simulations—developed directly from scrum-based software development, a core labor process. Through adopting gamification techniques (e.g., mythological narratives, storylines, and heroic characters), managers simulate the artificial video-gaming environment in the software development process and interpellate engineers' gamer subjectivity. Once engineers' gaming subjectivity is mobilized, they take the initiative and create many playing strategies to invest in these simulation games and use those strategies to solve problems that emerge in the scrum development process.

For example, engineers developed a blurring gaming strategy to solve an inherent paradox embedded in the scrum process. On the one hand, by adopting a permanent-beta ethic, scrum development embraces significant instability, which is characterized by ongoing product pivots and team reorganizations. On the other, the process's high demand for collaboration requires engineers to establish trustworthy and rapport-driven relationships that are easier to create in a stable team environment. Facing this dilemma, white engineers mobilize their gamer subjectivity, retreating to the video-gaming world to build rapport through gaming relationships with their scrum team coworkers and extending these gaming relationships to the workplace. As shown in Chapter 3, white engineers' self-started strategy of blurring the line between work and video-gaming relationships effectively resolves the inherent paradox of scrum development.

Peasant coders invest in simulation games more actively than they do other games. Some structural factors preface these coders' consent. For one thing, the online video-game industry has been booming in India and China since 2005, accompanied by the rapid proliferation of internet cafés. As a result, games like *League of Legends* and *World of Warcraft* were imported to these two countries about the same time that they were released in the West (Messner 2019; Stang, Osterholt, and Hoftun 2007; Singh 2020). In short, while the growing-up experiences between white engineers and peasant coders were quite different, their online gaming experiences have converged since 2005—which is why my white and Asian interviewees reported that online gaming memories have become the most important topic of discussion. Due to this background, it is not difficult to understand why peasant coders genuinely enjoy simulation games compared to racing, crowdsourcing, and pranking games.

Many peasant coders consented to white engineers' blurring strategies and authentically enjoyed bonding with their colleagues in the online gaming space. However, these peasant coders were keenly aware that their play served work interests as well. Recall a particular section in Chapter 3, where the emphasis is on the self-initiated blurring of lines between gaming and work relationships among engineers. In this context, I introduce the story of Chuan. As a Chinese engineer who once was a part of the Knight team, Chuan provides insight into balancing personal gaming preferences with work-related interests. Despite his preference for games like *League of Legends* and *World of Warcraft*, Chuan was convinced by his teammate, Fei, to participate in *CS:GO*, recognizing its social benefits. Upon creating an account and informing Mike, the leader of their gaming team, Chuan noted Mike's apparent satisfaction and consented to adhere to Mike's strategies in the game. From Chuan's narrative, we can tell that he prioritizes social function over personal interest: if he went by his personal preference, he would play the other two games instead. However, as we discussed in Chapter 3, playing *CS:GO* was how the Knights chose to resolve the problems caused by their frequent team reorganizations from 2013 to 2015. To speed up the establishment of rapport, a majority of the Knight team decided to play *CS:GO* every Wednesday and Thursday night as a group. By choosing to play the game his team preferred, Chuan made it clear that this participation was less for off-hours enjoyment and more for improving relations between coworkers.

Even so, peasant coders were likely to be victimized in their simulation game investment. When playing video games, peasant coders more readily displayed their aggressive, dominant, and competitive sides. Asian engineers' aggressive and competitive gameplay formulated a mismatch with the stereotypical traits perceived to be associated with their peasant coder subjectivity (characterized by stereotypical adjectives like "humble," "modest," "conservative," and "submissive"). This dissonance challenged white gamers' commonly held views about their Asian colleagues and sometimes stirred up their resentment.

Jammar's story illustrates this tension. Like all other Pipe Org teams, the Ranger team organized game nights. Jammar's aggressive gaming style caught his teammates' attention, and they grew fond of sharing their "surprising" findings about Jammar's gaming personality with nonplaying colleagues— tirelessly broadcasting Jammar's "domineering" and "self-centered" gaming behaviors, such as his preference for playing leader roles and avoidance of support roles, his quitting midgame with no regard for a team loss, and his ban from the gaming platform due to his constant abuse of teammates and opponents. Over time, his teammates provided varied interpretations of why Jammar (a Level 4 engineer) was so "self-centered": one widespread speculation was that Jammar was an only child.[7] Ultimately, Jammar's lack of team spirit led other Ranger team players to begin excluding him from their game night, and they secretly invited Benjamin (white, male, Level 4) from their sister team to join the team as a replacement.

Worse still, Jammar's teammates' negative interpretations and exclusionary attitudes toward him, which arose in the video-gaming world, were carried into the workplace. The blurring of boundaries between working and gaming activities creates a venue in which engineers can draw on gaming characteristics to judge their teammates' working characteristics. An unidentified assailant once used the Ranger team manager Paulo's unlocked account to send out a donut email titled "Ranger is ready to trade Jammar with Benjamin" to the Pipe Org email list. Although everyone knew this was a donut email and not a serious trade offer, Jammar's unpopularity among the Ranger team was exposed to the whole organization. Ultimately, Jammar was transferred to a small, newly established team linked to the Rangers during Pipe Org's latest reorganization.

White engineers' attitudes to Jammar are very representative. Some white engineers described peasant coders' video-gaming play with phrases like "crazy fights," "bloody play," "aggressive as fuck," and "as if in a deathmatch." Peter, a white engineer on the Wizard team, once joked to me that I should try playing *LoL* with Amir and JW, and then I would know that "it's just so damn hard to not curse at them because of how aggressive they are. . . . They just don't give a fuck about towers,[8] vision, team. . . . They just fight . . . like crazy." A few peasant coders admitted to their slightly aggressive performance in simulation games, but they also said that they did not want to play "friendly" against their will. Peasant coders felt they did not intentionally play aggressively but were mimicking their favorite Asian esports team. JW once told me that his best youth memory involved gathering around a computer screen with his college friends to watch livestreams of *LoL* competitions and the International (an annual gaming competition for *Defense of the Ancients*). Then JW concluded, "After like ten years' mimicking [his favorite team's fight], that fighting style just gets into my bloodstream."

A sizable group of peasant coders recognized their awkward position within white engineers' simulation games; in response, this group sought gaming partners within their own ethnic community. For peasant coders, there are plenty of advantages to retreating to their ethnic community. For example, this choice reflects peasant coders' determination to separate their work and gaming lives; when playing with friends from the same ethnic community who aren't coworkers, these coders can feel more relaxed and reveal their gaming identities and authentic selves. For example, Chuan, who gave up his favorite game (*LoL*) to join his team's *CS:GO* group, eventually quit that game and went back to playing *LoL* with his Chinese friends. He later told me that it felt more exciting to play games that he authentically enjoyed and was good at playing. For other peasant coders, being their authentic selves implied that they could curse whenever they wanted and use their own language. As J. Sun put it, "I am not proud of it . . . but it feels more blunt when you bust out curse words using your native language, right?"

It is worth mentioning, however, that these peasant coders' choice to separate work and gaming relationships and activities ran counter to white engineers' playing strategies in simulation games, which blurred gaming and work activities. Furthermore, since white engineers' blurring strategy essentially serves corporate interests (e.g., by increasing the effectiveness of collaborative innovation and removing obstacles endangering the permanent-beta mode), to some extent these peasant coders' behaviors dampened the functionality of simulation games in boosting collaborative innovation.

Concluding Remarks

This chapter illustrates how Asian engineers' lack of gamer subjectivity determines their difficulties in integrating into Behemoth's gameful environment. Indeed, Asian engineers' peasant coder subjectivity, which is characterized by the precarious self, hardworking self, and providing self, profoundly contradicts white engineers' gamer subjectivity. Guided by their peasant coder subjectivity, Asian engineers interpret engineering work as the serious business of achieving upward mobility, maintaining legal immigrant status, and supporting families; they hesitate to treat work as a mode of gaming or having fun.

After laying the foundation, this research discusses how peasant coders draw on their subjectivity to develop distinct playing strategies for the three major game types developed in the tech firm to target three critical elements of engineering work. Specifically, peasant coders worry that participation in pranks creates hostility toward colleagues and enhances their precarious status; therefore, these coders develop a perfunctory approach to cope with pranking games, one that attempts to minimize the humiliation of their colleagues. Additionally, peasant coders draw on their hardworking self and refuse to romanticize serious maintenance working processes into collecting and sprinting games. Finally, peasant coders' attitudes to simulation games are complicated: some peasant coders embrace simulation games wholeheartedly and blur the boundaries between video-gaming and working activities, relationships, and spaces; however, this group of peasant coders then encounters a dilemma in which their white colleagues conflate their aggressive gaming characters with their working characters. Other groups of peasant coders try to resist white engineers' blurring play strategies by completely separating their video-gaming relationships from their working relationships.

Finally, this chapter tries to point out a disconnect between the gameful working environment constructed by the tech firm and Asian engineers' prescriptions about engineering work that are guided by their peasant coder subjectivity. The gaming strategies developed by peasant coders, in general, constitute a certain level of resistance. For example, peasant coders' efforts to minimize humiliation in pranking games weaken the games' mutual surveillance capacities. Similarly, their skepticism toward romanticizing maintenance work into racing games reduces Behemoth's ability to extract extra knowledge, labor, and skills from them. One thing, however, must be emphasized: such resistance from peasant coders is very limited and highly individualistic, and it can hardly bring substantive challenge to Behemoth's gamified system design. Instead, this resistance contributes to peasant coders' disadvantaged position and outsider status at the firm.

7

CONCLUSION

Innovation is indubitably the central ethos of the technology industry. In the two decades since the dot-com bubble, two significant economic forces have escalated the intensity and frequency of technological innovation. First, lower entry barriers into the tech sector for competitors and copycats have made it more challenging for companies to maintain advantageous positions at the national or global level. As a result, tech capitalists have feverishly pursued the most disruptive and transformative ideas in an effort to preserve their leading-edge status (Bulut 2021; Gandini 2019; Huws 2014). Second, the increased financialization of the U.S. economy has meant that tech companies continuously need to iterate and update their technological products to satisfy the expectations of their investors and secure successive rounds of venture capital investment (Bulut 2021; Neff 2015; Neff and Stark 2004; Shestakofsky 2018).

The tech industry's desperate pursuit of innovation produces a puzzling paradox. On the one hand, informational capitalists' gamble on technological innovation endows engineers with inherent power. Due to the high demand for creative workers, engineers can move between companies and seek better work conditions and higher wages, giving them significant bargaining power in the labor market. On the other hand, a permanent-beta production mode means intense and precarious work lives for these engineers, involving long workweeks, heavy maintenance burdens, and constant product pivots and team reorganizations. Under pressure from competitors and investors, the tech industry strives to realize this modus operandi, pushing to accelerate continuous technological novelty and the cycle of designing, developing, and testing products.

Despite the drawbacks of this intense production mode, software development engineers continue to try to rise to the challenge. Some engineers, like Charles, portrayed in Chapter 4, self-organize ticket marathons and work around the clock, attempting to fix as many bugs as possible in the shortest time. Others, like Ben, discussed in Chapter 3, devote most of their leisure time to developing work-team rapport to reduce the negative impact on collaboration of constant team reorganizations. Yet a common consequence of unlimitedly compressing production time is quick burnout, as experienced by Ben and others. The question then becomes, Why does this seemingly powerful worker group submit to such an intense production mode?

From Normative Control to Game Control

A response requires reflection on labor control, an issue that has long engaged labor scholars. Since the writings of Marx, studies have sought to understand how capitalists gain control over workers. Harvey Braverman's seminal 1974 work, *Labor and Monopoly Capital*, has been particularly influential, reviving and advancing labor process analysis by highlighting the separation of conception and execution as the key mechanism by which capitalists can gain control over the labor process. Specifically, through monopolizing central knowledge and standardizing processes, capitalists maximize the extraction of surplus value while reducing workers' skills required and making them easier to replace.

Yet, when it comes to creative and knowledge industry workers, traditional labor process theory proves inadequate. Indeed, the complexity and difficulty of standardizing these workers' knowledge and abilities makes it hard for capitalists to obtain control over them. In Chapter 3, Lei's story provides a concrete example of how innovation can disrupt standardization and challenge classic labor control methods.[1] Lei's algorithm updated the original standardized computing process by finding shortcuts and bypassing the original process. The creative element of Lei's "smarter" algorithm was, in fact, precisely its ability to challenge the standardized process.

Researchers have gradually come to the consensus that effective control of knowledge workers requires aligning workers' interests with those of capitalists. In this regard, Kunda's (2006) insightful study of engineers convincingly demonstrates how corporate culture can become a powerful mechanism for aligning engineers' and organizational interests, a form of "normative control" that ensures the internalization of corporate discourse and interests. A large body of work has since confirmed the effectiveness of normative control in manipulating the knowledge class (Clarke, Brown, and Hailey 2009; Kunda 2006; O'Donnell 2009; Perlow 1998; Peticca-Harris, Weststar, and McKenna 2015; Sturges 2013; Tse and Li 2022; Weststar and Dubois 2022).

The paradigm of normative control has, however, become less applicable in recent years, as creative workers have become more mobile and less likely to identify with a specific corporate culture (Bulut 2020; Neff 2012; Thompson and Smith 2010, 17). In fact, occupational and generational elements are, for these workers, more influential than organizational ones. Notably, the cultural elements most engineers identify with—freedom as the foundation of creativity, heroic and adventurous spirit, and gamified fun—originate from gaming culture and were cultivated long before they entered the tech industry. This rupture between individualist and organizational interests invalidates normative control. As Danny commented in Chapter 4, the badge game is a "corporate trick." His resentment of such managed fun derives from his disappointment with Behemoth's inauthentic mimic of video games' badge system, giving him the impression that the company disrespects gaming culture.[2] Generally, a new dynamic has put an end to the mediator variable of a stable and durable organizational culture and weakened or led to the failure of normative control.

Nonetheless, the fundamental logic of controlling knowledge workers through an alignment of interests remains valid: via the theory of labor game control, capitalists manage to align workers' interests with their own. Namely, by luring workers into investing in workplace games, managers lead them to believe that their gaming strategies serve their interests of winning and "making out" (Burawoy 1979). However, this interest in making out also aligns with managers' own interest in expropriating more labor power.[3]

From Labor Games to the Field of Games

Behemoth's story serves as a vivid example of the ongoing relevance and complexity of labor game theory, a classic area of study frequently revisited by scholars (Burawoy 1996, 296). The evidence presented in previous chapters reveals that gaming has become a fascinating and complex phenomenon at Behemoth. Labor games, in particular, have emerged as a potent means by which managers exert control over their engineers. However, while Burawoy's framework for labor games provides valuable insight, it is insufficient for fully comprehending the gaming phenomenon on Behemoth's engineering floor. Indeed, as work has become increasingly complex and hybrid (McCabe 2014), a single labor game no longer captivates workers. This book introduces the concept of a field of games to describe the shift from a labor process governed by a single game's rhythms and logic to one characterized by a multiplicity of games.

Firms construct a field of games and effectively gamify labor control through four categories of labor games: simulation games, crowdsourcing games, racing games, and pranking games. Each game genre has its own distinct set of rules and serves different purposes, is embedded in discrete segments of the work process, values specific technological skills and gamer traits, and creates varied subjectivities. For example, a series of simulation games (analyzed in detail in Chapter 3) is firmly rooted within the scrum development process. By transposing video games' mythological storylines and heroic characters into workplace culture, Behemoth creates an environment that engineers find not only exciting but familiar enough to generate legitimate and authentic self-exploitation. In contrast, crowdsourcing games and racing games (Chapter 4) both adopt gamification mechanics to enhance engineering performance in maintenance work, though the former aims to appropriate engineers' knowledge and skills for volunteer maintenance work, while the latter mobilizes their competitiveness in performing routine maintenance. Pranking games (Chapter 5) pervade daily work communication: in organizing pranks, workers articulate and internalize the corporate culture, as well as monitor and discipline each other's behaviors. If, on the surface, pranking games seem to contribute a layer of chaos to Behemoth, in reality they represent and maintain a veiled order.

A field of games better simulates real life than a single game, reflecting the countless games that permeate nearly every aspect of social life (Bourdieu 1998; Huizinga 1950). Moreover, in penetrating every corner of work life, a field of games offers engineers a more immersive and authentic gaming experience on the engineering floor. Engineers can, however, become so busy switching between different gaming fields and adjusting their strategies to enhance their chances of winning that they lose sight of why they invested in these games in the first place. Specifically, such immersion can obscure the fact that what they lose through gameplay—time and labor—is won by the capitalist class.

Gamification: Another Piece of the Puzzle

The field of games concept highlights the diverse and hybrid nature of games, building on reflections concerning gamification's dysfunction (Mollick and Rothbard 2014; Statler 2011; Trittin, Fieseler, and Maltseva 2019). While some scholars argue that gamification mechanics cannot evolve into potent discipline mechanisms in the workplace (Whitson 2013, 173), I caution that the field of games does create an environment in which gamification mechanics can be successfully integrated into labor games to attract engineers' participation. The ticket games described in Chapter 4 exemplify this point, where a top-down gamification approach utilizing countdown bars and a leaderboard generates urgency and competitiveness. Meanwhile, engineers' self-organized ticket sprint marathons and gaming strategies represent a bottom-up concept ensuring the games' absorption of engineers' investment. This combination of competitive challenge and a feeling of control creates a compelling gaming experience for engineers.

Captivating mechanisms are, in addition, central to the theory of labor games, and their evolution and sustainability are of particular interest. Scholars agree that games attract players through the pull of tension that arises from uncertainty. Maintaining a balance of uncertainty is crucial, as too little or too much can deter players from investing (Burawoy 1979, 1987). Competition between workers and the level of strategic discretion also play a vital role in absorbing players.

Gamification mechanics bring new dynamics to labor games' absorption of players. On the one hand, specific gamification mechanisms enhance tension and adjust the games' level of uncertainty, further luring workers to invest. In fact, due to the instability and permanent-beta nature of the scrum software development, simulation games may even have too high a level of uncertainty for management's comfort. Behemoth has, however, normalized and even romanticized uncertainty by incorporating game characters, storylines, and artifacts from board games, video games, and fantasy movies into simulation games. On the other hand, racing games may face the opposite challenge of being less exciting and intense than software development. To increase tension and uncertainty, Behemoth has incorporated gamification elements, such as leaderboard ranking and countdown timers, into racing games. While the countdown timer considerably enhances urgency and thus the tension level of the game, the leaderboard ranking induces competitiveness between engineers and teams, likewise enhancing tension as well as uncertainty.

While under certain circumstances gamification can be a practical add-on to labor game design, it can also hinder absorption under others. For example, the badge system in the crowdsourcing game is rigid, diminishing uncertainty and contributing to the game's failure. These observations call for attention to gamification elements in future studies of labor games, as well as an awareness of the complexities and ambiguities they bring to labor control. In sum, though captivating mechanisms remain central to labor games, and gamification mechanics bring new dynamics to game design, gamification's impact on absorption can nevertheless be nuanced and context dependent, necessitating careful analysis.

Interpellating Gamer Subjectivity
in the Field of Games

Behemoth workers clearly possess a unique subjectivity and agency, an examination of which clarifies their perceptions, attitudes, and strategies toward games. While Burawoy's classic labor game theory considers workers' subjectivity within a class structure and emphasizes the role of class identity in shaping their strategic gaming behaviors, other types of subjectivity play a more important role in determining creative and information workers' investment in games. I highlight, in particular, the importance of gamer subjectivity.

Having grown up with technology and computer devices, engineers in Silicon Valley born between 1979 and 2000 belong to the gamer generation. Especially in the tech industry, many engineers strongly identify as gamers (derived from video-game consumption) and take pride in possessing gamer traits. As observed in Chapter 2, 43.9 percent of the interviewees in this book are gamers. These gamer traits are constructed under the demand of the video-game industry and are more contextualized and contingent compared to class, race, or gender identity.

The game industry has a history of commodifying play and expropriating unpaid innovative ideas from game hobbyists, thus blurring the line between play and labor (Kücklick 2015; Woodcock 2019). Given this tradition, the feeling of accomplishment among engineers when playing games they programmed themselves is perhaps unsurprising. Recall, in Chapter 2, Bill proudly narrating how he programmed his bomb-dropping game even while playing Nintendo. Such overlap between programming and gaming plays a strong role in ensuring engineers' investment in simulation games (i.e., where work and video-game teams become indistinct) and racing games (i.e., conflation of gaming marathon with ticket marathon). Video-game consumption thus predisposes engineers' gamer subjectivity, functioning as both cause and consequence, and lures engineers into labor games and self-exploitation.

Gamer subjectivity is culturally specific, its principal characteristics being rooted in the development of the gaming industry in the Western world in the 1980s (Kirkpatrick 2012). That said, as illustrated in Chapter 6, many Asian engineers—a majority group within tech—cultivated their gamer traits in an entirely different video-game industry development context. The boom in the Asian game industry accompanied by the rapid proliferation of internet cafés in the mid-2000s linked Asian gamer identity with online video gaming and esport culture, and a notable aggressiveness and competitiveness. Gamer subjectivity also exists in relation to other social identities, such as gender, race, age, and sexuality. At Behemoth, racial identity was especially intertwined with gamer subjectivity, to the point that racial minorities found it difficult to enter mainstream tech game culture. Asian engineers consequently resorted to their peasant coder subjectivity to withdraw from labor games organized by their white counterparts.

Labor game organization is a process of marking and interpellation that makes explicit reference to gamer subjectivity. In the panorama painted throughout this book, we saw many such fluid, contingent, and yet substantive gamer traits interpellated through the game-playing process. For instance, the gaming-programming blurring permeates most labor games organized on the engineering floor. Simulation games aim to mimic the gaming relations within a work environment, achieved by commingling a video-game battle team with a software development team and taking advantage of engineers' retreat to the virtual gaming world to solidify their work team rapport. In addition to clouding the difference between work and gaming teams, the use of gaming tricks to solve work problems is rife. For instance, engineers mobilize their gaming tricks to boost their team's ranking in the ticket-solving game. Some use the marathon sprint trick, where a video-game team gathers and opens the back door to play video games for a relatively long and uninterrupted time. Others skim through the firm's internal video-gaming forum to learn practical tricks to collect game badges.

Modding traits, or hacker traits in a more general sense, frequently appear in narratives of gameplay, as demonstrated by Amir's two-day hack to solve a difficult issue, which earned him the title of "Tier 1 warrior" in simulation games. Similarly, Ben was recognized as a legend in ticket-solving games for having spent forty-eight hours hidden in a meeting room to solve a ticket, entirely losing track of time in the process. These "killer" or "bad-ass" moves in games distinguish engineers like Amir and Ben as the true modders and hackers on their teams, making them ideal workers in the broader tech industry, as defined in Chapters 3 and 4.

A heroic ethos is a vital motivator for engineers, who express their adventurous selves through nicknames, game characters, and artifacts in simulation games. This ethos can stimulate creativity in the development of gaming strategies for defending their teams, such as Philip's trash-talking tactics in racing games. It can also serve as a means of encouraging gamers to embrace risk and repeatedly save their team from danger, as depicted in the engineering survival guide, "A Dungeon Master's Guide to SCRUM."

Yet the impact of gamers' actions and decisions in gaming is unpredictable. At Behemoth, the notion of what constitutes a "good gamer" shapes the very essence of gaming. Managers play a critical role in this process, claiming that a good player requires an "obsession with programming," a "heroic ethos to save teams from life-and-death moments," or a "modder mentality to stimulate flow." A good video-game player with these traits cannot be a bad engineer according to these managers. These claims are strongly reiterated in the organization of labor games.

Finally, a detailed unpacking of the relations between gamer subjectivity and gaming outcomes allows the theorization of a more fluid conception of gamer subjectivity, where sets of practices continuously reconfigure the dynamics of labor games and open up the possibility of varied gaming outcomes.

How Is the Extraction of Creativity Achieved in the Field of Games?

Like previous studies on labor games, this book closely examines the practices of capitalists in securing and obscuring labor extraction via labor games, with a particular focus on the extraction of creative labor. Creativity does not solely rely on prolonged labor duration but also on increased intensity within a given time. Chapter 3 describes Lei's invention of an innovative algorithm, which resulted in a soaring surplus value rate of 1,897 percent. The key to this burst of inspiration within the office legend was complete immersion in solving the problem rather than the amount of time he spent working on it. In fact, it took Lei only half a day to transform his innovative idea into codes. Many engineers recounted similar moments: Amir's immersion in the fight for Q4's spikes of errors, Charles's racing against system downtime, Ben's "killer move" of indulging himself in solving a tricky ticket and losing all sense of time. Scholars have shown that this immersive mentality, defined as "flow," enhances concentration, innovation, and productivity (Csikszentmihalyi 1990; Siciliano 2022), and the culture of the tech workplace seeks out and valorizes this burst of productivity. Yet scant attention has been paid to how flow moments generate enormous labor power in the form of creativity, drawing tech capitalists' interest in appropriating it. As discussed in the empirical chapters of this book, tech companies like Apple, Facebook, Yahoo, Google, and Amazon have all eagerly experimented with various strategies to stimulate such a flow mentality.

Labor games and their blurring of working and gaming processes have become a vital mechanism in tech companies' efforts to obtain flow moments and secure the exploitation of innovation. Given their yearlong gaming experiences and cultivated gamer subjectivity, engineers are likely to immerse themselves in these gamified work processes. Recall Amir's immersion in the fight for Q4's spikes of errors. The precondition for his deep immersion in the Q4 fight was his complete absorption in simulation games. Similarly, the precondition for Charles's indulgence in racing against system downtime was his absorption in racing games. These instances illustrate how labor games have become a powerful means for tech companies to appropriate engineer innovation.

Notably, labor games help tech companies increase their innovation appropriation not only by providing an immersive experience but also by eliminating obstacles that prevent innovation. The paradox between a permanent-beta instability and the workers' need for stable and trustworthy relationships can cause feelings of uncertainty that ultimately block their inventive and innovative spirit. However, simulation games organized in the scrum process provide a channel through which engineers can retreat to the gaming world and build trustworthy team relationships; this can then be reintegrated back into the work process, largely diminishing anxiety and insecurity.

Conflicting interests between managers and workers, manifested as managerial priority for profit making over technological perfection versus workers' opposite prioritization, could discourage engineers from developing innovative measures to fix or patch the system. However, gamification elements incorporated in the ticket games, such as leaderboards and countdown timers, successfully distracted workers' attention from these conflicting interests. As a result, engineers contributed their most creative moves to the ticket-solving game to boost their team's ranking and their own social status in the game.

Theorization of Varied Gaming Outcomes

In this book, I have examined the complexities and variations among the outcomes of games in the tech workplace, particularly labor games. How do gaming outcomes vary across different labor games? What are the factors that shape and determine variations among gaming outcomes? In seeking to answer these questions, I argue that two attributes stand out as key determinants of gaming outcomes: the alliance between managers and workers, and engineers' productive gamer subjectivity (respectively the x- and y-axis in Figure 7.1).

Alliance between managers and workers is crucial in determining game outcomes, measurable through the gaming mechanism of conflict navigation. In the case of Behemoth's scrum development, conflicts arose from the divergent interests of managers and engineers. While managers sought to maximize the flexibility, instability, and uncertainty necessary to maintain a culture of precarity and innovation in the workforce, engineers prioritized stability in an effort to establish trustworthy collaborative relationships. These conflicts were disguised in simulation games, where uncertainty was reframed as an "exciting" adventure. The engineers who embraced challenges and welcomed them as opportunities were deemed the most competent "adventurers." Engineers therefore took responsibility for establishing collabo-

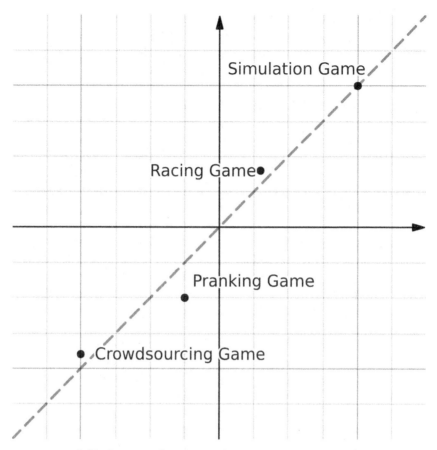

Figure 7.1 A field of games and its two attributes

ration and simulating video-gaming relationships to facilitate the latter. In short, alliance between managers and workers was achieved through engineers' internalization of managers' interests.

In routine maintenance work, conflicts arose between managers' prioritization of profit over technological perfection and, on the contrary, engineers' prioritization of technological perfection over profit. This tension was deflected by playing racing games. Managers incorporated gamification elements, such as leaderboards and countdown timers, to mobilize engineers' competitiveness and incite them to beat other teams. This redirected attention from vertical conflicts between managers and engineers toward horizontal ones between different development teams and resulted in a medium-high level of alliance between managers and workers, albeit less effective than the complete conflict disguise in simulation games.

Pranking games meanwhile approximated classic working-class teasing. Engineers organized and patrolled these games in routine tasks such as stand-up meetings and email communications. Some pranking games, such as newcomer hazing games, were organized to celebrate workers' chaotic fun and, in doing so, realized a manager-worker alliance because they normalized uncertainty for new workers. Others, such as the whistle-blowing donut hacks, expressed resistance toward surveillance, thus exposing the tensions between managers and workers. The swinging pendulum of alliances formulated through pranking games was therefore much less stable than those through simulation or racing games.

Crowdsourcing games rarely achieved any alliance. Managers' attempts to appropriate workers' extra efforts through a shallow and rigid mimicry of video-gaming setups (e.g., badges) instead elicited resentment among engineers. Behemoth's choice of rewarding engineers' modding efforts with virtual badges only further intensified conflicts between managers and workers. Finally, managers' attempts to point out engineers' perfunctory strategies of collecting badges exposed the tensions between a managerial goal of maximum labor appropriation and engineers' aim of minimizing time spent on extra labor.

The second key determinant of gaming outcomes consists of the degree of game interpellation in engineers' productive gamer subjectivity. When game practices and gamer subjectivity are in alignment, the latter becomes an essential component for ensuring the game's functionality, as seen in simulation and racing games. The allure of both is increased by gamer subjectivity, although it operates in distinct ways. Simulation games highly evoke gamer subjectivity, serving as the primary power source for engineers' self-internalization of gamified discourse and self-governing behaviors, which are pivotal to establishing gamified governmentality. Meanwhile, gamer subjectivity is more moderately invoked in racing games, leading to engineers' consent to game rules rather than complete disempowerment. The establishment of hegemony in racing games involves concessions made by managers and coordination with engineers and is not solely due to the mobilization of gamer subjectivity. Despite this, both games reflect how labor games generate a relationship between agents and structures that tends toward a fusion and adjustment of subjectivity to the structure.

There are, however, instances where gamer subjectivity and game structures do not match, and games have low, close to nonexistent, matching or even counter effects. As we saw in Chapter 5, for example, most pranking games closely resemble classic working-class games, where engineers' gamer subjectivity is hardly mobilized. Consequently, playing pranking games can generate tension and resistance, intensifying a perceived contradiction between hacker traits emphasizing technological freedom/autonomy and gaming practices monitoring work progress and misbehavior. In such cases, gamer subjectivities are counteranacted, leading engineers whose hacker subjectivity has been interpellated to develop resistance strategies, such as creating false alarms, to the detriment of productivity. Mismatches between subjectivity and games occur more frequently in crowdsourcing games. In Chapter 4, I illustrated how the rigid gamification setup is generally contradictory to gamer traits, which highly value freedom, autonomy, and creativity. Such mismatches frequently elicit engineers' resentment, leading to tension.

The effectiveness of gaming for both their success with the engineers and the usefulness to firm goals relies on the intersection of these two main factors, as depicted in Figure 7.1: collaboration between managers and workers (x-axis) and the embodiment of subjectivity (y-axis). Based on the interplay of these principal determinants, four distinct gaming outcomes have been delineated: gamified governmentality prevalent in simulation games, gamified hegemony identified within racing games, occasional hegemony associated with pranking games, and mock hegemony observed in crowdsourcing games.

The Toxic Work Environment and Workers' Minimal Resistance

The gamification of engineering work in the tech industry creates a challenging work environment that intensifies labor rhythms. This is sometimes the direct result of gamification setups, such as countdown timers. Other times, engineers' competitiveness, simulated by the game setup, amplifies this intensity. Games at Behemoth also exacerbate overwork—already a severe issue in the tech industry, with workweeks ranging from seventy to one hundred hours (Bulut 2020; Ó Riain 2009)—as evidenced by engineers participating in ticket sprint marathons, where they work nonstop for forty-eight or even seventy-two hours to troubleshoot and solve tickets.

Furthermore, when working and gaming activities become blurred, engineers lose the ability to separate themselves from their jobs. Gaming used to be an escape from work, a way for engineers to disconnect from the space of *production* and engage in a precious nonwork space of *reproduction*. When, however, work invades the video-gaming world and gaming strategies are utilized at work, the boundaries between production and reproduction collapse. In other words, the gamified working world engulfs the engineers' reproduction.

The labor games developed at Behemoth do make development work more pleasurable and exciting, increasing engineers' enthusiasm to innovate. Behemoth's engineers admire their colleagues' disruptive project designs, enthusiastically learn from one another, and are incentivized to be more creative. Yet this self-driven innovation can also diminish workers' well-being. Creativity requires deep reflection, but the industry's permanent-beta mode and perpetual innovation cycle, combined with the engineers' self-driven push for invention, leave little time for reflection and rejuvenation. The thirst for constant novelty risks harming the workforce's welfare.

The consequences of intense labor rhythms and the blurred boundaries between work and gaming activities can be severe. Engineers may experience quick burnout and leave their jobs, as in the case of Ben, the Knight team's rising star at Behemoth, who quit abruptly and left his colleagues with the words "couldn't do this anymore." Ben is not alone. Many engineers respond to poor work-life balance by quitting, as evidenced by the short average job tenure at Behemoth: 1.88 years among sixty-six interviewees, a number even lower than the average of 3.8 years in the tech industry in Silicon Valley (Charles 2018). A tight labor market in the tech industry means some engineers can quickly find a position in another company. This also means they are more likely to address their work crises via job hopping than by seeking to improve their current situation.

Engineers' quitting should not, however, be considered an expression of dissatisfaction, let alone resistance. They view this exit strategy with a "take it or leave it" attitude combined with a belief in meritocracy. The general sentiment is that if you want to survive in this work environment, you must force yourself to become more creative and efficient. If your level of competence makes it challenging to thrive in this environment, you have to leave. Other more rebellious practices, such as acts of sabotage like hacking into the donut email system, happen very infrequently. Moreover, these are largely individual undertakings (far from the formulation of collective resistance and grievance) that do little to change the fundamental problems within tech: toxic work environments and an unhealthy work-life balance.

Engineers' reluctance to contest or rebel may be related to the ludic discourse constructed through the field of games. As mentioned, one new and distinct feature of the field of games is its perception of games as a technology of governance. Yet, once labor games are positioned to enable free play and perceived as an expression of individualistic interests—and once engineers internalize such a discourse—there is little or no space for them to organize resistance, especially large-scale, collective resistance.

The discourse constructed through the field of games reinforces engineers' perceptions of libertarianism and individualism, both linked to the high-risk nature of software development work. According to such a worldview, engineers' status is connected to individual merit, whether in the virtual gaming world or the workplace. Similarly, games romanticize and celebrate the unstable nature of development work, further undermining collective efforts to promote job equality and stability.

Engineers may moreover fall into the trap of believing that their passion for games leads to overwork rather than recognizing that this overwork is rooted in exploitation. Games are often embedded in the work process, and winning can enhance an engineer's status and respect in their workplace. As a result, they can become willing conspirators in their own exploitation as long as they are winning gaming and work-related challenges. This reinforces their skepticism of collective appeals and contributes to negative perceptions of group actions.

Although factors associated with gamification contribute to engineers' indifference to united resistance, there are other influential elements as well. Engineers' high mobility (Bassett and Cave 1993; Milton 2003), occupational nature, and weak ties to any particular tech company (Barely and Kunda 2006) also hinder the formulation of collective interests. Combined, these aspects result in very low rates of unionization in the high-tech industry (Bulut 2021; Legault and Weststar 2015; Milton 2003).

New Dynamics, Activism, and the Future of the Tech Industry?

Nonetheless, the tech industry has, since 2018, seen the emergence of two prominent activism trends. The first concerns gender equality, with Google employees' demonstration serving as a prime example. On November 1, 2018, employees at Google walked off the job to protest the company's treatment of its female staff, demanding equal pay and opportunities and transparency in sexual harassment reporting. The second trend relates to the struggle to improve working conditions, particularly after massive layoffs by major game companies (e.g., Blizzard dismissed eight hundred employees in 2018). Game workers began to realize that collective struggle might offer a powerful strategy for improving labor conditions. Notably, the group Game Workers Unite (GWU) was founded in March 2018 during the Game Developer Conference (Frank 2018; Perez 2019). These two activism trends have significant implications for the tech industry. They not only revitalize older traditions of collective action within the tech industry (previously considered a utopian idea) but have made many workplace issues visible, such as gender inequality, sexual harassment, poor working conditions, and problematic contracts.

Further momentum has seen tech labor activism expand its influence. A noticeable uptick in unionization attempts occurred in 2022, in part buoyed by protests during the COVID-19 crisis related to the increased stress placed on service workers to enforce pandemic codes, such as implementing mask mandates and checking vaccination documents (Sallaz and Trongone 2023). The tech industry also experienced massive layoffs in 2022, further fueling worker grievances.

Several tactics might enhance tech activism's influence. To begin, workers could form broader alliances across different companies, working groups, and individual activist organizations. Indeed, as capital aims to divide and atomize tech workers, uniting is crucial for greater control. Gender equality movements might accordingly seek supportive partnerships beyond geographic location, while Game Workers Unite could expand beyond the game industry, promoting better working conditions for all tech workers or popularizing and sharing their experience of organizing online campaigns with other software engineering communities. Several scholars have illustrated how the strong social network and virtual community organized among game developers has helped to remove obstacles to collective action (e.g., difficulties related to information sharing or the constraints of physical gathering) and has proved to be an efficient means of enhancing collective expression (Legault and Weststar 2015; Shirky 2008). Finally, building on the momentum of 2022, activists might expand workplace struggles to the broader political arena. For example, labor movements that aim to promote gender equality at work could seek supportive alliances with other feminist movements (e.g., the #MeToo movement), thus making their voice louder and gaining more influence.

Finally, a recent trend in the U.S. tech industry following the pandemic is worth discussing. Four major players—Google, Amazon, Meta, and Microsoft—have experienced multiple rounds of layoffs, announcing more than fifty thousand job cuts in 2022. Instead of aggressively recruiting new talent, tech companies are now focused on obtaining more productivity from their current employees. Illustrative of this point is Google CEO Sundar Pichai's mid-2022 call for enhanced performance and creativity on the part of employees, as well as increased focus time and productivity, to make each "headcount" worth it (Elias 2022; Hobson 2022; Karaian and Kelley 2022).

Whether these circumstances reflect short-term turbulence or indicate a turning point potentially leading to the complete transformation of the existing tech industry structure remains uncertain. It is similarly hard to predict whether this new dynamic will invalidate or further strengthen the labor regime identified in this book: the field of games. In may be that gaming hegemony will dissipate, and a more despotic regime will return to the stage. It could also well be that games closely related to productivity will remain intact.[4] Regardless, there is no guarantee that workers' playing strategies will remain the same as described in this book. Will they continue to invest in games driven by their gamer subjectivity, or will they play due to a fear of job loss?[5] As with any production model, it is difficult to know whether the game regime will remain or disappear. As labor ethnographers, we are only able to document the current game model and analyze the forces underlying its construction at particular historical junctures.

Although ascertaining future developmental trends relative to the field of games is challenging, it is likely that labor conditions and worker's grievances will only worsen under the current circumstances. Activists must accordingly unify workers, solicit collective interests, fight for their rights, and support one another. Hopefully, in their efforts to navigate these troubling times, engineers will realize that collective struggle, rather than individualist resolutions, offers a more powerful weapon to end the industry's toxic work environment.

Appendix A

Overview of a Field of Games

TABLE A.1 SIMULATION GAMING GROUP

Games	Game description	Gamification elements	Gamer skills/traits/ subjectivity	Gaming outcome
Game of Security	Adopting fantasy movie language to romanticize security engineers' work as "a game of security," "a fight of security," "maintaining security in a hostile world," and "keeping the security club together"	Battle and adventure simulations; mythological storylines	Interpellate heroic characters; adventurous gaming self; rapid adaptability	Normalize uncertainty; reduce anxiety; governmentality/gamified governmentality
Video-gamify work teams	Blur the relationships, space, and activities between video-game teams (e.g., CS:GO team, WoW team, LoL team) and work teams	Battle and adventure simulations	Heroic characters	Collaboration; reduce anxiety; governmentality; heterotopia; autonomy
Nicknaming	Use video-game or sci-fi-movie characters to nickname teammates, such as "Zach of the North" and "DKP"	Adventure simulation; mythological storylines	Interpellate heroic characters; adventurous gaming self	Gamified governmentality
Weaponize the team	Every member in the Wizard team is asked to be "weaponized" (equipped with Nerf guns, bows, sword) and has to be always ready to use their weapon to put up a fight with other teams	Battle simulation	Competitiveness	Heterotopia; autonomy
Wearing the characters' hats	Materialize the metaphoric roles (e.g., people wear role-related hats to reveal their work roles)	Adventure simulation; mythological storylines	Interpellate heroic characters	Collaboration; gamified governmentality
Project-naming games	Teams draw on movie series or video-game series to name their development projects (e.g., naming each project with one thief in Ocean's Twelve, naming project as "George Martin Program")	Adventure simulation	Heroic characters; adventurous gaming self	Gamified governmentality; enhance autonomy
Code Review Roulette	Use the Russian roulette game to decide who perform code-review tasks ("who gets the bullets will do the code review")	Bets and games of chance	Algorithmization of the issue; "Theorycraft"	Solve labor division problem; increase collaboration; autonomy
Code Ninja Chronicles	Behemoth organizes online events (e.g., "code ninja time challenge") to recruit "the army of code ninja;" if participants pass the test, they can receive rewards and be contacted for telephone interviews	Adventure simulation, mythological storylines; online contests, timely feedback	Heroic characters; adventurous gaming self	Formulate mind flow; extract creative ideas and extra labor efforts

Four-Hour Ninja Contest	The four-hour contest invites participants who can be either employees or job applicants; participants are encouraged to solve as many technical issues as possible within four hours	Battle simulation; progress bars, virtual rewards	Heroic characters; complex problem solving ability	Increase competition; formulate mind flow
Ninja CodeSprint	Engineers can organize teams outside their team at their will to participate in the sprint and tackle the company's toughest technical issues	Heroic characters; mythological storylines	Heroic characters; adventurous gaming self; rapid adaptability	Increase competition; formulate mind flow; extract creative ideas and extra labor efforts
Monkey Master dice game	The monkey is a scream toy to remind engineers of standup meetings; engineers roll dice and decide who becomes the monkey masters and responsible for taking the minutes for the standup meetings	Dice rolling	Board game playing skills	Solve labor division problem; enhance autonomy
Trading games	Engineers adopt video-game "trading" in work and develop trading games such as "trading player" and "trading on-call hours"	Transparency	Trading and bargaining skills	Enhance autonomy and community cohesion; increase engagement
Anti Corporate Borg games	"Corporate Borg" borrows from *Star Trek* and refers to the evil corporate entity that removes worker individuality; Behemoth engineers organize Anti Corporate Borg groups (email list) to regularly propose and conduct Anti Corporate Borg gaming ideas	Mythological storylines	Disruptive creativity	Community cohesion; autonomy achieved through subverting rules
Encrypting game ("Crack the code!")	Sometimes wizard team members exchange/communicate messages using encrypted code only team members know; Knight team engineers also create their own codes to encrypt all members' names	Adventure simulation; crisis simulation	Adventurous gaming self	Team cohesion
Customizing Cards against Humanity	Wizard team orders Cards against Humanity game card deck and customizes it for the team (e.g., putting team members' name on it and coming up with member-specified rules)	N/A	Card game play	Enhance community cohesion; increase team rapport
Nerf gun shooting / laser attack	Nerf gun / laser attack fights organized between two sister teams or between two subgroups within one development team (sometimes involves disarming or destroying enemy teams' weapons)	Battle simulation (migrate CS:GO shooting game onto the engineering floor)	Theorycraft (WoW)	Cooperation; competition

TABLE A.2 RACING GAMING GROUP

Games	Game description	Gamification elements	Gamer skills/traits/ subjectivity	Gaming outcome
Ticket-sprint marathons	Engineers self-organize weekend ticket marathons to boost their team's ranking on the ticket dashboard	Timely feedback; leveling up	Theorycraft; modding skills	Mind flow; enhance concentration; extract extra labor; autonomy
Ticket-ranking competitions	Incorporate leaderboard into the dashboard; publicly display and rank all teams' ticket-solving performance	Leaderboard, ranking, timely feedback, countdown timer	Competitive self; quantifying self; crisis mentality	Increase competition; enhance productivity; autonomy
Behemoth Hackathons	Team up with coworkers to create a functioning software/service within a limited period; finalists will be supported by the company to implement the designed product	Virtual rewards, transparency; competition	Competitive self; modder traits; timely feedback; disruptive creativity	Mind flow; enhance concentration; extract creative ideas; collaboration
Coding-Testing-Debugging Triathlon	Organize a triathlon consisting of coding, testing, and debugging	Leaderboard; timely feedback	Competitive self; modder traits (modding skills); grinding	Mind flow; enhance concentration; extract extra labor
Dart-challenge games	Transform the dart-shooting activities into a competition; members calculate the speed, angle, and distance to enhance the chance of winning	Ranking	Calculative self; competitive self, mathematical and algorithmic thinking ability	Team cohesion
Board game tournaments	Board game nights are organized in varied formats (organize game night within their development teams; find coworkers outside their teams)	Virtual rewards	Calculative self; competitive self, mathematical and algorithmic thinking ability	Community cohesion
Texas Hold'em tournaments	Behemoth organizes Texas Hold'em poker tournaments in annual reinvention meetings, postholiday parties, and summer picnics (rewards are offered to the best players—the person who pulled a good play with poor hands)	Leaderboard	Calculative self; mathematical and algorithmic thinking ability	

			Mathematization/ algorithmization of the issue	
Betting on-call hours	Use on-call hours to gamble and bet (e.g., engineers who lose a bet will cover the winner one- to two-hour on-call time)	Points; bets and game of chances		Community cohesion; autonomy; collaboration and interdependence
Pumpkin pie scalability dilemma	Propose the dilemma on how to divide a pumpkin pie and attract engineers' solution	Narrative gamification	Calculative self; algorithmic thinking ability; problem-solving skills	Nudging behaviors; normative control
Snatching party	Organize party at other company's territory to snatch potential teammates	Competition	Competitive self; crisis mentality; quantifying self	Commitment; community cohesion; normative control
Pipe Org Cup	Organize development teams for different competitions (laser tag, escape room, cricket, football competitions)	Timely feedback, virtual rewards	Competitive self; problem solving skills	Competition and cooperation; team cohesion
Ping-Pong competitions	Divide up teams along racial lines and compete (e.g., China vs. U.S. competition; Asian vs white competition)	Competition	Competitive self	Community cohesion
Cricket matches	This match is organized every few months to absorb teammates who are not from India to team up with their Indian teammates to play cricket together	Leaderboard; virtual rewards; competition	Competitive self	Commitment; communication; community cohesion
Eating challenges	Organize different eating challenges, such as eating different Chinese restaurants without repeating for a week, going to different bars in a row in a week, and trying all milk tea shops in town	Challenge	Competitive self	Community cohesion
Drinking challenges	Many teams designed varied types of drinking challenges (e.g., drinking in different bars for a whole week without repetition, taking shots while solving tickets)	Challenge	Competitiveness	Reduce fatigue and relieve boredom

TABLE A.3 CROWDSOURCING GAMING GROUP

Games	Game description	Gamification elements	Gamer skills/traits/ subjectivity	Gaming outcome
Phone-tool icons collection games	Give virtual rewards (i.e., phone-tool icons) to engineers who complete volunteer work, such as providing feedback for other teams' products	Badges; phone-tool icon display platform	Modder traits; grinding skills	Obscure the extraction of surplus; external bricolage tasks to volunteers
PC-Building "shenanigans"	Engineers organize interest groups to custom build computer (parts) together	Online forum	Skills of modding hardware	Optimize hardware; enhance productivity and creativity
Reverse virtual reality (VR)	Materialize elements on Behemoth's virtual world places (e.g., virtual phone tools, countdown timers, virtual coins) and bring them back into the real world	N/A	Modder traits; hands-on skills; creative thinking	Increase autonomy; enhance creativity
Team optimization	Encourage engineers to propose fun and unique ideas to optimize team setup and collect these ideas to pose as action items to be discussed in the retrospective	Timely feedback	Problem-solving skills	Enhance team collaboration; increase autonomy and satisfaction
Puzzle trophy collection	The puzzle trophy is a trophy in the shape of puzzles and is awarded engineers' patent ideas; the more patent ideas they submit, the more puzzle trophies they can collect and piece together	Level up; display to offer bragging rights	Creative thinking; collecting habits	Extracting and crowdsourcing ideas; increase creativity
Collecting funny cause of errors	A forum where engineers can search, contribute, and discuss funny causes of errors (COEs)	Online forum	Knowledge sharing; quick-learning ability	Familiarize work system; enhance community cohesion; extract extra knowledge

Tier 1 resolver games	A forum where engineers share tips they believe are helpful to solve technical problems, hardware issues, and get through a tough stage of software deployment	Online forum	Knowledge sharing; quick-learning skill	Extract extra knowledge, and efforts; enhance; community cohesion; familiarize work system
Online voting games	Polling on the dashboard to help with decision-making (e.g., collect and count votes to decide organization logos, picnic places, after-party activities)	Online forum, voting plugin; timely feedback	N/A	Increase engagement; demonstrate democracy
All-hands live polls	Use live poll apps to facilitate voting during all-hands meetings	Live poll apps; timely feedbacks	N/A	Increase engagement; demonstrate democracy
Scavenger hunts	Organize scavenger hunts for different purposes (e.g., to help engineers familiarize the work campus, Behemoth asks development teams to gather all items hidden in different places on campus)	Narrative gamification	Problem/puzzle solving; collaborative ability	Increase collaboration; enhance community cohesion
Meowstanding Achievement Award	Rewarding people who contribute cat-related conversation, images, and discussions to an email lists	Badges	N/A	Increase communication; enhance community cohesion

TABLE A.4 PRANKING GAMING GROUP

Games	Game description	Gamification elements	Gamer skills/traits/ subjectivity	Gaming outcome
Donut email pranks	When engineers fail to lock their computers when leaving their desks, colleagues can hijack their email account and send embarrassing emails; as a penalty, the one who forgets to lock the computer purchases donuts for colleagues	N/A	N/A	Mutual surveillance; resistance occasionally emerges; chaotic fun
Newcomers hazing games	Newcomers to the engineering floor had to negotiate a series of humiliation initiation ceremonies	N/A	Occasional mobilization of cyber satire	Reduce boredom; construct horseplay; heterotopia; normative control
Welcome-back games	When engineers return to the office from a long vacation, they are likely to be teased with a welcome-back prank	N/A	N/A	Reduce boredom; construct horseplay; heterotopia
Funny skit	Behemoth designs funny skit (e.g., vice president wears a miniskirt and dances) before a big event (e.g. all-hands meetings; post-holiday parties)	N/A	N/A	Relieve boredom; construct horseplay; valorize culture of casual fun
Farewell pranks	When engineers leave Behemoth, they sometimes ritually pull a last prank on their teams as a way to say good-bye	N/A	N/A	Reduce boredom; resistance occasionally emerges; chaotic fun
Detective game ("Who is the traitor!")	Some teams convert the discussion on who is hopping into a detective game; teammates deduce who is the traitor (hopper) according to clues and follow a script to name the suspect	Scripting	Board game playing skills	Discipline; mutual surveillance

		Rank and competition	Competitiveness	
Who is the latest to come to work?	The Wizard team keeps a list on the whiteboard to document who is the latest to come to work	N/A	N/A	Discipline; mutual surveillance
Snap a napping picture	Many engineers like to go to the conference room to take naps; sometimes their napping behaviors will be photographed by their teammates, sending out team email lists and being teased	N/A	Occasional mobilization of cybersatire	Discipline; mutual surveillance
Ridiculing patent ideas	Sometimes engineers submit ridiculous patent ideas, not for winning the trophy but for fun	N/A	N/A	Chaotic fun; enhance creativity; resistance occasionally emerges
Ridiculing action items	Engineers incorporate ridiculous action items during their scrum planning meetings for fun	N/A	N/A	Reduce fatigue and relieve boredom; enhance creativity
Costume play	Engineers wear costumes on special occasions as a way of conducting pranks and expressing themselves	N/A	N/A	Reduce fatigue and relieve boredom
Joking mentor-mentee relationship	Joking about the mentor-mentee relationship (e.g., act as if the relationship was the same as a dating relationship or a married couple)	N/A	N/A	Reduce fatigue and relieve boredom; valorize the flattened structure

Appendix B

Basic Information on Interviewees

TABLE B.1 BASIC INFORMATION OF INTERVIEWEES

Pseudonym	Age	Gender	Race/ ethnicity	Immigrant status	Degree	University	Team	Level	Work length	Gamer identity
GY	25	Female	Chinese	H1-B	MS	Indiana University	Assassin	Level 4	8 month	No
Huong	27	Female	Vietnamese	H1-B	MS	University of Florida	Day 1	Level 4	1 year	No
Jie	25	Male	Chinese	H1-B	MS	Cornell University	Portal	Level 4	1.3 year	No
JW	26	Male	Chinese	H1-B	MS	NYU	Wizard	Level 4	8 month	Yes*
Ah Hao	31	Male	Chinese	H1-B	MS	University of Pennsylvania	Machine Learning	Level 4	1 year	No
Javier	27	Male	Hispanic	N/A	MS	University of Pennsylvania	Launcher	Level 4	4 month	No
Fang	27	Male	Chinese	H1-B	MS	Carnegie Mellon University	Tablet Application	Level 4	1 year	No
ZH	27	Male	Chinese	H1-B	MS	University of Pennsylvania	Knight	Level 4	8 month	No
SJ	28	Female	Chinese	LPR[1]	MS	University of Washington	Finance	Level 5	2 years	No
WZH	27	Male	Chinese	H1-B	MS	University of Pennsylvania	Assassin	Level 4	8 month	No
Michael	26	Male	Singaporean	H1-B	BS	Purdue University		Level 4	2 years	No
Naji	31	Male	Indian	H1-B	MS	Columbia University	Database Service	Level 5	2 years	No
Dinesh	29	Male	Hispanic	Canadian resident	BS	University of Toronto	Wizard	Intern	3 months	No
Qifan	25	Male	Chinese	H1-B	MS	Columbia University	Tablet Application	Level 4	1 year	No
J. Sun	25	Male	Chinese	LPR	MS	Columbia University	Shopping Recommendation	Level 5	1.5 years	Yes
Boss Lei	25	Male	Chinese	H1-B	MS	Oregon State University	Credit	Level 4	2 years	Yes*
Qian	25	Female	Chinese	H1-B	MS	Rensselaer Polytechnic Institute	Subscriptions	Level 4	1.5 years	Yes
Yuan Liang	25	Male	Chinese	H1-B	MS	Columbia University	Credit	Level 5	1 year	Yes*
Ben	24	Male	White	N/A	BS	Oregon State University	Knight	Level 4	1.5 years	Yes*
Andi	28	Female	White	N/A	BS	Seattle University	Knight	Level 4	3.5 years	No
Little Zach	22	Male	White	N/A	BS	N/A	Knight	Intern	6 month	No
Philip	23	Male	White	N/A	BS	University of Buffalo	Knight	Level 4	7 months	Yes*
Danny	23	Male	White	N/A	BS	University of Michigan	Wizard	Level 4	1.5 years	Yes*

(continued)

TABLE B.1 BASIC INFORMATION OF INTERVIEWEES (*continued*)

Pseudonym	Age	Gender	Race/ethnicity	Immigrant status	Degree	University	Team	Level	Work length	Gamer identity
Mark	23	Male	White	N/A	BS	University of Michigan	Wizard	Level 4	1.3 years	Yes*
Amir	24	Male	Pakistani	H1-B	BS	Illinois Wesleyan University	Wizard	Level 4	1.5 years	Yes
Peter	25	Male	White	N/A	BS	Lehigh University	Wizard	Level 5	2.5 years	Yes*
Chuan	28	Male	Chinese	H1-B	MS	NYU	Knight	Level 4	1.3 years	No
Little Hao	25	Male	Chinese	H1-B	MS	University of Pennsylvania	EBS	Level 4	1.25 years	No
Jassie	29	Female	Korean	H1-B	MS	University of Washington	AIV	Level 4	6 months	No
Andrea	34	Female	White	N/A	BS	Illinois Wesleyan University	Documentation Build	Level 5	9 months	No
Sylvia	26	Female	White	N/A	BS	University of Washington	Vendor Express	Level 5	3.5 years	No
Hasini	30	Female	Indian	H-1B	MS	N/A	Network engineering	QA engineer	1 year	No
Jai	26	Female	Indian	H-1B	MS	Northeastern University	Digital Book Store	Level 4	1 year	No
Bill	29	Male	White	N/A	MS	Minnesota University	Knight	Level 5	3 years	Yes*
Old Jack	38	Male	White	N/A	BS	N/A	Wizard	Level 5	6 years	No
Matt	35	Male	White	N/A	MS	University of Michigan	Wizard	Level 5	3.5 years	Yes*
Tony	24	Male	White	N/A	BS	University of Waterloo	N/A	Level 4	1.5 year	Yes
Kim	24	Male	White	N/A	MS	University of Pennsylvania	Email Platform	Level 4	3 months	No
Ricky	27	Male	White	N/A	MS	N/A	N/A	Level 4	2 years	No
Wei	30	Male	Chinese	H-1B	MA	N/A	N/A	Level 5	4 year	No
Yang	32	Male	Chinese	L-1B	MA	University of Pennsylvania	Pipeline One	Level 5	1.5 year	No
JJ	48	Male	White	N/A	MA	Bowling Green State University	Config Storage	Level 5	1 year 3 month	Yes*
Jun	25	Female	Chinese	H-1B	MA	UCLA	Serverless	Level 5	1 year	Yes
AL	26	Male	White	White	BS	Virginia Tech	Could Run Admin	Level 4	1 year 8 month	Yes
Min	31	Male	Chinese	H1B	MS	UC Irvine	N/A	Level 5	4 years	No
Guang	27	Male	Chinese	H-1B	MS	Brown University	Supply Chain Management	Level 6	3 years	No
Carlos	29	Male	Hispanic	N/A	MS	Minnesota University	Billing Account	Level 5	3 years	No

Name	Age	Gender	Race	LPR	Degree	University	App Engine Flex	Level	Duration	
Andras	39	Male	White (Hungary)	N/A	MS	N/A		Level 5	3.5 year	No
Eric	23	Male	White	N/A	BS	Duke University	Shepherd	Level 4	1 year	Yes
Zhou	27	Female	Chinese	F-1 Visa	MS	UCLA	Unified Auth	Level 5	1 year 11 month	Yes
Manjuf	31	Male	India	H-1B	MS	University of Buffalo	Scable	Level 5	4 years	No
Qin	28	Female	Chinese	H-1B	MS	University of Pennsylvania	N/A	Level 5	1 year	No
Umish	27	Male	Indian	H-1B	MS	Holland	N/A	Level 5	1 year	Yes
Elizabeth	27	Female	White	N/A	MS	UCLA	Unified Auth	Level 4	2 years	Yes*
Shannon	31	Female	White	N/A	MS	University of Massachusetts Amherst	Grocery	Level 4	2.5 years	No
Jonathan	40	Male	White	N/A	MS	University of Washington	Pipe Org	Level 8 (manager)	8 years	No
Paul	30	Male	White	N/A	BS	N/A	Ranger	Level 6 (manager)	N/A	No
Charles	24	Male	White	N/A	BS	Western Washington University	Ranger	Level 4	1.5 years	Yes*
YR	25	Male	Chinese	H1-B	MS	University of Arizona	Wizard	Level 4	7 months	Yes
Jack the North	24	Male	White	N/A	BS	UCLA	Wizard	Intern	6 months	Yes*
Vikram	30	Male	Indian	LPR	BS	University of Michigan	Wizard	Level 6 (manager)	4 years	Yes
Vicky	27	Male	Chinese	H1-B	MS	University of Michigan	Wizard	Intern	6 months	Yes
Creepy	31	Male	White	N/A	N/A	N/A	Wizard	Level 4	2 years	Yes
Jammar	27	Male	Indian	H1-B	MS	Boston College	Ranger	Level 4	1.5 years	Yes
Howard	30	Male	Chinese	H1-B	MS	University of Pennsylvania	Shepherd	Level 6 (manager)	4 years	Yes
Anandit	35	Male	Indian	LPR	MS	University of Michigan	Pipe Org	Level 7 (manager)	6 years	No

* Implies "self-labeled" gamer.
1. LPR is the abbreviation for "lawful permanent resident."

APPENDIX C

Demographic Questionnaire

1. Age _____ (years)
2. Gender _____
3. Race (check one)
   ☐ White
   ☐ African American (Black)
   ☐ American Indian (Alaska Native)
   ☐ Asian: Indian
   ☐ Asian: Chinese
   ☐ Asian: Other Asian
   ☐ Hispanic (Latino) (e.g., Mexican, Puerto Rican, Cuban)
   ☐ Other _____
4. Immigrant Status
   Are you currently? (check the one that applies)
   ☐ F-1 Visa holder
   ☐ H-1B holder
   ☐ Green card holder
   ☐ First-generation American (foreign-born immigrant who has relocated to the United States and been naturalized as a U.S. citizen)
   ☐ 1.5 generation American (foreign-born immigrant who has relocated to the United States before adolescence)
   ☐ Second-generation American (children of first-generation immigrants)
   ☐ Other _____
5. What is the highest level of education you have achieved? (check one)
   ☐ Associate's Degree or Technical/Vocational Degree (2-year)
   ☐ Some College
   ☐ Bachelor's Degree
   ☐ Master's Degree

☐ Doctoral Degree
☐ Professional Degree (MD, JD, etc.)
☐ Other _____

6. [Please answer if this question applied to your situation.] What level of education did you achieve before moving to the United States? From which university? What level of education did you achieve in the United States (if applicable)?
   From which university?
   _____

7. How long have you worked in this corporation? What is your level/position in
   this corporation?
   _____

8. Have you been promoted in this corporation? When did that happen?
   _____

9. What is the name of your current team? How many people are in your team?
   How long have you worked in your team?
   _____

10. What is the racial/ethnic status of your team leader/manager (check one)?
    ☐ White
    ☐ African American (Black)
    ☐ American Indian (Alaska Native)
    ☐ Asian: Indian
    ☐ Asian: Chinese
    ☐ Asian: Korean
    ☐ Asian: Japanese
    ☐ Asian: Vietnamese
    ☐ Asian: Other Asian
    ☐ Hispanic (Latino) (For example: Mexican, Puerto Rican, Cuban)
    ☐ Other _____

11. If you could describe your corporate culture in three words, what would they be?
    _____

12. What was your approximate income last year? (check one)
    ☐ Less than $100,000
    ☐ $100,000–$149,999
    ☐ $150,000–$199,999
    ☐ $200,000–$249,999
    ☐ $250,000–$299,999
    ☐ $300,000–$349,999
    ☐ $350,000–$399,999
    ☐ $400,000–$449,999

Notes

CHAPTER 1

1. I acknowledge that—despite my efforts to avoid sample bias and create a diverse interview pool that included white, Latino, and Asian individuals—I was unable to collect interviews from the Black community. I recognize that the underrepresentation of Black individuals is a serious issue in the U.S. tech industry, as evidenced by diversity reports from major tech companies. While I understand that this lack of participation may be influenced by larger societal and historical factors, I also recognize that it may indicate potential biases in my own recruitment and interview processes, which need to be acknowledged here.

2. An "incremental model" refers to the deployment of a minimum viable product instead of a perfect end product, which is then continuously improved through repetitive testing and optimizing.

3. "Computational power" denotes the ability of a computer to perform work, often with reference to how much random-access memory (RAM) it has. Chapter 3 offers a more detailed discussion on how tech firms take advantage of engineers' creativity to save computational power.

4. One key informant provided this insight, explaining that most companies told their employees about a desired "resource trade-off" equation; most companies encouraged their engineers to adopt a 2:1 "saving-to-effort ratio" when thinking about their work. A software development project is practicable only if the engineer's one-year effort (defined in hypothetical working hours as 9 hours / 5 days a week / 235 weeks a year) can save the company computers two years of running power (defined as 24 / 7 / 365). According to this informant, a very creative project is highly recommended, since it pushes the ratio to its higher bound—3:1, 4:1, or even higher.

5. In classic writing, *bricolage* refers to the activity of "making do" with the materials at hand to concoct whatever tools are needed to accomplish certain tasks (Lévi-Strauss 1966). Baker and Nelson (2005) adopt this concept to contemporary business settings and illustrate that bricolage is a crucial mechanism for spawning entrepreneurship and en-

suring innovation: they discuss how entrepreneurial companies engage in bricolage by maximizing use of resources like personal knowledge, technical skills, and open-access technology/tools. Whether innovation can occur is closely related to whether the bricoleur can flexibly use and recombine their technical knowledge and get access to open-source technology (e.g., open-source software).

6. Inspired by bricolage theory, I define bricolage tasks as those in which engineers are encouraged to accomplish by utilizing whatever technological resources/knowledge they can access and concocting the necessary tools with minimum cost. Bricolage tasks are viewed in contrast to the type of tasks that require engineers to carefully plan ahead to access everything that is needed to handle them.

7. In Friedman's typology, direct control resembles Bravermen's deskilling control, which is built on separation of conception and execution. The strategy of responsible autonomy, according to Friedman (1977, 78), stems from the attempt "to harness the adaptability of labor power by giving workers leeway and encouraging them to adapt to changing situations in a manner beneficial to the firm."

8. In Edwards's theoretical framework, simple control prevailed during the competitive capitalism of the nineteenth century and was characterized by harsh penalty policies implemented by supervisors. Technical control was developed after Ford's innovation of the assembly line in 1913 and involved "designing machinery and planning the flow of work to maximize the problem of transforming labor power into labor as well as maximize the purely physical-based possibilities for achieving efficiencies" (Edwards 1979, 112). Finally, bureaucratic control was established to ensure the "impersonal force of company rules or company policies as the basis for control" (152).

9. According to Huws (2014), in an era of rapid deregulation and upgrading of telecommunications networks around the world, the formation of the International Telecommunications Union (ITU) in 1992 was an iconic event.

10. Scholars in this vein largely follow Braverman's (1998) view that labor process issues suffered by manual workers will also be encountered by knowledge workers like technicians and engineers. Indeed, Braverman hinted that knowledge workers as we call them today, such as "draftsmen, technicians, engineers, and accountants, nurses and teachers, and the multiplying ranks of supervisors, foremen, and petty managers," also encountered the same labor process issues experienced by blue-collar workers, such as automation and deskilling (282).

11. The year 2000 was a watershed year. The year 2000 problem (also known as the millennium bug or the Y2K problem) signaled the enhanced significance of the IT sector and increasing demand for tech workers (Huws 2014; Xiang 2007).

12. For example, in his work on knowledge-intensive workers, Alvesson (2000) illustrates that these workers are very motivated by the work they perform but not by their loyalty to specific companies. Being a knowledge worker, he argues, means being a hardworking individual committed to delivering high-quality service.

13. All workers agreed to "make out" at an acceptable percentage output, that is, not higher than 140 percent or lower than 125 percent.

14. According to Huizinga (1949, 10), a founding scholar of games, people are drawn into play due to the pull of "tension." The latter arises from uncertainty, closely associated with chances, risks, and players' limitations.

15. Gramsci draws on his working-class experience in Turin in 1919–1920, a time when exploitation was hardly hidden.

16. The emphasis on the generation of subjectivity at the point of production means that Burawoy's depiction of subjectivity is more malleable than Pierre Bourdieu's game

metaphor. While Bourdieu's players make moves based on deeply ingrained dispositions, Burawoy argues that players engage in conscious calculation and strategizing directed by their subjectivity. As such, in Bourdieu's study their habitus is merely a reproduction of the social structure and thus much more stable than in Burawoy's portrayal (Burawoy and Von Holdt 2012; Sharone 2013).

17. It was in this historical context that researchers began to explore why women workers and gendered subjectivity were preferred by global manufacturers.

18. Scholars working on aesthetic labor have found that people who embody the "right" type of aesthetic (i.e., the right look)—usually cultivated through consumption—are more likely to be recruited by service capitalists. Furthermore, capitalists who hire based on the "right look" expropriate workers' consumption as part of their labor power.

19. According to Burawoy (1979, 60), the entire plant made out at an average of 133.5 percent of the standard rate.

20. Purcell and Brook try to bridge the Foucauldian notion of governmentality and Burawoy's concept of "hegemonic despotism" to explain how domination is established in platform work (Purcell and Brook 2022).

21. Certainly, there is no one way to define and perceive gamers' subjectivities. Early studies attempted to associate gamers with a stereotypical image of a young, white male, perpetually viewed as nerdy, socially awkward, indoorsy, introverted, and overly intellectual (Dill and Thill 2007; McClure and Mears 1984). Later game scholars have problematized this image, pointing out the ambiguities, mutability, and heterogeneity embedded in the gamer identity (Chess 2017; Juul 2009; Shaw 2012; Williams 2006). Kirkpatrick (2012), for example, stresses that gamer identity is socially constructed and should not be perceived as static. Drawing on his study of the UK gaming industry, he illustrates that gamer identity shifted from an association with hardcore and technologically sophisticated players to youth culture and consumerism when the industry experienced a radical shift after 1985. Some game scholars insist that gamer identity exists in relation to other social identities, such as gender, race, age, and sexuality (Chess 2017; Shaw 2012; Shaw and Chess 2016). Others highlight different gamer identities (e.g., hardcore gamers, casual gamers, cool gamers, purists, moderates), present distinct gaming capital or traits embodied by different gamers (e.g., some gamer identities are associated with heroism and crisis conquering, others with data-driven fact-finding and technical proficiency), and explore the ways in which these differences are socially and culturally constructed (Chess 2017; Consalvo 2009; Dovey and Kennedy 2006; Juul 2009).

CHAPTER 2

1. In fact, "player trading" is another game engineers developed at Behemoth, inspired by video-game trading activities. In video games, players trade in-game items (e.g., character skins, weapons). Engineers borrowed this concept and developed trading games for at-work items, such as on-call hours and teammates.

2. As is shown in later chapters, nongamers regularly team up with their gamer colleagues to play video games during "game nights" organized in many software development teams.

3. A gamer who is addicted to massive multiplayer online (MMO) games.

4. *PCf*g* is a term used to describe a gamer who is obsessed with games run on Windows PCs and who has no other social life but PC gaming life. Because the term makes use of a slur, I've elided it in this book.

5. Inspired by Adriene Shaw (2014), I draw on both interviews and participant observations to identify these implicit gamers. For example, when I visited some interviewees' apartments, I found that they have more than two shelves of gaming console collections. During my conversation with some informants, I learned that they spend more than six or seven hours playing video games every day after work, which implied that these engineers basically did nothing but gaming during their off time. Furthermore, while some informants were silent about their gamer identities, they were well known at my field site for their addictive gaming behaviors, like "secretly" spending a fortune hiring pro gamers as coaches to improve their gaming records and skills or repeatedly quitting certain games and rejoining after a few days or weeks. Although these engineers did not explicitly identify themselves as gamers, they possessed traits associated with dedicated and even hardcore gamers (Juul 2010). Therefore, they are labeled as "implicit gamers" in this study.

6. Nintendo is one of the world's largest video-game companies by market capitalization, having created some of the best-known and top-selling video-game franchises, such as Mario and Pokémon.

7. A digital distribution platform that provides multiplayer gaming, video streaming, and social networking services.

8. "Playbor," a hybrid form of "play" and "labor," is a concept coined by Kücklich (2005). Kücklich draws on this concept to alert scholars to the type of free labor that fits neither the traditional definition of labor nor the categories of play.

9. These new frameworks are not developed by Mark but by other teams and thus beyond Mark's responsibilities.

10. As discussed in the introduction, bricolage tasks are defined as the tasks that are encouraged to be accomplished by utilizing whatever technological resources/knowledge that engineers can access (a.k.a., the work activity of "bricolaging"). Therefore, the bricolage tasks are seen as contrasting with the type of tasks that require engineers to carefully plan ahead and gain access to all that is needed to accomplish.

11. Nexus Mods, CurseForge, and Mod DB are gaming modification websites that allow gamers to upload or download mods for certain computer games.

12. Soft modding involves changing software or codes to achieve a goal, while hard modding focuses on hardware.

13. OpenMW is an open-source game engine that refers to game engine remastering practices for reimplementing and rewriting the *Morrowind* game from scratch.

14. A Gentoo package is a type of software used in the Gentoo Linux operating system. Gentoo Linux is different from most other operating systems because it is built directly from the source code on the user's computer. This means that the software can be customized to fit the user's needs and is often fine-tuned to work best with their specific computer. The name "Gentoo" comes from the gentoo penguin, known for being the fastest swimming penguin species. This name was chosen to highlight Gentoo Linux's speed and efficiency, which are key characteristics of this operating system.

15. The Atari 2600 was a home video-game console released by the Atari company in 1977.

16. Typically, the company adopts a conservative approach toward the development of new features in the fourth quarter (Q4), recognizing that such initiatives may compromise system stability during the critical holiday season. Contrary to this practice, Amir's team implemented a new feature at the end of a Q4 development sprint. This action introduced a heightened risk of a significant increase in system errors. Consequently, Amir was tasked with rapidly addressing these errors to mitigate potential damage to the system

during this peak period. It was under these circumstances that Amir experienced considerable pressure, compelling him to envision himself as a heavily armed warrior to cope with the challenges.

17. This term, which originated in the *StarCraft* community, describes the dedication of video-game players to delving into the game's interior to discover its optimal strategies and tactics. Theorycraft involves drawing on mathematical and programming skills to analyze statistics, hidden systems, or underlying game code (Karlsen 2011; Mortensen 2010). Or, if we adopt the definition from the website wowwiki.com, "theorycraft is the attempt to mathematically analyze game mechanics in order to gain a better understanding of the inner workings of the game."

18. The Borg are the recurring antagonists in the *Star Trek: The Next Generation* TV series in the early 1990s, which are depicted as the main threat in the film *Star Trek: First Contact*.

19. In this section, I use "Task-Rabbiting" as a metaphor to capture the essence of Behemoth's crowdsourcing games' initiative, which is characterized by the mobilization of volunteer labor. TaskRabbit, a well-known online marketplace, connects individuals seeking freelance labor with those offering local services, covering a wide range of tasks including personal assistance, furniture assembly, and delivery. Similarly, Behemoth's crowdsourcing games organize activities where tasks are allocated to a group of volunteer engineers. These engineers, comparable to "taskers" on the TaskRabbit platform, freely choose to take on various tasks, contributing their skills and time without financial compensation.

20. A Nixie tube is a device composed of fine tungsten and a phosphorus anode, which creates light when heated by an electrical current. The light can be used for displaying numerals. A Nixie countdown timer displays the countdown time.

21. Determining COEs is a work task that asks engineers to write a report to describe and analyze serious software errors, issues, and crashes.

CHAPTER 3

1. As the RAM for a MacBook Pro usually is 16 GB, it would be more straightforward (if approximate) to think of the cost of an engineer's annual labor time as equal to the cost of buying 3,200 MacBook Pros as well as the electricity costs incurred in letting them run for a year.

2. This equation was disclosed by the Behemoth engineer Lei, who mentioned that he learned this equation from his previous employer.

3. Specifically, Lei's new algorithm allowed the feature (the webpage link) to save resources totaling 8,700 GB each year. According to Lei, the newly improved feature has already run for four years and would run at least another year, so it helped the company save 43,500 GB (8,700 * 5) computational resources, equal to 43.5 terabytes (TB).

4. As defined by the equation provided by Lei's previous employer, an engineer hypothetically worked 235 days a year and 5 days a week.

5. 1 GB is equal to 0.001 TB.

6. Marx defined the rate of surplus value (r.s.) as surplus labor / necessary labor. Marx assumed workers' necessary labor was 5 hours and surplus labor was 5 hours, thus calculating the rate of surplus as 100 percent (r.s. = 5/5 = 100%). Moreover, Marx also called to attention that the rate of surplus value was the degree of exploitation. While Marx calculated in labor hours (and British pounds), I calculated in TBs of RAM, following tech industry tradition. Therefore, the calculation should look as follows: necessary labor = 2.178 TB;

surplus labor = 43.5 TB − 2.178 TB = 41.322 TB; rate of surplus value (r.s.) = 41.322 / 2.178 = 1897.245%. Although it is a very simplistic calculation and a coarse application of Marx's theory on the rate of surplus value, it gave me a sense of the enormous surplus value obtained through Lei's creative work.

7. In the tech world, *pivot* is used to describe a substantive change in direction to a software design, a service, or even a business model. When explaining the idea of pivot to me, several engineers cited the pivotal case of Instagram as an example. Apparently, before pivoting, Instagram was a location-based check-in app.

8. Tech lead is a role between scrum master and project owner: it is usually adopted by senior engineers, who should possess extensive technical knowledge about their scrum team's projects and enough leadership skills to guide scrum members and delegate tasks to the right engineers.

9. *Game of Thrones* is an American fantasy drama television series adapted from *A Song of Ice and Fire*, George R. R. Martin's series of fantasy novels, the first of which is titled *A Game of Thrones*.

10. Although Chuan realized the negative effects of his participation and chose to quit the game, it is worth pondering what might have happened had Chuan chosen to devote more time to the game and "grind" his shooting and escaping skills. This option implied the essence of the importation of gaming relationship to work—an engineer's sacrifice of his interests to this kind of team-building activity—and a further conflation of off-work and work activities.

11. Additionally, many junior engineers expressed that they were very resentful of doing CRs for senior engineers. It took these junior engineers a long time to understand senior engineers' codes. Furthermore, when these engineers encountered difficulties in understanding the codes, they felt timid about asking their senior colleagues to explain them. On the one hand, the junior engineers worried that these senior engineers would "laugh them out of the room"; on the other hand, they did not want their senior colleagues to feel like they were being interrogated.

12. Indeed, the design of Code Review Roulette largely alleviated the intensified conflicts emerging from the CR process. Think about it this way: without the game, engineers who were not assigned to review Deron's codes would feel nothing but normal. By participating in the game, however, engineers who did not catch the bullet and were not tasked with Deron's code review would feel "rewarded" by a very fair system they themselves had constructed. On the contrary, the only engineer who fired the bullet—Charlie—might feel it very reasonable to surrender to the odds system and his bad luck.

CHAPTER 4

1. The reason why the icons are called phone-tool icons is that they are displayed on the phone-tool page. The phone tool has two functions: one is to be used as a communication platform that includes instant messaging, video chat/conferencing, and phone call features; the other is as a personal website to display an employee's basic information (e.g., their level, reporting managers, length of time at Behemoth, and teams) and personal achievements in icon format. None of the people I interviewed was aware of a monetary reward or promotion/advancement advantage tied to obtaining Behemoth phone-tool icons; instead, the reward lay simply in the bragging rights and social status that accompanied the achievements.

2. As discussed previously, Baker and Nelson (2005) illustrate that bricolage is a crucial mechanism to spawn entrepreneurship and ensure innovation. For example, they dis-

cuss how entrepreneurial companies engage in bricolage by maximally using resources, such as personal knowledge, technical skills, and open-access technology/tools at hand to facilitate their production and innovation process. In this book, I define bricolage tasks as tasks that are to be accomplished by utilizing whatever methods and tools engineers can get access to.

3. Bricolage knowledge is defined as knowledge that the company encourages enigneers to share and contribute and that is considered potentially usable knowledge resources for bricolaging activity.

4. Hannah is the pseudonym for Behemoth's voice assistant, just like Siri (Apple) or Alexa (Amazon).

5. The issue of practicality is particularly noteworthy. Some of my interviewees explained that their video-gaming experience teaches them that no matter how well they comprehend gaming strategies (e.g., killing, battling, and dueling), those mean nothing until they start practicing them on the "battlefield." The same holds true for programming skills. Rather than spend a long time reading an entire book or chapter to learn a coding skill, they would rather get started quickly after briefly reading a simple tip page and then read more specific tips that target particular problems they encounter during the code implementation process.

6. The way to get the Security Badge icon is to take a test involving questions on thirteen security protection scenarios. If workers pass the security test, they will be awarded the badge.

7. I do not know if it is just a coincidence that the Wizard team engineers' joke imagining Hannah as a "real lady" was adopted by Behemoth's later advertisement campaign for its e-speaker. In a series of advertisements, Behemoth portrayed its speaker as a shy girl with a very "humble personality" that people enjoyed talking to. Behemoth even portrayed this girl, Hannah, as experiencing certain common human situations, such as losing her voice, in order to distance this image from that of a cold-blooded and technologically sophisticated software application.

8. SEVIS denotes the hierarchy of ticket severity at Behemoth. This categorization is subdivided into five levels, with SEVIS V representing the least severe and urgent, and SEVIS I signifying the most critical level, which requires immediate attention from high-level managers, such as subdivision directors. Notably, SEVIS II indicates a scenario of significant urgency, wherein on-call engineers are required to initiate resolution procedures within fifteen minutes of being paged.

9. In the realm of multiplayer video games, it is common for battle teams to be formed randomly through online matchmaking. However, the dynamics of gameplay alter significantly when teams are organized through inviting close friends to gather in a shared physical space. Such arrangements foster enhanced competitiveness, attributable primarily to the efficiencies of face-to-face communication and the deeper rapport established among teammates. Within gaming communities, this practice is referred to as "opening the back door." This term encapsulates the strategic advantage gained through direct, real-time communication, offering a comparative edge in the gaming experience.

10. "Account trading" implies that players lend their accounts to players with greater expertise to enhance their rankings.

11. Hiring professional "boosters" is a practice whereby a high-level player is paid to increase the rank of the buyer's account. This practice has become increasingly problematic, since it impedes the possibility of fair play. In fact, South Korea started to make commercial boosting services illegal in 2018. Professional boosting, however, reveals how desperate these engineers are to obtain advanced video games positions.

12. A "premade team" is the opposite of a "random team." A random team is assigned by the online gaming system. Players randomly selected to a random team do not know each other; therefore, the rapport of the random team is lower than that of a premade team, which significantly affects the team's gaming performance. The premade team has a playing advantage due to team rapport and frequent interaction (as the players work together within the same sitting). Thus, a premade team's gaming score and performance are usually higher than those of a random team.

CHAPTER 6

1. In 2014, the Equal Employment Opportunity Commission (2014) reported that the high-tech sector employed a larger share of Asian Americans than private industry overall (14%–5.8%).

2. In the context of this study, Asian engineers present in the fieldwork comprised Indian, Chinese, Pakistani, Korean, and Vietnamese individuals.

3. According to a 2017 Goldman Sachs report, while H1-B workers hold about 12–13 percent of the jobs in the U.S. tech industry, they only hold 0.6–0.7 percent of jobs in other industrial sectors (Torres 2017). In addition to the tech industry's favorable migrant policies in comparison to other industries' recruiting processes, which place a strong emphasis on cultural fit, high-tech recruiting processes for junior engineers are some of the most objective: all of the interview questions revolve around programming and mathematics. As long as the interviewees can write down the correct codes and provide reasonable solutions for the math puzzle on the whiteboard, they can prove their engineering competencies and thus get the jobs.

4. "Eating bitterness" describes a Chinese value system that believes people should make enormous efforts to survive, especially in the toughest circumstances.

5. OOTO stands for "out of the office."

6. As defined by Confucianism, the class-based society of imperial China was composed of four ranks: literati, peasants, craftsmen, and merchants. Craftsmen in fact had a rather low social status and were ranked third, even lower than peasants.

7. I found out this fact through an unexpected conversation with Matt. After one lunch, I followed the Wizard team back to their team area. As we walked, Matt (white, male, Level 5) started to criticize Jammar's behavior, attempted to associate his self-centeredness with the "one-child policy," and commented, "Jammar is not the worst 'one-child' baby. . . . I have seen more spoiled and bossy ones." I could not help but remind Matt that Jammar probably was not the only child in his family as he came from India, where a "one-child policy" had not been implemented. Matt seemed surprised and told me that he thought Jammar came from Pakistan and that somehow he'd had the impression that Pakistan followed China and had a "one-child policy."

8. Towers are a type of self-defense mechanism in many video games, in which teams attack any enemy team that gets within range.

CHAPTER 7

1. Lei's creativity saved 43.5 TB of computational power for the company and contributed to an impressive 1,897 percent surplus rate. If Behemoth had instead followed the Taylorism tradition and encouraged the standardization of development, Lei's innovative algorithm would not have been possible.

2. Similarly, when the company's cultural ritual runs counter to the gaming culture, it can easily lead to resistance on the part of engineers. As shown in Chapter 5, when the donut email prank strongly promoted mutual surveillance and damaged freedom, hardcore gamers would adopt strategies, such as "false alarm" and "terminal hack," to disrupt the cultural rituals set up at Behemoth.

3. This book acknowledges that various types of control mechanisms coexist on the engineering floor in addition to game control. For instance, time control and mechanisms designed to standardize the coding process are evident in the preceding empirical chapters. Despite the implementation of the game control mechanism, the book aims to emphasize the significance of other forms of control mechanisms that are still in practice.

4. As reported by the media, multiple types of score games, such as "focus scores," "point ranking systems," "idle time," and "productivity scores," were rampant in 2022 (Kantor and Sundaram 2022).

5. If the latter occurs, then a new type of regime—hegemonic despotism—will be formulated on the floor (Burawoy 1985). If this regime becomes mainstream, can we then predict that engineers will have minimum space to withdraw but will be forced to participate in games that now render unsuccessful, such as the crowdsourcing games?

References

Alexandersson, A., & Kalonaityte, V. (2018). Playing to dissent: The aesthetics and politics of playful office design. *Organization Studies, 39*(2–3), 297–317.

Alfrey, L., & Twine, F. W. (2017). Gender-fluid geek girls: Negotiating inequality regimes in the tech industry. *Gender & Society, 31*(1), 28–50.

Alvesson, M. (2000). Social identity and the problem of loyalty in knowledge-intensive companies. *Journal of Management Studies, 37,* 1101–1123.

American Institute of Stress. (2020). *Are you experiencing workplace stress?* https://www.stress.org/workplace-stress

Andrews, C. K., Lair, C. D., & Landry, B. (2005). The labor process in software startups: Production on a virtual assembly line? In R. Barrett (Ed.), *Management, labour process, and software development* (pp. 45–75). Routledge.

Attewell, P. (1987). The deskilling controversy. *Work and Occupations, 14*(3), 323–346.

Baerg, A. (2009). Governmentality, neoliberalism, and the digital game. *Symploke, 17*(1), 115–127.

Baker, T., & Nelson, R. E. (2005). Creating something from nothing: Resource construction through entrepreneurial bricolage. *Administrative Science Quarterly, 50*(3), 329–366.

Banks, J., & Humphreys, S. (2008). The labour of user co-creators: Emergent social network markets? *Convergence, 14*(4), 401–418.

Banks, J., & Potts, J. (2010). Co-creating games: a co-evolutionary analysis. *New Media & Society, 12*(2), 253–270.

Banks, M., & O'Connor, J. (2017). Inside the whale (and how to get out of there): Moving on from two decades of creative industries research. *European Journal of Cultural Studies, 20*(6), 637–654.

Barley, S. R., & Kunda, G. (2006). Contracting: A new form of professional practice. *Academy of Management Perspectives, 20*(1), 45–66.

Barley, S. R., & Kunda, G. (2011). *Gurus, hired guns, and warm bodies: Itinerant experts in a knowledge economy.* Princeton University Press.

Barnett, L. A. (2007). The nature of playfulness in young adults. *Personality and Individual Differences, 43*(4), 949–958.

Barrett, R. (Ed.). (2005). *Management, labour process, and software development.* Routledge.

Bassett, P., & Cave, A. (1993). Time to take the unions to market. *New Statesman and Society, 6*(268), 16–17.

Beck, J. C., & Wade, M. (2006). *The kids are alright: How the gamer generation is changing the workplace.* Harvard Business Press.

Bogost, I. (2007). *Persuasive games: The expressive power of videogames.* MIT Press.

Bogost, I. (2014). Why gamification is bullshit. In S. P. Walz and S. Deterding (Eds.), *The gameful world: Approaches, issues, applications* (pp. 65–79). MIT Press.

Boltanski, L., & Chiapello, E. (2005). The new spirit of capitalism. *International Journal of Politics, Culture, and Society, 18*(3), 161–188.

Bourdieu, P. (1998). *Practical reason.* Stanford University Press.

Braverman, H. (1974). *Labor and monopoly capital: The degradation of work in the twentieth century.* Monthly Review.

Bulut A. (2020). *Precarious game: The illusion of dream jobs in the video game industry.* IRL Press.

Bunchball. (2010). *Gamification 101: An introduction to game dynamics.* https://jndglobal.com/wp-content/uploads/2011/05/gamification1011.pdf

Burawoy, M. (1979). *Manufacturing consent: Changes in the labor process under monopoly capitalism.* University of Chicago Press.

Burawoy, M. (1996). A classic of its time. *Contemporary Sociology, 25,* 296–299.

Burawoy, M., & Von Holdt, K. (2012). *Conversations with Bourdieu: the Johannesburg moment.* NYU Press.

Butler, J. (1997). *The psychic life of power: Theories in subjection.* Stanford University Press.

Cappelli, P. (2000). *Managing without commitment.* Organizational Dynamics.

Carli, L. L., Alawa, L., Lee, Y., Zhao, B., & Kim, E. (2016). Stereotypes about gender and science: Women ≠ scientists. *Psychology of Women Quarterly, 40*(2), 244–260.

Carroll, J. M. (2014). Games as design archetypes. In S. P. Walz and S. Deterding (Eds.), *The gameful world: Approaches, issues, applications.* (pp. 197–200). MIT Press.

Cavallero, D. J. (2017). *Choose your identity: gender identity formation through video game characters.* [Master's thesis, California State University]. https://scholarworks.calstate.edu/downloads/4t64gp81q

Charles, D. (2018, October 1). Here's the average length of employment at the biggest Silicon Valley tech companies and it ain't long. Brobible. https://brobible.com/culture/article/how-long-employees-stay-tech-companies/

Cheryan, S., Plaut, V. C., Davies, P. G., & Steele, C. M. (2009). Ambient belonging: How stereotypical cues impact gender participation in computer science. *Journal of Personality and Social Psychology, 97*(6), 1045–1060.

Chess, S. (2017). *Ready player two: Women gamers and designed identity.* University of Minnesota Press.

Chess, S., & Shaw, A. (2016). We are all fishes now: DiGRA, feminism, and GamerGate. *Transactions of the Digital Games Research Association, 2*(2), 21–29.

Christensen, C. M., Baumann, H., Ruggles, R., & Sadtler, T. M. (2006). Disruptive innovation for social change. *Harvard Business Review, 84*(12), 94–101.

Clarke, C. A., Brown, A. D., & Hailey, V. H. (2009). Working identities? Antagonistic discursive resources and managerial identity. *Human Relations*, *62*(3), 323–352.

Clawson, D., & Fantasia, R. (1983). Beyond Buraway: The dialectics of conflict and consent on the shop floor. *Theory and Society*, *12*(5), 671–680.

Colbert, A., Yee, N., & George, G. (2016). The digital workforce and the workplace of the future. *Academy of Management Journal*, *59*(3), 731–739.

Collinson, D. L. (1988). Engineering humour: Masculinity, joking, and conflict in shop-floor relations. *Organization Studies*, *9*(2), 181–199.

Conger, K. (2021, Jan. 4). Hundreds of Google employees unionize, culminating years of activism. *New York Times*. https://www.nytimes.com/2021/01/04/technology/google-employees-union.html

Connell, R. W. (2005). *Masculinities*. University of California Press.

Connell, R. W., & Messerschmidt, J. W. (2005). Hegemonic masculinity: Rethinking the concept. *Gender & Society*, *19*(6), 829–859.

Consalvo, M. (2009). *Cheating: Gaining advantage in videogames*. MIT Press.

Costas, J., & Fleming, P. (2009). Beyond dis-identification: A discursive approach to self-alienation in contemporary organizations. *Human Relations*, *62*(3), 353–378.

Crain, M., Poster, W., & Cherry, M. (Eds.). (2016). *Invisible labor: Hidden work in the contemporary world*. University of California Press.

Csikszentmihalyi, M. (1990). *Flow: The psychology of optimal experience*. Harper & Row.

Deterding, S. (2014). The ambiguity of games: Histories and discourses of a gameful world. In S. P. Walz & S. Deterding (Eds.), *The gameful world: Approaches, issues, applications* (pp. 23–64). MIT Press.

Dill, K. E., & Thill, K. P. (2007). Video game characters and the socialization of gender roles: Young people's perceptions mirror sexist media depictions. *Sex Roles*, *57*(11), 851–864.

Dovey, J., & Kennedy, H. (2006). *Game cultures*. McGraw-Hill Education.

Dyer-Witheford, N., & de Peuter, G. (2006). EA spouse and the crisis of video game labour: Enjoyment, exclusion, exploitation, exodus. *Canadian Journal of Communication*, *31*(3), 599–617.

Dyer-Witheford, N., & de Peuter, G. (2009). *Games of empire: Global capitalism and video games*. University of Minnesota Press.

Edery, D., & Mollick, E. (2008). *Changing the game: How video games are transforming the future of business*. Financial Times Press.

Edwards, Richard. (1979). *Contested terrain: The transformation of the workplace in the twentieth century*. Basic Books.

Elwood, S., & Leszczy, L. (2010). Privacy, reconsidered: New representations, data practices, and the geoweb. *Geoforum*, *42*, 6–11. https://doi.org/10.1016%2Fj.geoforum.2010.08.003

Fernández-Kelly, M. P. (1983). *For we are sold, I and my people: Women and industry in Mexico's frontier*. SUNY Press.

Fleming, P. (2005). Workers' playtime? Boundaries and cynicism in a "culture of fun" program. *Journal of Applied Behavioral Science*, *41*(3), 285–303.

Fleming, P. (2009). *Authenticity and the cultural politics of work: New forms of informal control*. Oxford University Press.

Fleming, P., & Spicer, A. (2014). Power in management and organization science. *Academy of Management Annals*, *8*(1), 237–298.

Fleming, P., & Sturdy, A. (2009). "Just be yourself!": Towards neo-normative control in organisations? *Employee Relations*, *31*(6), 569–583.

Foucault, M. (1991). Governmentality. Translated by Rosi Braidotti and revised by Colin Gordon, in G. Burchell, C. Gordon and P. Miller (Eds.), *The Foucault effect: Studies in governmentality* (pp. 87–104). University of Chicago Press.

Foucault, M. (2010). *The government of self and others: Lectures at the Collège de France 1982–1983.* Macmillan.

Foucault, M., Davidson, A. I., & Burchell, G. (2008). *The birth of biopolitics: Lectures at the Collège de France, 1978–1979.* Springer.

Frank, A. (2018, March 22). *Pro-union voices speak out at heated GDC roundtable.* Polygon. https://www.polygon.com/2018/3/22/17149822/gdc-2018-igda-roundtable-game -industry-union

Friedman, M. (1977). *Industry and labour: Class struggle at work and monopoly capitalism.* Macmillan.

Fuchs, C. (2010). Labor in informational capitalism and on the internet. *Information Society, 26*(3), 179–196.

Fuchs, C. (2014). *Digital labour and Karl Marx.* Routledge.

Gandini, A. (2019). Labour process theory and the gig economy. *Human Relations, 72*(6), 1039–1056.

Gramsci, A. (1971). *Selections from the prison notebooks,* edited and translated by Quintin Hoare and Geoffrey Nowell Smith. International Publishers Co.

Greenhaus, J. H., & Powell, G. N. (2006). When work and family are allies: A theory of work-family enrichment. *Academy of Management Review, 31*(1), 72–92.

Gregg, M. (2013). *Work's intimacy.* John Wiley & Sons.

Gunn, S. (2006). From hegemony to governmentality: Changing conceptions of power in social history. *Journal of Social History, 39*(3), 705–720.

Harvey, D. (1990). *The condition of postmodernity: An enquiry into the conditions of cultural change.* Wiley-Blackwell.

Hibbins, R. (2005). Migration and gender identity among Chinese skilled male migrants to Australia. *Geoforum, 36*(2), 167–180.

Hobson, N. (2022). *Google has a productivity problem that has stumped managers for 113 years. Will Sundar Pichai be the first to solve it?* Inc.com. https://www.inc.com/nick -hobson/googles-productivity-problem-has-stumped-managers-for-113-years-will -sundar-pichai-be-first-to-solve-it.html

Hochschild, A. R. (2012). *The managed heart.* University of California Press.

Huizinga, J. (1950). *Homo ludens: A study of the play-element in culture.* Beacon.

Huws, U. (2014). *Labor in the global digital economy: The cybertariat comes of age.* NYU Press.

Jansz, J., & Martis, R. G. (2007). The Lara phenomenon: Powerful female characters in video games. *Sex Roles, 56*(3–4), 141–148.

Juul, J. (2010). *A casual revolution: Reinventing video games and their players.* MIT Press.

Kalleberg, A. L., & Vallas, S. P. (2018). Probing precarious work: Theory, research, and politics. *Research in the Sociology of Work, 31*(1), 1–30.

Kantor, J., & Sundaram, A. (2022). The rise of the worker productivity score. *New York Times,* 14.

Karaian, J., & Kelley, L. (2022, Jan. 21). Layoffs at tech giants reverse small part of pandemic hiring. *Spreeny Times.* Spreenytimes.com/2023/01/21/business/tech-layoffs .htm

Karlsen, F. (2011). Theorycrafting: From collective intelligence to intrinsic satisfaction. In *DiGRA Conference 2011,* 6.

Kelly, T. (2012, Nov. 17). *Everything you'll ever need to know about gamification*. Tech Crunch. http://techcrunch.com/2012/11/17/everything-youll-ever-needto-know-about -gamification/November

Kerr, A. (2017). *Global games: Production, circulation and policy in the networked era*. London: Routledge.

Kim T., Peck, D., & Gee, B. (2020). *Race, gender, and the double glass ceiling: An analysis of EEOC National Workforce Data*. Ascend Foundation.

Kirkpatrick, G. (2012). Constitutive tensions of gaming's field: UK gaming magazines and the formation of gaming culture 1981–1995. *Game Studies, 12*(1), 3. https://gamestudies .org/1201/articles/kirkpatrick

Kirkpatrick, G. (2013). *Computer games and the social imaginary*. Polity.

Kline, S., Dyer-Witheford, N., & De Peuter, G. (2003). *Digital play: The interaction of technology, culture, and marketing*. McGill-Queen's Press.

Knight, F. H. (1921). *Risk, uncertainty, and profit*. Houghton Mifflin.

Kraft, P. (1977). The routinization of computer programming. In P. Kraft, *Programmers and managers: The routinization of computer programming in the United States* (pp. 97–107). Springer Science & Business Media.

Kücklich, J. (2005). Precarious playbour: Modders and the digital games industry. *The Fibreculture Journal* (5).

Kücklich, J. R. (2009). Virtual worlds and their discontents: Precarious sovereignty, governmentality, and the ideology of play. *Games and Culture, 4*(4), 340–352.

Kunda. G. (2006). *Engineering culture: Control and commitment in a high-tech corporation*. Temple University Press.

Kunda, G., and Van Maanen, J. (1999). Changing scripts at work: Managers and professionals. *Annals of the American Academy of Political and Social Science, 561*(1), 64–80.

Land, C., & Taylor, S. (2010). Surf's up: Work, life, balance, and brand in a new age capitalist organization. *Sociology, 44*(3), 395–413.

Lee, C. K. (1995). Engendering the worlds of labor: Women workers, labor markets, and production politics in the South China economic miracle. *American Sociological Review*, 60(3), 378–397.

Lee, C. K. (1998). *Gender and the South China miracle: Two worlds of factory women*. University of California Press.

Legault, M. J., & Weststar, J. (2015). The capacity for mobilization in project-based cultural work: A case of the video game industry. *Canadian Journal of Communication, 40*(2), 203–221.

Leidner, R. (1993). *Fast food, fast talk: Service work and the routinization of everyday life*. University of California Press.

Lemke, T. (2001). The birth of bio-politics: Michel Foucault's lectures at the College de France on neo-liberal governmentality. *Economy and Society, 30*(2), 190–207.

Lévi-Strauss, C. (1966). *The savage mind*. University of Chicago Press.

Lin, Y., Evans, J. A., & Wu, L. (2021). Novelty, disruption, and the evolution of scientific impact. arXiv:2103.03398v4 [cs.DL] https://doi.org/10.48550/arXiv.2103.03398

Littler, C. (1990). The labour process debate: A theoretical review, 1974–88. In D. Knights & H. Wilmott (Eds.), *Labour process theory* (pp. 46–94). Macmillan Press.

Lucas, K., and Sherry, J. L. (2004). Sex differences in video game play: A communication-based explanation. *Communication Research, 31*(5), 499–523.

Lupu, I., & Empson, L. (2015). Illusion and overwork: Playing the game in the accounting field. *Accounting, Auditing & Accountability Journal, 28*(8), 1310–1340.

Ma, Y. (2020). *Ambitious and anxious*. Columbia University Press.

McCabe, D. (2014). Making out and making do: How employees resist and make organisational change work through consent in a UK bank. *New Technology, Work, and Employment, 29*(1), 57–71.

McClure, R. F., & Mears, F. G. (1984). Video game players: Personality characteristics and demographic variables. *Psychological Reports, 55*(1), 271–276.

McDonald, D. (2013). *A new masculinity for a new millennium: Gender and technology in David Fincher's The Social Network*. English Seminar Capstone Research Papers.

McGonigal, J. (2011). *Reality is broken: Why games make us better and how they can change the world*. Penguin.

McKay, S. C. (2006). *Satanic mills or silicon islands? The politics of high-tech production in the Philippines*. ILR Press.

Mears, A. (2015). Working for free in the VIP: Relational work and the production of consent. *American Sociological Review, 80*(6), 1099–1122.

Messerschmidt, J. W. (1993). *Masculinities and crime: Critique and reconceptualization of theory*. Rowman & Littlefield.

Messner, S. (2019). Censorship, Steam, and the explosive rise of PC gaming in China. *PC Gamer*. https://www.pcgamer.com/its-time-to-pay-attention-to-china-inside-the-worlds-largest-pc-games-industry/

Milburn, C. (2018). *Respawn: Gamers, hackers, and technogenic life*. Duke University Press.

Milton, Laurie. (2003). An identity perspective on the propensity of high-tech talent to unionize. *Journal of Labor Research, 24*(1), 31–53.

Mollick, E., & Rothbard, N. (2014). *Mandatory fun: Consent, gamification and the impact of games at work*. Wharton School Research Paper Series.

Mollick, E., & Werbach, K. (2014). Gamification and the enterprise. In S. P. Walz & S. Deterding (Eds.), *The gameful world: Approaches, issues, applications* (pp. 439–458). MIT Press.

Moore, P., & Robinson, A. (2016). The quantified self: What counts in the neoliberal workplace. *New Media & Society, 18*(11), 2774–2792.

Mortensen, T. E. (2010). Training, sharing or cheating? Gamer strategies to get a digital upper hand. *E-Learning and Digital Media, 7*(1), 79–89.

Muñoz, C. B. (2011). *Transnational tortillas*. Cornell University Press.

Munro, G. D., & Munro, C. A. (2014). "Soft" versus "hard" psychological science: Biased evaluations of scientific evidence that threatens or supports a strongly held political identity. *Basic and Applied Social Psychology, 36*(6), 533–543.

National Center for Education Statistics. (2012). 2009–10 through 2018–19. https://nces.ed.gov › digest › tables › dt20_318.45.asp

Neff, G. (2012). *Venture labor: Work and the burden of risk in innovative industries*. MIT Press.

Neff, G., & Stark, D. (2004). Permanently beta: Responsive organization in the internet era. In P. N. Howard & S. Jones S. (Eds.), *Society online: The internet in context* (pp. 173–188). SAGE Publications.

O'Donnell, C. (2009) The everyday lives of video game developers: Experimentally understanding underlying systems/structures. *Transformative Works and Cultures, 2*. http://journal.transformativeworks.org/index.php/twc/article/view/73

O'Donnell, C. (2014). Getting played: Gamification and the rise of algorithmic surveillance. *Surveillance & Society, 12*(3), 349–359.

Ong, A. (1988). The production of possession: Spirits and the multinational corporation in Malaysia. *American Ethnologist, 15*(1), 28–42.

Ó Riain, S. (2001). Networking for a living: Irish software developers in the global work-place. In *A Critical Study of Work: Labor, Technology and Global Production*, 258–282.

Orlikowski, W. J. (1988). The data processing occupation: Professionalization or prole-tarianization? *Research in the Sociology of Work, 4*, 95–124.

Otis, E. (2012). *Markets and bodies: Women, service work, and the making of inequality in China*. Stanford University Press.

Otis, E. (2016). China's beauty proletariat: The body politics of hegemony in a Walmart cosmetics department. *Positions: East Asia Cultures Critique, 24*(1), 155–177.

Ouellet, L. (1994). *Pedal to the metal: The work life of truckers*. Temple University Press.

Paap, K. (2006). *Working construction: Why white working-class men put themselves—and the labor movement—in harm's way*. Cornell University Press.

Perez, M. (2019, Feb. 12). Activision Blizzard to lay off nearly 800 people as its 2019 looks bleak. *Forbes*. https://www.forbes.com/sites/mattperez/2019/02/12/activision-blizzard-to-layoff-nearly-800-employees/#1383866f76f5

Perlow, L. A. (1998). Boundary control: The social ordering of work and family time in a high-tech corporation. *Administrative Science Quarterly*, 328–357.

Peticca-Harris, A., Weststar, J., & McKenna, S. (2015). The perils of project-based work: Attempting resistance to extreme work practices in video game development. *Organization, 22*(4), 570–587.

Pierce, L. (1996). *Gender trials: Emotional lives in contemporary law firms*. University of California Press.

Prassl, J. (2018). *Humans as a service: The promise and perils of work in the gig economy*. Oxford University Press.

Pun, N. (2005). *Made in China: Subject, power, and resistance in a global workplace*. Duke University Press.

Purcell, C., & Brook, P. (2022). At least I'm my own boss! Explaining consent, coercion, and resistance in platform work. *Work, Employment and Society, 36*(3), 391–406.

Radhakrishnan, S. (2011). *Appropriately Indian: Gender and culture in a new transna-tional class*. Duke University Press.

Ranganathan, A., & Benson, A. (2020). A numbers game: Quantification of work, auto-gamification, and worker productivity. *American Sociological Review, 85*(4), 573–609.

Rangaswami, J. P. (2014). When peers select tasks and teams. In S. P. Walz & S. Deter-ding (Eds.), *The gameful world: Approaches, issues, applications* (pp. 459–462). MIT Press.

Reeves, B., & Read, J. L. (2009). *Total engagement: How games and virtual worlds are chang-ing the way people work and businesses compete*. Harvard Business Press.

Reich, A. D. (2010). *Hidden truth: Young men navigating lives in and out of juvenile pris-on*. University of California Press.

Rose, N. (1996a). Governing "advanced" liberal democracies. *Anthropology of the State: A Reader* 144162 (1996).

Rose, N. (1996b). *Inventing our selves*. Cambridge University Press.

Rosenblat, A., & Stark, L. (2016). Algorithmic labor and information asymmetries: A case study of Uber's drivers. *International Journal of Communication, 10*(27), 3758–3784.

Ross, A. (2004). *No-collar: The humane workplace and its hidden costs*. Temple Univer-sity Press.

Roy, D. (1959). "Banana time": Job satisfaction and informal interaction. *Human Orga-nization, 18*(4), 158–168.

Sallaz, J. (2009). *The labor of luck: Casino capitalism in the United States and South Af-rica*. University of California Press.

Sallaz, J. J. (2015). Permanent pedagogy: How post-Fordist firms generate effort but not consent. *Work and Occupations, 42*(1), 3–34.

Sallaz, J. J., & Trongone, S. G. (2023). Toward a field of labor activism. *Work and Occupations, 50*(3), 428–435.

Salzinger, L. (2003). *Genders in production: Making workers in Mexico's global factories.* University of California Press.

Schrape, N. (2014). Gamification and governmentality. In M. Fuchs, S. Fizek, P. Ruffino, & N. Schrape (Eds.), *Rethinking gamification* (pp. 21–46). Meson Press.

Scott, A., Kapor Klein, F., McAlear, F., Martin, A., & Koshy, S. (2018). *The leaky tech pipeline: A comprehensive framework for understanding and addressing the lack of diversity across the tech ecosystem.* Kapor Center for Social Impact.

Seaborn, K., & Fels, D. I. (2015). Gamification in theory and action: A survey. *International Journal of Human-Computer Studies, 74*, 14–31.

Sharone, O. (2002). Engineering consent: Overwork and anxiety at a high-tech firm. *Berkeley Collection of Working and Occasional Papers, 52.*

Sharone, O. (2013). *Flawed system/flawed self: Job searching and unemployment experiences.* University of Chicago Press.

Shaw, A. (2012). Do you identify as a gamer? Gender, race, sexuality, and gamer identity. *New Media & Society, 14*(1), 28–44.

Shaw, A. (2014). *Gaming at the edge: Sexuality and gender at the margins of gamer culture.* University of Minnesota Press.

Sherman, R. (2007). *Class acts: Service and inequality in luxury hotels.* University of California Press.

Shestakofsky, B. (2017). Working algorithms: Software automation and the future of work. *Work and Occupations, 44*(4), 376–423.

Shirky, C. (2008). *Here comes everybody: The power of organizing without organizations.* Penguin.

Siciliano, M. L. (2022). Effort in absence: Technologically mediated aesthetic experiences of the culture industries' routine workers. *Ethnography* (Sept. 14), 1–23.

Sihvonen, T. (2011). *Players unleashed! Modding the Sims and the culture of gaming.* Amsterdam University Press.

Singh, H. (2020, Sept. 11). Growth of cyber cafes declining sharply. *Economic Times.*

Sørensen, B. M., & Spoelstra, S. (2012). Play at work: Continuation, intervention and usurpation. *Organization, 19*(1), 81–97.

Stang, B., Osterholt, M. A., & Hoftun, E. (2007). *The book of games* (Vol. 2). Book of Games.

Statler, M., Heracleous, L., & Jacobs, C. D. (2011). Serious play as a practice of paradox. *Journal of Applied Behavioral Science, 47*, 236–256.

Sturges, J. (2013). A matter of time: Young professionals' experiences of long work hours. *Work, Employment and Society, 27*(2), 343–359.

Takeuchi, H., & Nonaka, I. (1986). The new product development game. *Harvard Business Review 64*(1), 137–146.

Taylor, P., & Bain, P. (2003). "Subterranean worksick blues": Humour as subversion in two call centres. *Organization Studies, 24*(9), 1487–1509.

Thomas, D. (2002). *Hacker culture.* University of Minnesota Press.

Thompson, E. P. (1967). Time, work-discipline, and industrial capitalism. *Past & Present, 38*(1), 56–97.

Thompson, P., & Smith, C. (2009). Labour power and labour process: Contesting the marginality of the sociology of work. *Sociology, 43*(5), 913–930.

Thompson, P., & Smith, C. (2017). *Working life: Renewing labour process analysis*. Bloomsbury.

Trittin, H., Fieseler, C., & Maltseva, K. (2019). The serious and the mundane: Reflections on gamified CSR communication. *Journal of Management Inquiry, 28*(2), 141–144.

Tse, T., & Li, X. (2022). Recoupling corporate culture with new political discourse in China's platform economy: The case of Alibaba. *Work, Employment, and Society*.

Turkle, S. (1994). Hackers: Loving the machine for itself. In C. Huff & T. Finholt (Eds.), *Social issues in computing: Putting computing in its place* (pp. 638–672). McGraw-Hill.

Turner, V. (1969) Liminality and communitas. In *The ritual process: Structure and anti-structure* (pp. 41–49). Cornell University Press.

U.S. Equal Employment Opportunity Commission (U.S. EEOC). (2014). *Asian-Americans in the US workforce*. EEOC.

U.S. Equal Employment Opportunity Commission (U.S. EEOC). (2016). *Diversity in high tech*. EEOC.

Virno, P. (1996). The ambivalence of disenchantment. In P. Virno & M. Hardt (Eds.), *Radical thought in Italy: A potential politics*, (pp. 13–37). University of Minnesota Press.

Visier Team. (2015). Four common tech ageism myths debunked. *VISIER*. https://www.visier.com/blog/four-common-tech-ageism-myths-debunked/

Wajcman, J. (2014). *Pressed for time. The acceleration of life in digital capitalism*. University of Chicago Press.

Wakabayashi, D., & Schwartz, N. D. (2017, Feb. 5). Not everyone in tech cheers visa program for foreign workers. *New York Times*.

Walz, S. P., & Deterding, S. (Eds.). (2014). *The gameful world: Approaches, issues, applications*. MIT Press.

Weststar, J., & Dubois, L. É. (2022). From crunch to grind: Adopting servitization in project-based creative work. *Work, Employment and Society, 37*(4), 972–990.

Weststar, J., & Legault, M. J. (2019). Building momentum for collectivity in the digital game community. *Television & New Media, 20*(8), 848–861.

Whitson, J. R. (2013). Gaming the quantified self. *Surveillance & Society, 11*(1/2), 163–176.

Whitson, J. R. (2014). Foucault's Fitbit: Governance and gamification. In S. P. Walz & S. Deterding (Eds.), *The gameful world: Approaches, issues, applications* (pp. 339–358). MIT Press.

Whitson, J. R. (2019). The new spirit of capitalism in the game industry. *Television & New Media, 20*(8), 789–801.

Wiener, A. (2020). *Uncanny valley: A memoir*. Farrar, Straus, and Giroux.

Wilkins, A. (2012). "Not out to start a revolution": Race, gender, and emotional restraint among black university men. *Journal of Contemporary Ethnography, 41*(1), 34–65.

Williams, C. L., & Connell, C. (2010). Looking good and sounding right: Aesthetic labor and social inequality in the retail industry. *Work and Occupations, 37*(3), 349–377.

Williams, D. (2006). A brief social history of game play. In P. Vorderer & J. Bryant (Eds.), *Playing video games: Motives, responses, and consequences* (pp. 197–212). Lawrence Erlbaum Associates.

Willis, P. (1977). *Learning to labour: How working class kids get working class jobs*. Routledge.

Wingfield, A. H. (2013). *No more invisible man: Race and gender in men's work*. Temple University Press.

Witz, A., Warhurst, C., & Nickson, D. (2003). The labour of aesthetics and the aesthetics of organization. *Organization, 10*(1), 33–54.

Wolf, D. L. (1992). *Factory daughters: Gender, household dynamics, and rural industrialization in Java*. University of California Press.

Woodcock, J. (2019). *Marx at the arcade: Consoles, controllers, and class struggle*. Haymarket Books.

Woodcock, J., & Johnson, M. R. (2018). Gamification: What it is, and how to fight it. *Sociological Review, 66*(3), 542–558.

Xiang, B. (2007). *Global "body shopping" An Indian labor system in the information technology industry*. Princeton University Press.

Yee, N. (2006). Motivations for play in online games. *CyberPsychology & Behavior, 9*(6), 772–775.

Zichermann, G., & Cunningham, C. (2011). *Gamification by design: Implementing game mechanics in web and mobile apps*. O'Reilly Media.

Zuboff, S. (1988). *In the age of the smart machine: The future of work and power*. Basic Books.

Zuboff, S. (2019). *The age of surveillance capitalism: The fight for a human future at the new frontier of power*. Public Affairs.

Index

Tongyu Wu is Assistant Professor of Sociology at Zhejiang University in China.